Sports Injuries

Written by a professional for the unlucky sportsman, whether professional, competitive or recreational, this book is the first effective guide to coping with injuries and getting back to sport. Vivian Grisogono passes on years of experience as a sports participant and physiotherapist in this accessible, fully illustrated, easy-to-read manual.

Injuries are described 'geographically', from foot to neck, and then down the arm. Arrowed drawings throughout help you identify the site of pain. The causes of injury are explained, to help you understand how and why a particular injury occurs, whether it is a sudden traumatic injury like the sprinter's hamstring tear or the squash player's Achilles tendon rupture, or a gradual overuse injury like tennis elbow or runner's shin soreness. Self-diagnosis is fraught with pitfalls, and this book aims to steer you clear of them by helping to identify the possible causes of your pain, in order to present a clear picture of the problem to your medical practitioner, so that he can make a speedy and accurate diagnosis.

The first-aid and immediate self-help measures you should take for any injury, before you manage to see your doctor, are described. Following diagnosis, rehabilitation principles for each injury are given, from the very early stages of recovery, through to your return to sport. For tendon and muscle injuries, the progression starts with passive stretching for flexibility, then you re-strengthen the injured muscle group, until the final stage when you work the muscles in co-ordination with the surrounding muscles. For joint injuries, you have to regain stability through strengthening exercises, then gradually mobilize the injured joint, before moving into the final phase of co-ordinating exercises. All the specific exercises for achieving these aspects of recovery are illustrated in detail, for each injury throughout the body.

The explanations of injuries and their recovery processes, as well as the amazing range of therapeutic exercises listed, will make this book indispensable not only to sportsmen and women of all types and ages, but also to coaches, P E teachers, and medical and paramedical practitioners interested in sports injuries.

Vivian Grisogono, chartered physiotherapist, set up the full-time sports injuries unit at the Crystal Palace Sports Centre, and has served as British team physiotherapist at the Winter and Summer Olympics, the World Student Games, and the Commonwealth Games.

In 1986 she was awarded an honorary lectureship to the London Hospital Medical College Sports Medicine Diploma Course. She has contributed chapters to many books on sport and sports medicine, including *Sports Injuries and their Treatment*, edited by Helal, King and Grange.

She does frequent lectures and seminars, in Britain and abroad, for PE teachers, coaches, sports players and sports medicine practitioners. She often appears on television and radio, including live phone-in programmes. She also writes articles on health issues in sports and general magazines such as *Running, Fitness, Sport and Leisure*, and *Performance Cyclist*.

She played tennis and squash to county level, and gained Blues in both sports at Oxford University. She was ranked in the British top twenty in squash in 1978 and 1980.

She has been in private practice since 1978. In 1991, she took up the post of chief physiotherapist at the Royal Masonic Hospital in West London, which includes a sports injuries clinic run in co-operation with two Olympic doctors.

Her other books include *Knee Health*; *Strokes and Head Injuries: A Guide for Patients, Families, Friends and Carers* (co-authored with Mary Lynch); *Children and Sport: Fitness, Injuries and Diet*, all published by John Murray.

Sports Injuries

A Self-help Guide

Vivian Grisogono

John Murray

For Andrew

Readers are advised to seek professional help in any case of
injury. The author and publishers cannot be held responsible
for readers' injuries under any circumstances.

First published 1984 by
John Murray (Publishers) Ltd
50 Albemarle Street, London W1X 4BD

Reprinted 1984, 1985, 1986, 1987, 1989, 1991, 1992, 1994 (twice), 1996,
1997, 2000

Set by Fakenham Photosetting Ltd, Fakenham, Norfolk
Printed and bound in England by
The Bath Press, Bath

British Library Cataloguing in Publication Data

Grisogono, Vivian
    Sports injuries.
    1. Sports - Accidents and injuries
    I. Title
    617'.1027   RD97
ISBN 0-7195-4111-5

Contents

Foreword 1

Acknowledgements 3

Introduction 4

Foot 20

Ankle 35

Shin 50

Calf Muscles and Achilles Tendon 70

Knee 80

Front-of-the-Thigh Muscles 126

Hamstrings 136

Adductors *(The inside thigh muscles)* 150

Hip Flexors *(The muscles at the top of the thigh)* 161

Hip Joint 168

Pelvis 176

Hip Abductors 185

Lumbar Spine *(Lower spine)* 189

Thoracic Spine *(Upper spine)* 213

Abdominal Muscles *(Stomach muscles)* 221

Chest Muscles 229

Rib Cage 235

Neck *(Cervical spine)* 238

Shoulder Joint 246

Arm Muscles 265

Elbow Joint 268

Forearm Muscles 275

Wrist Joint 278

Hand 283

Index 289

Foreword

Sportsmen are highly sensitive to wobbles in their fitness equilibrium. It is not because we are more conscious of pain than normal beings but rather because our bodies are so well tuned that the slightest piece of dust in the mechanism is instantly noticeable – and needs to be explained and rectified. Getting a sensible explanation is not always possible, even when an occasional niggling pain becomes chronic enough to inhibit the most dedicated from going out training.

Sports injuries are peculiar, in that they happen to people who are obsessed with achieving rapid, if not instant, recovery. 'Give it a rest for a couple of weeks', is a non-answer to the keen runner. Yet this is the normal prescription handed out by a G.P. to the injured.

What sportsmen need is an easily followed 'diagnostic manual' with cross referenced advice on prevention and maintenance, so that a minor ache can be identified and cured in the home-workshop.

My friend Vivian Grisogono has now produced such a work based on many years experience at the medical centre in the Crystal Palace Sports Centre. Here she has had an unrivalled opportunity to catalogue the trials and tribulations of all kinds of sportsmen – from the famous elite to the struggling tyro, and to chart their response to treatment and exercise. Miss Grisogono is a great advocate of self-help and like the army sergeant believes that it is a court-martial offence if a runner falls sick again after being appraised of the routine of preventive exercises that are necessary for healthy living.

Her book does not seek to pre-empt the skills of the medical practitioner, in fact, Vivian works very closely with sports medicine doctors in her professional life, but it does give us the means of recognizing the effect and to take appropriate early action to remove the cause when we are suffering from a strain or annoying limitation of movement. Her practical advice is invaluable to the thinking sportsman and should ensure that many more of us stay on the road longer and avoid those expensive major services which so detract from the simple pleasure that we find in doing sport.

John I. Disley CBE,
Chairman, Crystal Palace National Sports Centre Committee,
Director, London Marathon, Olympic Medallist

1

Acknowledgements

Among the many people I have to thank for their help are the patients who showed me the endlessly fascinating number of ways in which people can hurt themselves in sport. For the continuing satisfaction I derive from practising my profession as a physiotherapist, I have to thank in particular Mr. W. J. Guest, principal of the West Middlesex Hospital School, who saw me through the difficult transition phase of training.

One person who helped me as a colleague in physiotherapy, and mentor in squash-playing is Claire Chapman. Of those who helped me understand sport from the organizational, giving, side, I would thank especially John Disley, Roger Bottomley, Dick Palmer, Charles Wenden and Derek Johnson.

Rehabilitation is simple, the complicated aspects of sports medicine being the province of the medical experts. Craig Sharp has patiently shared with me a little of his vast knowledge of exercise physiology. Among the doctors and surgeons I have worked with, I have to thank Basil Helal, John King, Noel O'Brien, Howel Jones, Peter Sperryn, David Perry, and, most specially, Frank Cramer, medical officer to Crystal Palace Sports Centre, who gives more to his colleagues, subordinates, patients and friends than he can know.

This book owes a great deal to Andy Etchells, through whom the idea for it originated; Roger Hudson, patient editor, who gave it shape; and Michael Bartlett, who gave it visual imagery. There is a special debt to John Maley, president of the Chattanooga Corporation, whose personal friendship and generous kindness played a major part in making the book possible.

Introduction

Injury prevention

This book aims to give you an outline of the injuries which can happen to the different parts of your body through doing sport; how to recognize what might have happened; factors you should take note of to help your doctor make an accurate diagnosis quickly; and finally, guidelines on the rehabilitation process appropriate to the various injuries, leading to full fitness and your return to your sport. It is a 'self-help' book, within strictly defined limits: a correct diagnosis is crucial to an uncomplicated recovery. The medical profession alone has the expertise and facilities for using objective diagnostic techniques like X-rays, blood tests, bone scans, and the innumerable other internal investigations. Self-diagnosis can be a pitfall that at best wastes time, at worst causes serious harm.

Once an injury has been diagnosed, it is usually best treated by a chartered physiotherapist, who can use various techniques to help you over the initial phase of pain and swelling, and then guide you through the phases of recovery. If you are given advice that conflicts with suggestions in this book, you must accept the word of the practitioner treating you, or seek further advice through your doctor.

Self-help must include an understanding of how injuries happen, and how they can be avoided. Not all risks are foreseeable: accidents *will* happen, so some injuries are unavoidable. Some sports, by their nature, carry a high risk of injury, like the body contact and combat sports, gymnastics, hang-gliding, ski-jumping and pole vaulting.

Injuries can be classified in two basic categories. *Traumatic injuries* are sudden happenings, in which you know something has gone wrong, and you feel the immediate effects of the injury, perhaps pain, swelling, bruising, or an open wound. The traumatic injury can be extrinsic, or due to some external cause, like a direct blow, a sudden twist as you change direction, or a fall. It can also be intrinsic, without an obvious cause, like the sprinter's sudden hamstring strain in a race, or the squash player's Achilles tendon rupture. *Overuse injuries* are more subtle, because they come on simply as a gradually increasing pain, directly associated with a particular, usually repetitive, activity. Tennis elbow and runner's shin soreness are examples of overuse injuries. Traumatic injuries are rela-

4

tively easy for the specialist to diagnose. Difficulties only arise if the injury is particularly severe, or if complications occur which are not apparent at first sight, immediately after the injury has happened. Over-use injuries need more careful assessment, because many diseases or inflammatory conditions can mimic this kind of pain pattern.

The way to avoid traumatic injuries is to minimize risk factors. The environment must be safe, so if the floor is wet or the pitch waterlogged, the game should be cancelled. Equipment should be checked: are the posts of the wrestling ring properly padded? Is there a crack in the shaft of your squash racket? Safety gear, like helmets, mouthguards, padded vests, groin boxes, and shin pads, must be worn when appropriate. The rules of the sport must be understood by the participants, and applied by the umpires or referees. This is especially important in contact sports like rugby, sports where collisions can occur, like squash, and combat sports like boxing, where the rules are designed to protect participants from harm.

Avoiding overuse injuries involves allowing your body to adapt to repetitive stress. If you make any sudden change in your training routine, perhaps by suddenly doing four hours of tennis serving after a winter's rest from the game, or increasing your running mileage from twenty to eighty miles per week, or even by some more subtle change like doing your sport every day instead of every second day, some part of your body may show the signs of overwork. Increasing training has to be a gradual process, building up in easy stages, allowing recovery days from hard training, and rest days if fatigue or pain set in. If you have to rest for illness or injury, you must be sure, firstly, that you make a complete functional recovery before resuming your sport, and, secondly, that you re-start very gradually, doing a little at a time. For any exercise session, you should always warm-up and warm-down thoroughly, and shower as soon as you finish, to avoid stiffness. Your warm-up should consist of four parts, and should last for about fifteen minutes. You should do passive stretching for your muscles; ballistic bouncing movements for your joints; 'pulse-warmers', consisting of six to ten sets of half-minute intervals of hard exercise, like sprints or squat-thrusts; and finally, skill rehearsal, in which you practise specific movements relating to your sport. Technically, you must try to develop the most efficient style you can, appropriate to your sport. Any equipment you use must be the right size and weight for you: a child, for instance, should not use a full-size racket until he has grown strong enough to handle it easily. Your sports shoes must fit you properly, without rubbing or cramping your feet, and you must replace the insoles, soles, or the shoes themselves, if they wear down.

Your diet plays an important part in your fitness and wellbeing. You must eat enough food for the energy you need. Carbohydrates are especially important for sportsmen. You should not exercise on an empty stomach, but you must wait up to four hours before exercising after a heavy meal. Try to eat at regular intervals, with two or three proper meals a day, and perhaps light snacks in between, if necessary. Avoid 'junk' foods, and try to balance your diet. Your weight is not a guide to your fitness, but most fit sportsmen have relatively low fat levels (except long-distance swimmers, in whom fat layers form an important protective covering against cold).

Your fluid intake is essential in avoiding cramp, dehydration and heat exhaustion. Drink plenty of plain water, complemented by moderate salt on your food. Avoid drinking too much tea, coffee, alcohol, or fizzy drinks, as these tend to be dehydrating. If you tend to get cramp, or you take exercise in hot weather, you can experiment with electrolyte replacement drinks, but only take salt tablets if your doctor advises you to, and if you are certain you are drinking enough plain water. When you experience muscle cramp, try to stretch the affected muscle gently. You can apply ice over it, to help the muscle relax. If you suffer from bad cramp at frequent intervals, especially at night, you should refer to your doctor, as you may have a circulatory problem. Muscle cramp symptoms can also be caused by damage to the muscle itself, or to the bone underlying the muscle.

Common sense, and the self-discipline of knowing when to stop, or when not to start, a session of physical activity are two essential factors in avoiding any kind of injury. Illness, fatigue, pain and stiffness are warnings that you should not be taking exercise. If you disregard them, you are taking unacceptable risks with your health and wellbeing.

Rehabilitation principles

There is never any point in trying to exercise through, or 'run off', the pain of an injury. When you have pain relating to a particular movement or activity, continuing the activity only causes further harm to the damaged tissues. After doing any necessary first-aid measures, your next priority is to obtain an accurate diagnosis of what damage has been done. Once the diagnosis has been made, you have to begin your recovery with specific exercises to help the injured part, under the guidance of your practitioner, and within the limits of pain.

In general, the pattern of recovery for tendon and muscle injuries is *passive stretching* to regain lost flexibility, followed by *specific re-*

6

strengthening exercises concentrating on the injured muscle group, building up to a final stage of *functional exercises*, in which the injured muscle group works in co-ordination with its surrounding muscles, and normal patterns of movement are re-established. Stretching the injured muscles remains an important routine for some time after you have recovered from the injury, to prevent the danger of the muscles becoming tight and then being re-injured. You have to continue stretching the muscles daily, and as the first part of your warm-up before exercising.

For joint injuries, the pattern of rehabilitation usually consists of *strengthening exercises* for the muscles round the joint, to regain stability, followed by exercises to regain the joint's *mobility*, leading to the final stage of *functional, dynamic exercises*. Again, you must continue to do specific exercises to protect an injured joint, even after you have recovered.

Stretching muscle groups involves positioning the muscles in their longest possible range, within pain limits, and holding the attitude for a count of ten, without moving at all. In this way, the muscles pay out, and you can gradually increase the amount they stretch, each time you repeat the exercise. To increase joint mobility, you have to stretch the surrounding muscle groups passively, and you must also do some bouncing, ballistic movements, to mobilize the joint structures. Strengthening exercises only improve muscle power if you work the muscles against an increasing load. You can increase the work by increasing the number of times you do a particular exercise; increasing the speed at which you do it; or using a gradually increasing weight-resistance during the movement. For home use, you can make a simple weight-resistance device from a double-sided oven glove, which you can attach over your ankle or wrist, or hold in your hand. You can use food cans of known weights in the pockets of the glove, and increase the weights as you get stronger. Other useful items for weight-resisted exercises include sandbags; strap-on wrist and ankle weight-bands; an iron weights boot, with a bar for adding on free weights; adjustable dumb-bells; and springs, attached to a strong fixed point, with straps or grips.

When you plan your programme of rehabilitation exercises, remember that *progression* is the key principle. Start with little, but often, then gradually increase the amount you do. If you are stretching a muscle group, do two or three stretching exercises at a time, about every hour, if possible, and then try to increase the number of exercises, perhaps doing one or two longer stretching sessions each day. From the lists of specific strengthening exercises in this book, you should select up to five exercises to start with, doing each one about five times. Try to build up to three sets of ten repetitions of each exercise, then increase the number of exercises you do, and then add in gradually increasing weights. In some of the exercise lists, suggestions are given for the amounts which should be done. These are guidelines only. You should compose your programme according to the time you have, and the state of your injury. If you work within pain limits, you do not risk doing further damage to your injured tissues. If you do overdo your exercises, to the extent of feeling stiffness and increasing pain, you must cut back the amount you are doing, but maintain small amounts of specific exercises for your injury throughout the day. You should only progress from the initial rehabilitation stage to the next when your injury feels improved, and the visible signs of damage are receding.

Alternative exercise is an important part of your rehabilitation programme. You will need to maintain your fitness, even though you have to stop doing your main sport. In principle, any form of exercise that does not cause pain over your injury is a good fitness substitute. Swimming and cycling may be good for general exercise. In the pool, you can do specific exercises for your injury, or you can devise training sessions, improving your endurance by doing steady-state timed swims, and improving your general fitness with interval sprints in the water, interspersed with short rest periods. You can apply the same training principles to exercise circuits. You may be able to incorporate some of your specific strengthening exercises into a circuit, which you then do to time, or in stop–start bursts of work. Progression remains an important principle, so you must aim to increase the work you do, either by doing more exercises, or increasing your exercise time.

Throughout the rehabilitation process, you must avoid painful activities, and concentrate on the exercises directed towards improving function in the injured part. You must not resume your sport until you are sure you can stress the injured tissues without any reaction of pain, swelling, or limitation of movement. When you do resume your sport, you must start with little, and gradually build up to full participation. Whenever you change the routine of your programme, you should allow rest days between your sessions, so that you do not stress your body on a daily basis, and you can assess whether a particular activity has caused an adverse reaction. For some time after recovery, you should maintain a daily routine of specific exercises, to guard against recurrence.

First-aid

RESUSCITATION

'Sudden death' is a hazard for sportsmen of any age. It happens rarely.

8

The statistics confound those who claim that sport, or hard exercise, increases the risk of you dropping dead at an early age. However, deaths related to exercise have been documented. Sometimes they appear inexplicable, like the fifteen-year-old oarsman who collapsed shortly after a normal training outing. Often, the death is linked to a known history of heart disease, meaning that exercise was not necessarily the main factor causing it. Sometimes, the victim has complained of being unwell, or is trying to exercise through an illness. Common sense is an important preventive measure. If you know you do not feel well, or you feel abnormally fatigued, you should not exercise until you feel better. Checking your pulse and temperature provides a good guide to your day-to-day fitness. If they are raised, due to a virus, or any infection like an abscess in a tooth, you risk overworking your heart if you exercise hard before you are back to normal.

Everyone associated with sport in any way should know what to do in an emergency. The only way to learn emergency resuscitation is to go on a standard first-aid course, where you can practise the techniques on resuscitation models until you perfect them. If the brain is deprived of oxygen it can survive normally for about four minutes before its cells die off, causing irreparable harm. However, when the person has been exercising hard, stimulating the cardio-respiratory systems, the time is considerably reduced – to about eighteen seconds. So you need to know how to act very swiftly to save a sportsman who has collapsed.

The principles of resuscitation are based on reviving an air flow through the lungs and restoring activity to the heart. The oxygen supply round your body can be cut off because you stop breathing, or because your heart stops pumping the oxygenated blood round your arteries. A variety of accidents can interrupt your breathing: you may choke on your chewing gum, if you take a sudden breath; you may be strangled by the cord if you fall in the water while water ski-ing; your lungs could be punctured by a broken blade in fencing. Blocked breathing, or asphyxia, may cause your heart to stop. Your heart beat can be checked by a heart attack, or a sudden shock inhibiting the nerve controlling it, for instance if you dive into icy water on a hot day. If you are knocked unconscious by a direct blow to your head, your heart and breathing systems may stop because of interference to their controlling systems in the brain.

The first priority in coping with this type of accident is to assess what has happened. You have to remove any obvious causes of the problem, and then check whether the victim is breathing, by watching for chest movements and feeling at his mouth and nose for air flow. Then check for heart function. If there is no beat directly over the heart, or in the throat behind the windpipe, or in the wrist artery, and if the casualty is pale or blue, with dilated pupils when you open his eyelids, you can be sure that his heart has stopped.

The standard practice is to start with breathing recovery, because you can safely do airway resuscitation even when the lungs are slightly active, whereas cardiac massage over a heart which is beating too faintly to be perceptible can actually stop it.

Airway resuscitation works because you breathe out some oxygen on expiration. You have to make sure that the casualty's mouth and throat are clear, and this involves pushing his head backwards so that his tongue does not roll across his throat. By covering the casualty's mouth with yours, and blocking his nose with your hand, or vice versa if you use the mouth-to-nose method, you can then breathe oxygenated air into his lungs. Cardiac resuscitation works on the principle of stimulating heart movement by direct pressure on the chest over it. If you alternate breathing stimulation with the cardiac massage, whether you are alone or have a helper who can co-ordinate one part of the process with you, you may be able to re-vitalize the casualty's systems. You should certainly keep trying to achieve this, until emergency help arrives. If the casualty does regain his breathing and heart beat, but stays unconscious, you must turn him into the *recovery position*, almost on his stomach, with his mouth and nose clear of the ground, and keep checking his pulse and breathing at frequent intervals, until help arrives.

IMMOBILIZATION

If an accident causes major damage, like obviously broken bones, the casualty should not be moved more than is absolutely necessary. This is especially true if the spine is damaged, as careless handling can cause irreversible paralysis.

Supports and splints

In most injuries, pain is greatly reduced if the injured part is immobilized correctly. Supportive bandaging or splinting reduces stress, prevents painful movements, and helps control the swelling which is produced when tissues of any kind are damaged. Inflatable splints are a very convenient method of providing a comfortable, removable, adjustable support to a leg or an arm.

A simple splinting method is to tie one injured part to a neighbouring uninjured part, with crepe bandages, cotton bandages, or scarves and towels or other materials to hand. You can tie a fractured leg to the other one, strap an arm against the chest, or splint two fingers together. For comfort, you should always remember to put padding between the two

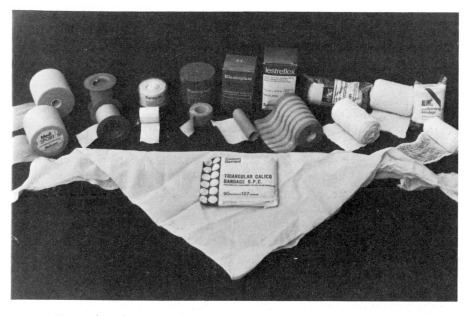

parts. Crepe bandages in themselves provide little support, but if you wrap the injured area in a wadding of cotton wool, and then bind over it with crepe bandages, the support is much firmer. Tubular or stocking bandage is an easy way of supporting a swollen joint: for firm support, the stocking bandage is applied double.

Whenever you apply support bandaging, you must make sure it achieves its end. To protect the lower leg from movement, for instance, you must immobilize the knee and ankle joints. To control joint swelling, you have to take into account the structure of the joint and the effect of gravity on the swelling. Therefore bandaging for the foot or ankle must extend from the toes to just below the knee, to prevent pooling of the excess fluid. A knee support should extend about ten centimetres above and below the joint, as the joint structures spread over this area.

Splints and bandages should never be tight, as they can constrict the blood flow and cause further damage. To check the circulation, you should press on the thumb-nail or toe-nail on the bandaged limb, to see whether the blood returns to the nail immediately after the pressure has turned it white. If the blood return is sluggish, the bandage must be loosened or removed immediately. Pressure in an inflatable splint should be reduced, by releasing some of the air, at the first sign of increasing discomfort or feeling of constriction inside it.

It is best not to use non-stretch strapping as a first-aid binding, unless you are certain you can use it properly. Swelling continues to gather for

11

some time after an injury has happened. If the injury has been enclosed in a non-elastic strapping (taping) there will be inevitable circulatory constriction. If the injury is bad enough, the casualty doctor will have to remove the strapping for X-rays, and he will probably apply a plaster-of-Paris cast in its place. If there is no choice but to use non-stretch strapping, you must check that the casualty is not allergic to this type of tape. It should only be applied over a film of pre-taping material. Failing that, the hairs must be shaved from the skin first, and the strapping should subsequently be removed with special fluid. Take care not to apply tape over broken, sensitive, or infected skin.

Non-stretch strapping should not be used to provide such firm support that the casualty can continue sport despite the injury. Further damage would probably be done. Sports medicine practitioners use strapping to provide 'feedback' support. By pulling on the skin, the strapping sends messages which re-activate the protective mechanisms in joints whose natural protective nerve messages have been impaired through injury. This is not a first-aid procedure, but part of rehabilitation.

MOBILITY

When a bad accident has happened, it is always best not to move the injured person until trained ambulance personnel arrive. They can then transport the casualty on a stretcher. However, if the injury is to an arm or a leg, and is not too severe, once it has been correctly supported in bandaging, the person may be able to move around provided the injured part is not moved or stressed by loading.

Slings and crutches

A sling is the best support for an injured arm or rib. If the injury is above the elbow, the sling is put on with the elbow bent to a right angle. The short end of the triangular bandage is placed under the elbow, and one long end is slipped under the forearm, up to the uninjured shoulder; the other long end is then drawn over the front of the arm to the injured shoulder, and the two long ends tied with a reef knot. If the injury is below the elbow, the hand should be supported upwards, to minimize the swelling. The sling is applied with the short end to the elbow, as for the normal sling, but over the front of it. The elbow is bent so that the hand rests up on the uninjured shoulder. The long end of the triangular bandage rests over the injured forearm, up to the uninjured shoulder. The other long end is slipped under the injured arm, round the back of the chest on that side, to be tied to the end over the uninjured shoulder in a reef knot. In both types of sling, the arm should rest comfortably in the

12

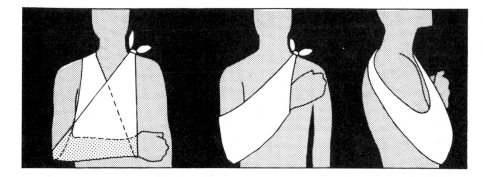

Slings. Left, *for an injury above the elbow.* Right, *for an injury below the elbow.*

material. You must, of course, check the circulation in the hand at frequent intervals.

Crutches provide support for mobility, when you cannot take weight through an injured leg. Immediately after an injury, you are probably safest if you rest on a companion's shoulder and hop. The principle of crutches is similar. Elbow crutches, which extend to the middle of your arm, are the most convenient kind, but if you are very tall you may have to use full-length, axillary crutches, which reach almost to your armpits.

To measure the correct height for crutches, you stand, balancing on your uninjured leg, with your arm resting straight down by your side. The handle part of the crutches has to be level with the small bump of bone on the outer side of your wrist. For full-length crutches, there must be at least five centimetres between the top of the crutches and your armpits. If you lean on the crutches through your armpits, you risk damaging the nerves supplying your arms and hands. If you change your shoes later on, you must remember to re-adjust the height of your crutches.

To avoid taking weight through your injured leg, you walk by putting your crutches a little way in front of you, and hop forward on your uninjured leg, up to your crutches, or just a little in front of them. Never put your crutches far away from you while walking, especially if the ground is wet. When you go up stairs, you hop up, and then bring your crutches up to the step you are standing on. Coming down, either use one crutch and the rail, or both crutches: put your crutches down to the step below, and then hop down to them. If you can take some weight through your injured leg, you use the crutches in the same way, except that every time you move the crutches, you also move your injured foot the same distance, placing it on the ground; you propel yourself forward by pressing down through the crutch handles to draw your other leg through.

13

If you use the crutches for any length of time, you must check that the rubber ends do not wear down, replacing them if necessary.

ELEVATION TO MINIMIZE SWELLING

A torn tissue releases fluid, which may be clear or coloured, according to the type of injury and the tissue damaged. If enough fluid is released, you see visible swelling, where the fluid is trapped between your skin and the underlying tissues. The trapped fluid may be blood, but this does not necessarily make your skin look red over the swelling. If the fluid tracks between the layers of your skin, you may see red or yellowish bruising, indicating a certain amount of internal bleeding.

If you aggravate the injured tissues, by doing stressful movements, more fluid will be produced. Even without this irritation, swelling, or fluid exudate, can be increased simply by the effect of gravity. The excess fluid lies outside the normal flow system which transports de-oxygenated blood back to the heart and tissue waste products into the lymph glands. Gravity promotes fluid flow vertically downwards, but opposes the flow in the opposite direction. In the normal way, your muscles act to press on your blood vessels and force their fluid upwards against gravity. Even normally, however, this action may not be sufficient, and you may find your feet, calves or hands swell after you have been on your feet all day, or worked with your arms downwards. After an injury, any excess fluid accumulates, unless you take active measures to promote its re-absorption into the normal flow systems.

One measure is to position the injured part so that gravity can help the return flow of the fluid. The aim is to stimulate circulatory flow in the direction of the heart, and of the main lymph glands, which lie, in the limbs, in your armpits and groins, with smaller glands in your knees and elbows. Therefore, for any swelling in your legs, you should try to rest as much as possible with your foot supported up above the level of your hip. Your leg should be comfortable on a soft support, like a pillow, as a hard surface would constrict the circulatory flow. If you have to sit in a chair with your foot down on the floor, you should try to straighten your knee and lift your leg upwards at intervals, to help the fluid flow. For swelling in the hand or the lower part of the arm, it is normally sufficient to support the arm in a sling holding the hand at shoulder level. If you have swelling in the upper part of your arm, you should try to lift the arm above your head at frequent intervals during the day, and flex the muscles, either isometrically, or by bending and straightening your elbow. For swelling over your abdomen or back, try to lie flat as much as possible, rather than sitting or standing.

14

Cold treatments (cryotherapy) are universally accepted as the simplest, safest immediate measure for relieving pain, reducing internal bleeding and bruising, and controlling swelling in injured tissues.

You can apply ice by rubbing ice cubes over the injured area, dabbing the skin dry at intervals. When the skin has turned pink (or darkened, if you are dark-skinned), you should stop, to avoid the risk of over-cooling the skin, or creating an 'ice burn'. You can use a bucket or bowl of iced water, to immerse an injured hand or foot. A wet towel containing ice cubes can be wrapped round the injury. If you use an ice pack, or packet of frozen food, you must protect your skin with olive oil, baby oil or a wet towel. If you put the pack directly onto the skin, it is likely to pull the skin away with it when you take it off. You can buy special freezer packs which have to be refrigerated. A useful form of cold therapy for carrying with you is a chemical freezer pack, which you strike hard to mix the chemicals, to produce an instant ice-pack. The advantage is that the pack does not need to be kept cold, the disadvantage being that these packs are not normally re-usable.

You should never apply cold to the skin if you have a circulatory deficiency, or if for some reason you cannot feel skin sensations properly. You must always remember that cold therapy can cause skin breakdown if it is used badly. So long as the skin is intact, you can safely apply ice at hourly or two-hourly intervals, to control the swelling and exudate which continues to form for the first day or two after an injury; but if the skin becomes uncomfortable, you must stop until it is back to normal. There is no set time for each ice application. If your skin is sensitive, you may only be able to tolerate a few minutes; some people can stand ice dips for half-an-hour at a time. Provided that you can see the skin colour changes after your ice application, you know you have achieved the effects you need.

CONTRAST BATHS

The aim of applying ice to an injury is to stimulate the blood flow in to and out of the area. A similar effect can be achieved by applying hot and cold alternately, and you may find this more comfortable than ice alone. You can use specially made hot-and-cold packs, taking care to protect your skin as for simple ice packs. The 'wet method' is to use two buckets or bowls of water, one iced, the other as hot as you can stand. You then dip the injured part (perhaps your ankle, wrist or elbow) into one bowl, for a few seconds; take it out, dab it dry with a towel, and dip it into the other bowl. Repeat the sequence for about ten minutes or so, until you see your skin changing colour.

As with ice, contrast baths should not be used if you have circulatory problems, or your skin is sore. Otherwise, they can be repeated at intervals, perhaps three or four times a day. When you are recovering from your injury, you may find that contrast bathing eases the part enough to allow you greater freedom of movement, so you may be able to start simple exercises first while you are using the technique.

APPLYING HEAT

Whereas cold therapy can be applied immediately to an injury, and continued through the rehabilitation phases for as long as there is swelling, bruising and pain, heat should only be applied, if at all, in the recovery phases of rehabilitation. Applying heat draws blood to the skin under the heat source. This tends to increase internal bleeding or fluid exudate (swelling) in an immediate injury. Therefore heat is not appropriate in first-aid.

Heat is used later on to relieve muscle tension, promoting relaxation. It is best for it to be applied only by qualified practitioners who can gauge whether it is necessary and suitable treatment for a specific case.

CREAMS

Massage, like heat, aggravates the situation when an injury has just happened. Heat creams have no part in first-aid. Any cream applied must be laid gently on the skin and allowed to soak in. If you rub it in, not only do you risk increasing internal bleeding, but you could stimulate blood clotting and bone formation in torn muscle fibres.

Heparinoid (anti-coagulant) creams are useful in first-aid, because they help promote blood flow, and disperse bruising. Arnica is the homoeopathic equivalent to a heparinoid cream, achieving similar healing effects.

DRESSINGS

Even a small skin cut carries the risk of infection. Every sportsman, especially in field sports, should have routine inoculation against tetanus. If he is not protected, he should go to his doctor for an anti-tetanus injection as quickly as possible after being cut.

Any skin wound must be carefully cleaned. Soap and water, or plain water, are the best cleansing agents, preferable to using antiseptics. Use sterile swabs or very clean material, to clean a wound: never use a swab more than once, and make sure you use a clean edge of it each time you touch the wound. Do not apply creams over a wound or skin burn, but dry it carefully and cover it with a clean or sterile dressing. Sticking plasters cover normal cuts: you must take care not to touch the gauze centre of the plasters, which go directly over the wound. Butterfly plasters are used to draw together the edges of a razor-type wound. For larger wounds, you should use sterile gauze swabs, held in place with cotton or loosely woven conforming bandaging. Specially prepared sterile dressings in different sizes are very convenient for dressing wounds, as they have their own cotton bandages attached. Try to spread the fixing bandages over quite a wide area, to avoid creating a garter constricting effect around the wound. If there is heavy bleeding, cover the wound with layers of dressings, and leave them in place until the bleeding has stopped, or the casualty gets to hospital and is checked by the accident specialist.

If there is a splinter in the wound which you can see, you can take it out with tweezers, if it is near the surface. If it is more deeply lodged, or not visible, do not dig around for it, as you risk creating an infection. Clean up the wound, cover it with a sterile dressing, and tell the casualty officer that you suspect there is a foreign body in the wound. If it is not possible to extract it, your body will reject it in due course, so the priority is to keep the area clean, and watch for signs of infection like pus, warmth, redness and pain.

Any wound must be dealt with immediately, because of the risk of infection. No sportsman should be allowed to continue a game with an open wound, as there is a risk not only to himself but, in contact sports, to other players. You should never allow a wound to come into contact with dirty materials or suspect water: oarsmen, for instance, have been known to suffer major infections as the result of dipping raw hand blisters into polluted river water.

Blisters vary in type and severity. They are caused by friction. Your hand may blister because of unaccustomed or prolonged rubbing against the handle of an implement; your feet may be blistered by your shoes. Blisters are more likely to occur if hot conditions make your hands or feet swell, creating different grip alignment, or extra compression in your shoes. For a minor blister, you can cover the fluid-filled patch with heparinoid cream, and protect it from further friction with a sticking plaster. For a large blister, or blood-blister, you can make two small holes on either side of the blister with a sterilized needle, and gently squeeze out the fluid. Make sure the area is clean, and protect it with a dressing. If the blister is raw, and has lost its top layer of skin, clean it with soap and

17

water or antiseptic solution. You can then protect the area with a healing gel, or 'plastic skin' covering, or you can simply cover it with a sterile dressing, held in place by tubular bandage or tape.

To prevent blisters, or their recurrence, you must firstly make sure that your shoes fit you properly, or that the handle of your equipment is the right size. When you know there is a special risk of blisters, you can protect your skin with strips of narrow, non-elastic taping, for instance over each finger before you do long sessions of bar work in gymnastics. Vaseline spread liberally over your toes and under the ball of your foot can help prevent blisters during a long-distance run. Changing the insoles of your shoes can reduce friction. Hardening up the skin in vulnerable areas can help prevent blistering, and you can do this by soaking the skin every day in a special solution. Surgical spirit is often used, but there are more effective products which your doctor or podiatrist may recommend. If you build up areas of hard skin following blisters, you must keep them pared down, using a special rasp and perhaps removing cream.

THE FIRST-AID KIT

You have to assess the particular risks associated with your sport, if you want to carry useful items. In all cases, you need items to help in major emergencies: possibly an airway for resuscitation, inflatable splints for

A useful basic first-aid kit. Included are: stocking bandage, cotton wool wadding, dressing strip, covering fabric, skin healing gel, covering tape, Thermos for ice, scissors, sterile dressings (lint), Brook airway, butterfly plasters, sterile dressings (gauze and film), heparinoid cream, sterile dressings (gauze).

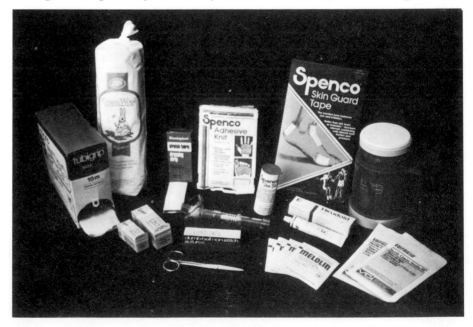

broken limbs, sterile dressings for major wounds. In contact and combat sports, you need a good supply of dressings and swabs. In repetitive sports, where there is little risk of trauma, but more risk of overuse injuries, you can carry the minimum emergency equipment, but you should have lots of ice, in a cold jar, or chemical ice packs.

If you are likely to be far from a source of clean, running tap-water, you should also carry a bottle of water. This is for cleansing purposes, not for drinking. Anyone who has suffered a major accident should not be allowed to eat or drink anything at all, in case he has to have emergency surgery. At the most, he can be allowed small sips of water, just enough to moisten his lips.

If you carry too much first-aid kit around with you, it hampers your speed of movement. However, you should have a comprehensive kit within easy reach, perhaps in your car, or in a box at the side of the court, pitch or track. As a bare minimum, you could carry a jar of ice, and a supply of sticking plasters.

The Foot

Bones

The foot normally consists of twenty-six bones, some tiny, some thick, some relatively long. Two 'extra' bones, called sesamoids, normally lie under the ball of the big toe. Your toes normally form a sloping line from your big toe to the tiny fifth toe, but the shape of your toes may vary. In many people the second toe is longer than the big toe. This variation is called 'Morton's foot'.

The arches

Your foot bones form functional arches for transmitting forces during movement. The inner side of your foot, from your heel to your big toe, is the medial arch. Its upward curve is not normally in contact with the ground. If it is flattened, lying close to the ground, the arch is said to have 'dropped', and you have flat feet. If the curve is exaggerated, you have high-arched feet. The lateral arch is the outside of your foot, from your heel to your little toe. It is not very curved, but lies flat to the ground. The ball of your foot is called the transverse arch, but it is functionally a 'pillar', linking the heads of the metatarsal bones.

Soft tissues

Many ligaments bind the foot bones together, but two are especially important. The spring ligament links the heel-bone to the navicular, and helps to support the medial arch. The long plantar ligament extends from the heel-bone, across the cuboid, to the near ends of the middle three metatarsals. It helps support the lateral arch. Four layers of little muscles lie under the foot, with one layer on top of the foot. Longer muscles, from the calf, also act on your foot and toes, and you can feel them working if you put your hands round your calf and move your toes. Underlying all the structures on the sole of your foot, and separating your skin from the muscles and tendons, is a strong band called the plantar fascia, which extends from your heel to the base of your toes.

FUNCTIONS

When you walk forward on a flat surface, your body weight is transmit-

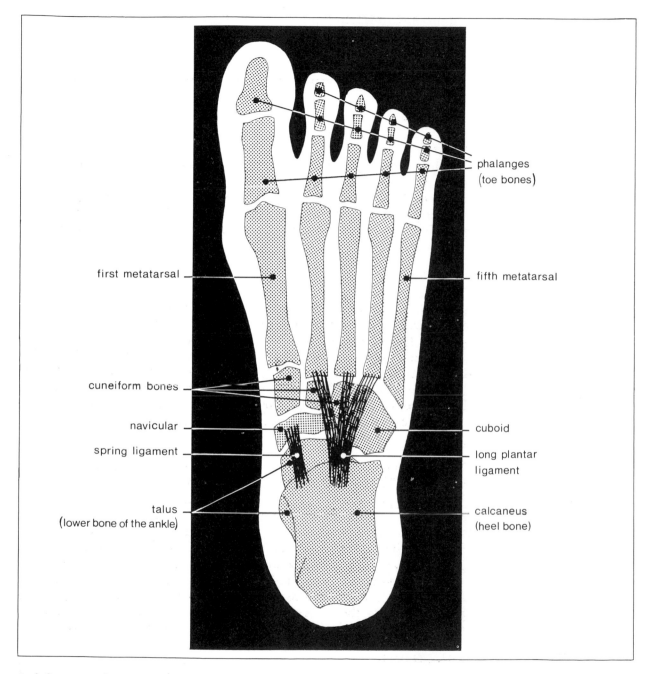

phalanges
(toe bones)

first metatarsal

fifth metatarsal

cuneiform bones

navicular

cuboid

spring ligament

long plantar
ligament

talus
(lower bone of the ankle)

calcaneus
(heel bone)

Left foot, seen from under the sole. Bones and major ligaments.

ted, ideally, from your heel, along the outer border, and onto the ball of your foot, from where you 'push off' to gain propulsion. The skin on the ball of your foot is hardened, usually behind the big toe, or behind the second toe if you have Morton's foot.

There is little sideways movement in your foot when you walk, and even less when you sprint, as you transmit your weight directly onto the ball of your foot, with propulsive force from your ankle and toe movements. But your foot joints can produce a great range of twisting (rotatory) movements, which allow you to adapt to uneven surfaces, or to run with sudden twists and turns. Inversion is the movement of turning your foot inwards under your ankle, while eversion turns your foot out. With your foot on the floor, you can roll your mid-foot to bring your medial arch close to the ground: this is pronation, while supination is the opposite movement which lifts the medial arch while you keep your heel down.

Your feet can be adaptable and pliable, or they can act as rigid levers. Sensory awareness, or proprioception, is essential to good function. It is impaired if you injure your foot, so adaptability and proper co-ordination with other joints are reduced. Bad shoes can also damage the foot's message systems, by working against normal movement. You need shoes wide enough to allow your foot to spread when you walk and run; soft enough to move with your foot; and thick-soled enough to prevent jarring. Clogs and platform shoes prevent normal foot movement. If you have to wear this type of shoe, try to spend some time each day walking barefoot or doing foot exercises. When you change from court shoes to sports shoes, allow your feet to adjust by doing foot movements barefoot before you put on your sports shoes.

FOOT PAIN

Gradual pain in your foot can be caused by an inflammatory joint problem; gout; ankylosing spondylitis (p. 180), which can cause plantar fasciitis (p. 25); and referred symptoms from a back problem (p. 207). You must keep an accurate record of how your pain came on to help your doctor make the correct diagnosis.

Foot injuries

LIGAMENT STRAINS

The many joints which comprise the foot are all bound together by ligaments, or thickened protective parts of the joint coverings. Any of these ligaments may be damaged by abnormal strains. Usually, the strain is the result of a sudden twist, perhaps when you run over a stone or rut, or you land awkwardly from a jump. In this case, you feel the strain as a sudden slight tearing feeling. The strain may occur gradually, from repeated over-stretching, if, for instance, you wear unsuitable or unaccustomed shoes. The pain then comes on after a space of time, perhaps only after you have stopped wearing the damaging footwear. In either case, once a ligament is damaged, it will set up a painful spot which will be aggravated each time you subsequently over-stretch that point, or apply pressure over it. Even a tiny ligament can give severe pain when strained, and the pain can persist for some months.

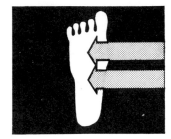

Treatment may consist of an injection from your doctor; rest; supportive strapping; underfoot supports to prevent stress over the damaged ligament; or electrical and exercise therapy from a physiotherapist. Any painful activities increase the damage and prolong the injury: the more you can rest the foot, the quicker it recovers.

STRESS FRACTURES

These may occur in any of the foot-bones, although they rarely happen in the first metatarsal. The cause is generally an increase in quantity of any repetitive activity using the feet. Squash players may suffer foot stress fractures if they suddenly take up running or skipping for endurance training – especially if they do this type of exercise on hard surfaces, wearing their thin-soled squash shoes. Long-distance runners may incur the problem if they step up their mileage, or train too intensively after a lay-off. Which bone is affected may be determined by your particular style of foot movement, or your activity. The heel-bone may suffer in a long-distance runner who tends to land heavily on it with each pace. The third or fourth metatarsal head, or both, may give way if you tend to land on the outer side of the ball of the foot while skipping, jumping or running for long periods. People with Morton's foot are very prone to stress fractures in the weight-bearing second metatarsal head, if they increase repetitive exercising. This stress fracture is known as a 'march fracture', because it was first described in army recruits doing unaccustomed long marches and drills. A high jumper may damage the navicular bone in the take-off leg during an extended practice session.

The first sign of damage is usually a slight pain, which gradually gets worse, if you continue to try to run or jump on the painful foot. The only evidence of bone damage is tenderness on pressure over the bone. X-rays will not reveal the damage in the early stage of a stress fracture, although a

23

bone scan will show increased activity in the bone. If in doubt, it is safest to treat any tenderness over a bone as a suspected stress fracture, especially if you are aware of having increased your activities or training immediately before you first felt the pain. If you ignore the pain, and continue exercising in the same way, the bone may eventually break completely. If you rest from any painful activities, but substitute painless activities such as swimming or cycling, the bone will normally heal within four to six weeks. When the bone is no longer sore to touch, and when your specialist says it has healed, you can resume your usual activities, but in small quantities only. Build up the amount you do very gradually, allowing rest days in between any exercise sessions. If you run, for instance, you should start with no more than half a mile, and build up in quarter-mile stages, preferably running on soft surfaces only at first, and then gradually including some running on harder ground. Check your shoes when you resume exercising, to make sure that they are cushioned enough, and flexible in the sole. If the pain recurs at any stage, you must rest again until it has subsided, and then resume training with a reduced quantity of exercise. If you try to build up too quickly, you risk a recurrence of the stress fracture, either in the same bone or another.

HEEL BRUISE

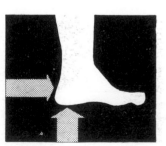

This can be caused by heavy landing on the heel, most often from jumping, but also from repeated heavy footfalls in running, or jarring from heel stamping in squash. Inflammation is set up in the protective fat pad which lies under the heel, so that the heel feels sore when pressure is applied. The condition is difficult to treat, and may last for some weeks. Specialist treatments may include injection and electrotherapy, but the most important factor is to protect the heel well with shock-absorbing cushioning, and to avoid activities which aggravate the pain.

BURSITIS

A bursa is a small sac containing fluid, which forms between two moving surfaces or tissues to provide friction-free movement. A bursa sometimes forms under the heel, and if this becomes inflamed, the symptoms are like those of heel bruising. More commonly, inflammation occurs in the bursa at the back of the heel which separates the bone from the insertion of the Achilles tendon (p. 73). This may happen because the tendon is prevented from moving normally, either by a direct strain, or by ill-fitting shoes. The back of the heel becomes tender to touch, but you do not have pain when you contract the tendon, for instance by standing on your toes. The treatment may be similar to that for heel bruising. You should also check the backs of your shoes for roughness or bad fit.

HEEL SPUR

If a tissue is repeatedly strained at its attachment onto a bone, it may cause inflammation, and eventually set up the reaction of new bone growth. This can happen to the plantar fascia where it joins the heel, and the new bone can be seen on X-rays as a small bony outgrowth on the front of the underside of the heel. It may eventually be necessary to have the tiny bone removed surgically, but in the first instance, treatment aims at relieving the repeated pressure on the plantar fascia which has caused the problem. If the heel is sore, heel pads should be used, while the arch and midfoot should be supported by a soft cushioned support or insole.

EPIPHYSITIS OF THE HEEL-BONE

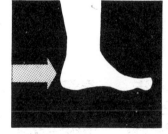

Like all other bones, the heel-bone is formed in parts which join together as a child grows older. If, for any reason, the blood supply to the bone is poor, the back edge of the heel-bone may fail to join the greater mass of the heel properly. The usual cause is repetitive jarring, perhaps because the child has been running too much, or jumping on hard floors in gymnastics. Pain is felt down the sides of the back of the heel. Any pressure on the heel, such as jarring, running or jumping, hurts. The problem usually happens to children between the ages of twelve and sixteen. It needs rest from any painful activities, and cushioned heel supports to reduce jarring during walking. If the child continues to do sport, the pain may persist for many months, whereas with rest it usually clears within a few weeks. Pain-free activities, such as swimming and cycling, can safely be continued during this time.

PLANTAR FASCIITIS

The plantar fascia may be strained by a change in shoes, or some alteration in the pattern of your foot movements, perhaps because you have taken up a new activity. When the fascia is strained, it usually becomes painful where the fascia is attached to the heel-bone, and the front of the heel-bone feels tender when you press it. The heel hurts on walking and running, and on standing up after you have been sitting down. It also hurts when the sole of your foot is put on the stretch, for instance if you pull your foot and toes backwards towards you with your hands. Specialist treatment may consist of an injection and/or electrotherapy. A

25

soft arch support will take the pressure off the fascia. Painful activities should be avoided. You can resume sport when the tenderness to pressure under the heel has disappeared.

'SPRING' LIGAMENT STRAIN

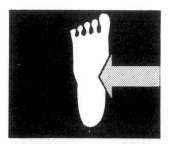

Like the plantar fascia, this ligament may be strained by a change in your normal activities which causes over-stretching of the ligament. The pain and tenderness are felt more forward on the sole of the foot, towards the inner arch. Treatment is similar to that appropriate for plantar fasciitis, with support for the arch playing an important part in reducing the immediate pain.

METATARSALGIA

This is a general term to describe pain in the forefoot, between the metatarsal heads. The pain may be associated with, or caused by, structural defects such as an excessively high arch. Treatment aims to correct the defects and improve overall foot function, usually by exercises to improve the balanced working of the muscles in the foot, and by foot supports to improve the mechanical alignment of the joints.

A more specific form of metatarsalgia is a condition called 'Morton's metatarsalgia', or interdigital neuroma. Rather than generalized pain, there is a severe localized pain, which occurs only occasionally, between two metatarsal heads in the forefoot. The pain is relieved if you take off your shoe and rub your foot. The cause of the pain is a swelling in the nerve which lies between the two bones. This results in the nerve occasionally 'catching' and being compressed between the bones, causing a knife-like pain in the area. If the swelling, or neuroma, is big enough, it will feel tender if you press the area between your fingers from above and below your foot, or if you squeeze the forefoot from either side. If the condition is not severe, it may be eased by a pad placed directly behind the affected metatarsal bone, which stops the bone rubbing over the enlarged part of the nerve. However, if the condition is very bad, giving frequent episodes of pain, it is usually necessary to have the swelling removed by an operation.

SESAMOIDITIS

Pain under the ball of the foot, behind the big toe, may be caused by damage to one of the sesamoids, the tiny extra bones lying in the tendon under the first metatarsal head. The bone can be broken by a direct force, especially if this happens when the toes are bent back. Or it may be bruised by persistent jarring, possibly associated with a change in footwear or foot movements. Treatment in the first instance is aimed at reducing pressure over the bones with padding, and improving the efficiency of the small muscles of the foot, especially those which act on the big toe. If the damage is great and the pain severe, it may be necessary to have the sesamoid removed surgically.

HALLUX RIGIDUS

The development of this condition, stiffness in the big toe joint, is a gradual process, often the late result of injury to the big toe or to its joint with the metatarsal head during the growth phase of adolescence. The joint may become painful when stressed, either by forceful bending movements, like those involved in sprinting, hopping, or landing from a jump, or by badly fitting shoes. Usually the pain will subside with rest from painful activities, a soft support under the inner arch, and foot exercises. As in all cases of pain under the front of the foot, it is important to avoid high-heeled shoes, which tilt your body-weight towards your toes. Similarly, you should choose sports shoes with good sole thickness, and avoid any with thick heel wedges but thin support under the front of the foot. If the problem of hallux rigidus becomes long-standing and causes a lot of pain, surgery may be necessary to trim down the bones and relieve pressure in the joint.

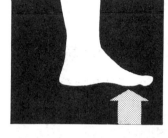

BUNION

In this condition, technically known as hallux valgus, the big toe is pulled towards the second toe, causing the big toe joint with the first metatarsal to form an angled protrusion on the inner side of the foot. The condition is caused by excessive pull inwards from the tendons acting on the toe. Shoes with pointed toes can contribute to the problem. The deformity may become severe, but it is not necessarily very painful. If it does cause pain, pads are used around the protruding bone, to try to prevent friction from shoes over it. Underfoot support, to try to re-balance the weight-bearing load, may be tried. If the joint becomes very painful, and especially if the second toe is crushed by the sideways drift of the big toe, an operation is needed to remove the protruding part of the bone and straighten the joint.

HAMMER TOES

If the tendons of the foot become shortened, possibly in association with

27

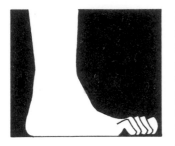

a high arch, or because of tight shoes, they can pull the toes into a deformity in which they are bent up in the middle, so that the ends of the toes are pressed downwards into the ground. This may be painless, and, if so, you should ignore it, beyond checking that you do not wear shoes which rub over the joints of the toes. If necessary, you can place a circle of padding around the bent joints, to prevent friction and blisters. If you also have a high arch, you can use an arch support to relieve excessive weight-bearing pressure over the ball of the foot. If the hammer toes cause severe pain, however, surgery may be neeed to correct the deformity.

TENOSYNOVITIS

The tendons over the top of the foot are vulnerable to this condition. A direct blow, friction from tight shoe-laces, or overuse strain, can cause irritation between these tendons and their covering sheaths. Over-stretching the tendons, by extending the ankle and pointing your foot down, is painful. If you touch the tendons and move your foot, you will feel a slight 'grating' sensation. Specialist treatment may include an injection, or various forms of physiotherapy treatment. You should check your shoes for tightness over the mid-foot, hard lacing eyelets, or roughness on the shoe tongues. If necessary, you should place a padding along the whole tongue. Painful activities and over-stretching should be avoided until the pain and grating have subsided.

BLACK TOE-NAILS

These occur because of a direct blow to the nail, or through friction from tight shoes, or from disruption of the nail, for instance if an inner seam in a shoe catches on the toe and lifts the nail away during movement. The blackness is blood and bruising under the toe-nail. If the nail is painful, with a feeling of excessive pressure, you can ease it by boring through the nail with a sterilized needle, to release some of the blood. If the nail is persistently painful, you should ask your doctor either to treat it, or to refer you to a chiropodist or podiatrist [foot specialist]. You should take care to trim all your toe-nails evenly, straight across the top of the toes, to avoid the further problem of ingrowing toe-nails. Make sure that all your shoes allow plenty of space over the toe-box, with no awkward seams to catch on the ends of your toes.

SKIN CONDITIONS

It is normal to have patches of hardened skin under the main weight-bearing areas of the foot. Your heel invariably has thick rough skin under it. If you play a sport which involves a lot of pivoting on your toes, such as squash, you normally find there is a round area of hard skin directly under the big toe joint. If you have a Morton's foot, you may find a similar callous under the second toe joint. These callouses are created by usage, and they reflect which areas of your foot are subjected to most pressure. They protect the skin from breakdown. However, if too much hard skin forms in one area, it can cause discomfort, and it may mask a skin infection, which might even have caused the excess skin to form. Therefore you should control the hard skin under your feet, by removing excess skin with a removing lotion, or a specially formed skin paring tool. If in doubt, refer to your doctor or podiatrist.

Where your foot is not protected by hardened skin, it may blister, if it is rubbed. Blisters are not dangerous, but you must avoid the risk of infection through them. Protect the skin with dry dressings, especially if the blister has broken, leaving raw skin. Keep your feet very clean, and avoid walking barefoot in dirty areas. Check your socks and shoes for rough edges or tightness which may have caused the blisters. Your shoes should allow plenty of room for foot spread, as your feet widen considerably during running and jumping. If you have blisters over the tops of your toes, your shoes are too narrow. Some sports shoes have reinforced material over the top of the fifth toe area, and this often causes blisters over the toe. If you do marathon running, and tend to get foot blisters only on long runs, you can protect your feet to a certain extent by smothering them in Vaseline. If you suffer from blisters under your feet, experiment with insoles of differing materials, and check that your shoes do not have too firm a grip in the sole, as this can create too much movement between your foot and the shoe in a fast-moving court game like squash.

The feet are very vulnerable to infection, especially among sportsmen, who tend to walk barefoot around communal shower areas. Verrucae, or warts, are a common type of highly contagious foot infection. On the sole of the foot they tend to form embedded painful spots, with a dark central spot surrounded by an extending area of infection. They should be removed, either by using a proprietary substance, or, preferably, by a chiropodist. Athlete's Foot, or fungus infection, is another common problem among sportsmen. It forms patches of white, scaly skin, especially between the toes and under the foot, with irritation and itchiness. It must be treated by a chiropodist, although there are various brand-name preparations which can be used against it. You must avoid spreading the infection, by avoiding ever treading barefoot in a communal area. If your foot infection gives you severe discomfort, and especially if you become

29

aware of a burning, sore irritation, you must check with your doctor immediately, in case you need antibiotics to control a more severe type of inflammation.

General care of your feet involves keeping them very clean. Do not wear your socks for more than one session of sport: wash them each time. Let your sports shoes dry out each time, and do not keep them in a plastic bag between games. Choose socks with as little synthetic material in them as possible. Avoid sports shoes with plastic linings or too much nylon in the uppers, as they tend to make your feet sweat. When you shower in shared facilities, wear rubber sandals, or 'flip-flops', to avoid contacting the floor. Dry your feet thoroughly, and perhaps dust them with medicated foot powder.

Self-help measures for foot injuries

• Contrast baths or ice applications (p. 15) once or twice a day will help relieve pain and swelling, but remember that you should not use these measures if you have any circulatory problem affecting your legs.
• If your foot is swollen put it up on a stool or support whenever possible, to help the fluid drain away.
• Check your shoes: make sure they fit you properly, and have not become tight through shrinkage of the upper, or because your feet have spread. Check for friction points inside, and make sure no stitching has come away to catch on your skin or toe-nails. Replace the insoles if they are worn down. Check for uneven or excessive wear on the outer soles.
• Check your foot mechanics: if your shoes are worn unevenly, your foot mechanics may have contributed to your injury, and it would be advisable to refer to a podiatrist for a specialist assessment. You can experiment with inserts, to see if supporting your foot can help, but you must be prepared to abandon the inserts immediately, if they aggravate the problem. You can buy ready-made 'orthotics' to mould, or soft insoles with arch supports. You can cut shapes from chiropodist's felt to support parts of your feet. To protect your heels there are pads ranging from simple foam to shock-absorbing polymers, or heel-cups in plastic or rubber. If you try out any insert, you must make sure that it does not unbalance your feet, or cause constriction in your shoe.
• Alternative exercise. You must avoid any activities which cause pain over your injury, so you will probably not be able to run or jump, or even walk very far. Swimming and cycling are useful alternatives for keeping fit, and you can do circuit and stretching exercises.
• Specific exercises. As soon as the acute pain of injury has subsided, you

must start doing exercises to strengthen the small muscles of your foot. Start with a few, at intervals during each day, and gradually increase the amount. If you have a tendon strain, you should start stretching the injured area passively as soon as possible, or when your specialist dictates.

Mobilizing and strengthening exercises involve more generalized, co-ordination, movements, and they form the next stage of recovery. You should avoid any of the exercises which cause pain. A daily routine of these exercises, correctly done, lasting about half-an-hour, will help restore function in your foot, and you can then progress gradually back to your sport.

The stretching exercises help to regain and maintain flexibility over the foot, and they can help to counteract cramp. After a tendon or muscle strain, stretching prevents the injured tissues from shortening as they heal.

Foot exercises

STRENGTHENING THE SMALL FOOT MUSCLES

1. With your feet flat on the floor, press your toes down into the floor, not letting them curl, and not moving your ankle. Repeat three times, every hour during the day, if possible. Preferably, do the exercise barefoot, but you can do it wearing shoes, if necessary.

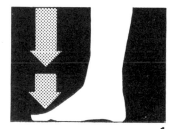

2. Sit with your feet flat on the floor, barefoot. Spread your toes outwards, then together again, keeping them in contact with the floor. (Do up to three sets of ten, twice daily.)

3. Sit barefoot, with your feet flat on the floor. Try to lift up each toe in turn, keeping the others down on the floor. (Three times each toe, twice daily.)

4. Sit barefoot, with your foot supported from the heel to the ball of the foot, and your toes resting on the edge of a weighing scale. Press your toes down onto the scale, keeping them straight, and see how much pressure you can generate. (Up to three sets of ten, twice daily.)

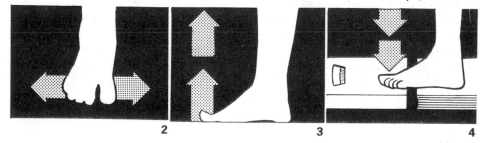

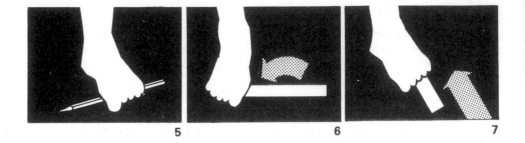

5. Pick up a pencil with your toes, hold it for a count of five, then put it down. (Up to three sets of ten, twice daily.)

6. Spread a string or strap, with one end under the ball of your foot, the other stretching out sideways (towards the other foot). Keeping your heel in contact with the floor, twist your forefoot to work the strap sideways until most of it has passed under the ball of your foot. Then work the strap back again. (Repeat ten times each way, twice daily.)

7. Lay a string or strap lengthways from your heel to your toes, and stretching forward in front of your toes. Keeping your heel in contact with the ground, work your toes down and backwards to pull the whole strap under your foot. (Ten times.)

8. Sit barefoot with your hand resting against the top of your toes. Keeping your ankle still, pull your toes only back against the resistance of your hand. Hold for a count of three, then relax. (Ten times.)

9. Sit barefoot, with your hand under your toes. Keep your ankle still, and push your toes down against your hand, holding for a count of three. (Ten times.)

10. Place a card between two toes, and bend your ankle up and down ten times, keeping hold of the card. Repeat between each pair of toes in turn.

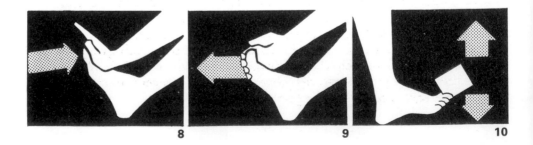

1. Sit, holding one foot in your hands. One hand holds the heel steady, while the other grasps across the ball of the foot. Keeping your foot quite relaxed, twist the forefoot round in circles, keeping your heel as still as possible. (Ten times, twice daily.)

2. Walk around barefoot, on your toes. Do up to six 15-second sets of walking, with 15 seconds of rest, twice daily.

3. Walk around barefoot on your heels, in 15-second sets, as (2).

4. Walk barefoot along a straight line, on the outside edges of your feet. Use a line about two metres long, and walk up and down it ten times.

5. Walk along the line on the inside edges of your feet.

6. Walk up and down stairs sideways, one stair at a time, barefoot. Do ten steps, first up to the right, then up to the left.

7. Walk up stairs sideways, barefoot, taking your lower leg up across the higher one to the stair above it. Come down one at a time. Ten steps each way.

8. Skip on your toes, on alternate feet. Start with half-a-minute, build up to five minutes of continuous skipping.

9. Hop forwards and backwards on your toes, barefoot. (Ten times on each foot in turn.)

10. Hop sideways on each foot in turn, barefoot. (Ten times in each direction.)

11. Alternate leg thrusts: crouch down and balance on your hands. Kick one leg (barefoot) straight out behind you, keeping the other knee bent up to your chest. Then bend up the straight leg, as you kick the other leg straight. Repeat the movements in quick succession, up to twenty times. This exercise is illustrated on p. 118 below, no. 1.

12. Run, barefoot if possible, or in light training shoes, over sand or soft ground. Do up to ten 30-second sets with 15-second rest periods.

13. Squat jumps. Barefoot, stand with one foot in front of the other. Squat down to touch the floor with your fingers, then spring up as high as you can, changing foot positions in the air, to land with foot positions reversed, crouching for the next spring. Repeat the movement without stopping, starting with five jumps, building up to twenty.

14. Heel-toe running. Barefoot, if possible. Jog lightly, landing on your heel, then rolling your weight forward onto the inside of the ball of your foot. Take twenty paces forwards, then ten back in a reverse motion, so that you roll from toes to heel. (Ten times.)

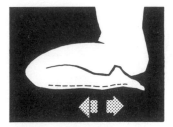

STRETCHING EXERCISES

1. Barefoot, kneel down on a soft surface and sit back on your heels, with the top of your foot resting against the floor. Feel a 'pull' over the top of your feet, and hold the position still for a count of ten. (Repeat three times, twice daily.)

2. If you find (1) easy, put a support under your toes, and kneel down as for (1). Keeping your toes on the support, and your ankle close to the ground, lift your knees to lean back as far as you comfortably can.

3. Sit, holding your foot in your hand. Gently pull your toes and foot downwards, stretching the top of the foot, so that you feel a pull over the toes. Hold to ten, then relax, and repeat the exercise three times.

4. Kneel down on a soft surface, barefoot, with your toes bent in contact with the floor. Sit back on your heels, pressing them backwards, so that you feel a pull under the soles of your feet. Hold for a count of ten, and repeat the exercise three times.

5. Sit, holding your foot in your hands. Gently pull your toes and foot back towards you, so that you stretch the sole. Hold to ten, and repeat three times.

6. Crouch down, with your toes held vertically against a block or step. Lean forwards over your feet, letting your heels come off the ground, but without moving your toes away from their support. Hold to ten, repeat three times.

The Ankle

Bones

The talus, which sits over the heel-bone (calcaneus) in the foot, is the lower part of the ankle. The lower ends of the shin-bone (tibia) and outer leg-bone (fibula) form an inverted U-shaped clamp over it. The bone ends, called malleoli, jut out on either side of the ankle.

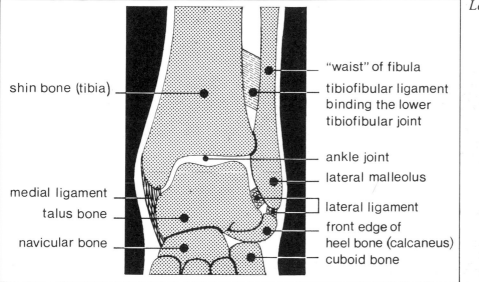

Left ankle, front view.

shin bone (tibia)

"waist" of fibula

tibiofibular ligament binding the lower tibiofibular joint

ankle joint

lateral malleolus

medial ligament

talus bone

navicular bone

lateral ligament

front edge of heel bone (calcaneus)

cuboid bone

Soft tissues

On its inner side, the ankle is guarded by the medial ligament, which fans out from the shin-bone to be attached to the navicular bone, the side of the calcaneus, and the back of the talus. On the outer side, the lateral ligament spreads out from the fibular malleolus to be attached to the talus and calcaneus. The least protected part of the ankle is the front. Above the ankle, but forming part of its structure, is the tibiofibular ligament, a strong band binding the shin-bone and fibula together. The ankle is further strengthened by surrounding tendons, which link the lower leg with the foot. You can see the tendons standing out as tense cords when you move your ankle.

FUNCTIONS

The talus acts as a rounded surface, over which the shin-bone and fibula rock backwards and forwards. The motion is hinge-like, as the bone shapes and ligaments prevent sideways movement. Pointing your toes down is called plantarflexion, and is achieved by your calf muscles. Pulling your foot up towards your shin is called dorsiflexion, and the movement is produced by your anterior tibial muscles on the front of your leg.

The ankle forms a stable link between the rigid lever of your lower leg, and your foot, which can be pliable or rigid. The joint works to produce propulsion. Sprinters and tennis players, who run on their toes, use a limited range of ankle movement, whereas long-distance runners who use heel-toe motion, work their ankles through a full range.

Your ankles also absorb shock. When you jump onto your feet from a

Left ankle ligaments. Medial

Lateral

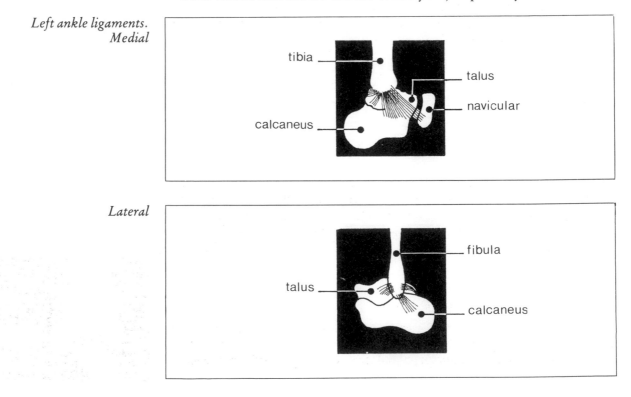

height, your ankles give, lessening the impact transmitted upwards into your back. If you have a stiff ankle, unabsorbed shock can cause joint damage in your legs or back. Restrictive taping often causes this problem in basketballers or gymnasts.

Your ankles are vital to your balance mechanisms. They have a rich nerve supply, which monitors the position of your joints, and provides in-built awareness or proprioception, which corrects you automatically, if you over-balance.

ANKLE PAIN AND SWELLING

If one or both ankles hurt and swell for no obvious reason, you could have an inflammatory or disease-related arthritis; or gout, even if it does not give the more common big toe pain; or a circulatory problem; or a back problem causing referred pain (p. 207). You must keep an accurate record of how the symptoms started, to help your doctor decide whether you need investigations like X-rays, blood tests or bone scans for a full diagnosis.

Ankle injuries

Inversion strain

This is the most common ankle injury because there is a greater range of movement in turning the foot inwards than in any other direction, in the normal foot and ankle joint complex. The outer parts of the joint suffer most, but other structures may also be damaged. The severity of the damage varies according to the amount and direction of the abnormal force applied to the joint.

OUTER LIGAMENT STRAIN

In a minor injury, the lateral ligament may be injured by itself. Although the injury can be painful, there is usually not much swelling at first. Swelling may appear gradually, increasing under gravity's influence.

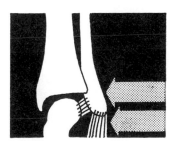

LATERAL LIGAMENT RUPTURE

A more severe injury may tear the lateral ligament completely. The ankle becomes unstable, as the talus is loosened from its restraining clamp, and is able to move too freely. The injury is always extremely painful, and the ankle swells greatly, either all round the joint, or just over its outer side.

SPIRAL FRACTURE OF THE FIBULA

If an inversion strain is severe enough, the fibula may crack, lengthwise. Bruising and swelling appear above the ankle, and the side of the leg is tender to touch. The tenderness indicates the extent of the crack, which may reach as much as fifteen centimetres above the lower tip of the fibula.

AVULSION FRACTURE OF THE FIBULAR MALLEOLUS

A severe strain may leave the lateral ligament whole, but wrench the tip of the fibula away from the rest of the bone.

STRAIN WITH FRACTURE OF BOTH MALLEOLI

An injury severe enough to wrench off the tip of the fibula may cause the talus to jar against the tibial malleolus, breaking that bone as well.

STRAIN WITH FRACTURE OF THE TIBIAL MALLEOLUS

The injury may break the lateral ligament instead of the fibular tip, and so allow the talus to press against the tibial malleolus and break it.

AVULSION FRACTURE OF THE FIFTH METATARSAL BASE

Attached to the end of the fifth metatarsal bone is a strong tendon which passes down from the leg, and lies behind the fibular malleolus at the ankle. If the tendon is over-stretched in a severe inversion strain, it may pull off the tip of bone to which it is attached. Bruising and swelling appear at the side of the foot, which is very sore to touch.

Eversion strain

This occurs where the foot turns outward under abnormal pressure.

FRACTURE OF THE FIBULAR MALLEOLUS

If the outward force on the ankle is hard enough, the talus may press against the fibular tip and break the end of the bone, causing bruising on that side, and swelling all round the joint.

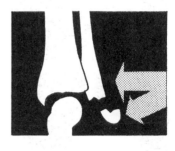

FRACTURE OF THE FIBULAR MALLEOLUS, WITH RUPTURE OF THE MEDIAL LIGAMENT

In a more severe injury, the medial ligament may tear when the fibular malleolus breaks, causing much greater instability in the ankle.

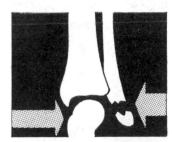

FRACTURE OF BOTH MALLEOLI

A severe injury, instead of breaking the medial ligament, may cause the medial malleolus to give way with the fibular malleolus. The joint becomes unstable, and tender to touch on either side.

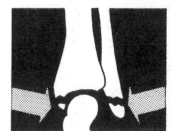

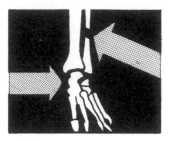

FRACTURE OF THE FIBULA, WITH RUPTURE OF THE MEDIAL LIGAMENT AND SEPARATION OF THE TIBIA AND FIBULA

A very severe eversion force may drive the talus against the fibula so hard that the bone is pushed sideways and breaks, fairly high above the ankle, while the medial ligament also gives way. As the fibula is broken, the ligament binding it to the tibia also breaks. This causes a great deal of swelling, bruising and pain around the ankle and leg, up to the level of the break in the fibula. The ankle may look quite deformed at the moment of injury, although this does not necessarily happen.

Dorsiflexion strain

This type of strain can happen if, for instance, you jump from a height and land flat-footed, with your knee bent and forcing your weight forward over your ankles. A moderate strain pushes the talus between the lower ends of the tibia and fibula, causing stress on the ligament between the two bones. A more severe injury may cause the ligament to break. A very severe injury may break the ligament and cause a crack in the top of the talus or the lower end of the front of the tibia.

Plantarflexion strain

This is the least common type of ankle injury, but it can occur, for instance if you catch the front of your foot while running. A moderate strain will simply over-stretch the front of the ankle. A severe strain, combined with a compression force, may cause a crack in the back of the lower end of the tibia, when the talus is driven against it.

Self-help first-aid measures for the ankle

A slight strain in the ankle can be extremely painful, whereas more severe damage, such as bone fractures or ligament ruptures, may not be evident in the first instance. After an ankle injury, if there is any danger that the damage might be severe, you must attend a hospital casualty department, or see your doctor, as quickly as possible. You may need X-rays and a specialist opinion.
• Ice. The wet towel method is probably the most comfortable for an injured ankle, as you can wrap the towel round the whole joint (p. 15).
• Keep your foot up. Do not sit or stand with your foot on the floor, but

try to rest with your ankle supported on a stool. Use a pillow, or soft support under the leg, to keep your foot higher than your hip. This will help any swelling to drain away, and will stop the swelling from gathering and increasing round the ankle.

- Support. Apply a bandage, extending from your toes to just below your knee. The simplest effective support is an elasticated stocking bandage, which you pull on like a sock, and which you can wear double if your ankle is very swollen. A crepe bandage is better than nothing, but it provides better support if you wrap your foot and leg in a layer of broad cotton wool first. If your ankle is very swollen, an inflatable splint may be used to support it, and contain the swelling (p. 10). Do not put on non-elastic strapping unless you are sure you know what you are doing. The swelling around your ankle may continue to increase for some time after the injury, and if it is held tightly in non-expanding material, the ankle will become painful and hot, and further (avoidable) damage may result.

Don't forget to check the circulation in your foot every fifteen minutes, once you have applied any kind of bandage. Squeeze the big toe-nail on the injured foot, and watch how quickly the redness returns to it. If the toe-nail remains white, loosen or remove the bandage immediately.

- Rest. If your ankle is too painful to walk on comfortably, keep your weight off it. Hop, if necessary, or preferably use crutches (p. 13). Avoid moving the damaged ankle, if possible. You should not try to use it for driving, if it is painful, as you would not be safe, and you would probably be legally liable, if you had an accident.

If you rest with your foot supported, you should try to move the ankle within its pain-free range, in a straight up-and-down direction. Do not try to circle your foot, as this would probably make the ankle more painful.

Phasing your recovery

When recovering from an ankle injury, remember not to try to put weight through your injured ankle, until the initial pain has receded enough to let you walk reasonably comfortably. This could be within three days or as long as two weeks after the injury, depending on how severe it is. You must start moving your foot, unloaded, in a straight up-and-down movement, as quickly as possible after the injury. Once you can bear weight through your ankle, you must start on the balance exercises, which you should continue to do as a routine for at least six months. If the pain and swelling go down enough, you can try to jog, in a straight line on a flat, even surface. Start with no more than about 200 metres, and gradually increase this distance. Allow rest days between running sessions, and gradually try to run faster, building up speed and distance over about four weeks. Stop at once if you find that your ankle becomes more painful or swollen. Reduce your running, and, if in doubt, refer back to your doctor. If you can progress your running without setbacks, you can try running and turning, or shuttle runs (p. 47), after about two or three weeks. At the same time, you should start the dynamic exercises, which will strengthen your ankles to protect them when you run over uneven ground. These exercises are a good test for your ankles. Once you can do them efficiently and without pain, you can consider yourself fully recovered from your ankle injury, and you can safely resume your normal sports.

Remember, during the phases of your recovery, that you must not exercise through increasing pain in your ankle. Stop any painful exercise immediately. To keep fit, meanwhile, you can do any forms of exercise which do not involve the ankle, or sports like swimming or cycling, provided they do not cause pain.

CONTROL PERSISTENT SWELLING

The ankle may continue to swell up after an injury, especially at the end of the day, and if you have to sit or stand still for long periods. It is important to control this swelling, partly because it will make the ankle throb and feel uncomfortable, and because it will interfere with the joint's normal function.

Try to support your leg with your foot up, above the level of your hip, as often as possible during each day. Sit with your foot on a stool, with a cushion supporting your lower leg. If you have to sit with your legs down, straighten out your knee at frequent intervals to lift your foot in the air. If your ankle swells badly each evening, try putting a bolster under the foot end of your bed, to help the swelling to drain overnight, provided that this does not interfere with your sleep.

Keep your foot moving as much as possible. When you are sitting, press your foot up and down at the ankle frequently. While standing, keep your legs moving by bending your knees slightly in turn, or going up and down on your toes, or lifting your toes off the floor by rocking on your heels one foot at a time. Foot and leg movements will help to promote good circulation, and so stop swelling from increasing in the ankle under gravity's influence.

Do a daily session of contrast baths or ice treatment (p. 15), preferably in the evening, or whenever you notice the swelling increasing. A compressive support, such as elasticated tubular stocking, stretching from your toes to your knee will also help to control the swelling. The support should be worn for as long as you have any swelling in the ankle, and especially if you have to stand or sit still for any length of time. If the ankle swelling is mild, with just a slight puffiness, the support need only extend from your toes to just below the fleshy bulk of your calf muscles.

SUPPORT BANDAGING

If your ankle feels weak, you should support it to protect the ligaments. It is never a good idea to strap up an ankle in order to do activities which would otherwise cause pain, as the pain is a warning that the ankle is not ready yet. If you immobilize the joint totally, you interfere with the co-ordinated action between all the joints from your hip and lower back downwards, and you risk damaging these other joints as a result. The purpose of strapping the ankle is to provide a measure of support, and to try to reinforce the natural message system which tells the joint to protect itself, when it is placed under stress. Tape applied to the skin will trigger this protective system, as the skin will hurt if the joint is stretched against the tape (p. 12).

To protect the outer ligament of the ankle, you can wind a two or three centimetre strip of zinc oxide tape from the inner side of the ankle, under the foot, and up the outer side of the ankle, along the line of the fibula, extending to about ten centimetres above the tip of the malleolus. Cover the first strip with two more, each slightly to one side of the first strip. Then cover the tape with a double 'stocking' of tubular bandage, up to the knee if there is a lot of swelling, or to the calf muscles. To protect the inner ligament, start the taping from the outside of the ankle, and reverse the procedure, so that the tape spreads up the inner side of the leg.

SPECIFIC EXERCISES

You should start simple foot movements as quickly as possible after an ankle injury, but you should avoid circular movements which rotate the foot at first. Your doctor or specialist will advise you on when you should start exercising your ankle, and how you should progress through the recovery phases.

Ankle exercises

1. Stand on one leg, keeping quite still and holding your balance. Count how many seconds you can hold the position, and try to increase your time on every repetition of the exercise. Start on your uninjured leg, for comparison, and then practise on the injured leg. (Six times, three to four times daily.)
2. Stand on one leg, holding your balance, with your eyes closed, increasing your time. (Three times, three to four times daily.)
3. Stand on one leg, holding your balance. Stretch your arms above your head, and do arm circles in the air, holding your body still and keeping your balance. Time yourself, aiming to increase your balance time. (Three times, twice daily.)
4. Stand on one leg, with a light football or object in your hands. Throw the ball up in the air and catch it as many times as possible while maintaining your balance. (Two to three times daily.)
5. Stand on one leg; go up and down on your toes as many times as you can. Count the maximum you can do without losing your balance, and aim to increase the number at least once a day. (Try the exercise three times, twice daily.)
6. Stand on one leg with your foot flat on the floor; keeping your foot flat, bend your knee forward over your ankle, then straighten the knee and go up on your toes; bend the knee again in a continuous movement, and continue the sequence six times, building up to fifteen consecutive movements. (Try the exercise three times daily.)
7. Stand on one leg with your toes on the edge of a stair, and your heel over the edge; let your heel drop downwards, then go up on your toes, then back down over your heel, in a continuous movement, starting with six consecutive movements and building up to fifteen. (Three times daily.)
8. Wobble board. A wobble board consists of a smooth flat upper surface, with a rounded rocker attached to its underside. A circular board with a hemisphere underneath is the ideal wobble board, and is available commercially. To make your own, simplified, board, attach a piece of wood, about thirty centimetres square, to a wooden rolling pin, with nails or glue.

Place your foot in the centre of the wobble board, and try to hold your balance, keeping the rim of the board off the floor, and standing perfectly still. Practise on your uninjured foot first, then try on the injured ankle. Time yourself, aiming to increase your balancing time. If you are using

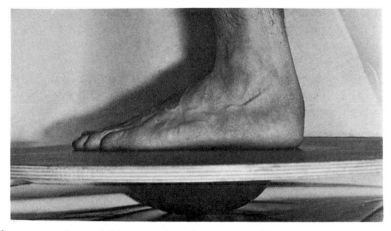

the home-made wobble board, place your foot first in line with the rolling pin, so that you are balancing in the sideways directions (inversion and eversion), and then across the rolling pin, balancing in the forwards and backwards directions (plantarflexion and dorsiflexion). Practise on the wobble board at least twice a day, trying to build up to twenty minutes of continuous perfect balancing.

9. When you can hold your balance on the wobble board for twenty minutes, you should make the exercise more difficult by balancing on the wobble board, and throwing a light ball against a wall, or to another person. Alternatively, you can do arm exercises while balancing, reaching sideways, forwards and above your head, to alter your centre of gravity. Finally, you can try to balance on the board with your eyes closed.

ISOMETRIC EXERCISES

These are useful strengthening exercises to do as alternatives, in situations where you cannot do the balance exercises. For instance, you can practise them sitting at your desk or table, during your working day. You can do them with your feet flat on the floor, or with your legs stretched out in front of you. You should not do isometric exercises, however, if you have a heart condition, or high blood pressure, as this type of static exercise can increase your blood pressure.

1. Place one foot on top of the other. Press the sole of the upper foot downwards, while pressing the lower foot upwards against it, so that the muscle work is balanced and no movement occurs. Hold the pressure for a count of five, then relax completely. Change over to reverse your foot positions, and repeat the exercise.

Ankle

2. With ankles crossed, place the outer edges of your feet together. Press the borders of your feet together for a count of five, then relax.

3. Place the inner borders of your feet together, press for a count of five, then relax.

DYNAMIC EXERCISES

Start doing these, after you have done at least one week of balance exercises, which should be continued as you add the more demanding, co-ordinated exercises into your rehabilitation programme. Leave out any exercise that causes pain. Every day, select six exercises for each of two specific exercise sessions, which should also include some of the balance exercises.

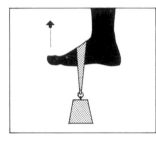

1. Dorsiflexion weights. Sit on a high chair or table, with your knee bent, foot down. Attach a weight over your foot; keeping your knee and ankle at right angles, lift your foot upwards and outwards so that the outer border lifts up. Count to three, then slowly lower your foot to neutral.

Do three sets of ten, starting with about a one kilogramme load, or as much as you can comfortably manage, and increase the weights each week.

2. Cross-legged stand-ups. Sit in a chair with your ankles crossed, feet at right angles to your knees. Stand up without shifting your feet, then lower yourself to touch your seat to the chair without sitting down. Do this as consecutive movements, starting with ten, and building up to thirty.

3. Side-steps. Walk sideways along a straight line, crossing one foot in front of the other. Do thirty paces to the right, then thirty to the left, then repeat the sequence reversing your foot placing.

4. Side-jumps. Keeping your feet together, jump sideways along a straight line, twenty times in each direction.

5. Hop forwards along a straight line for twenty hops, on one leg.

6. Hop sideways on one leg, twenty hops in each direction.

7. Draw two parallel lines, a foot apart. Hop from one line to the other on one leg, moving forwards, thirty times.

8. Alternate leg thrusts. Crouch down on the floor, resting on your hands. Kick one leg straight out behind you to touch the floor, then bend it up to the crouch position again, while you kick the other leg behind you, in a continuous movement. Repeat twenty times.

9. Kicking. Kick a rubber ball against a wall, continuously, twenty times, then do the same with the other foot. Start about two metres from the wall, and gradually increase the distance you have to kick the ball.

46

10. Sideways kicking. Stand sideways to the wall, and kick the ball with the outer part of your foot, continuously, twenty times. Repeat, kicking with the other foot. Start about twelve metres from the wall, and gradually increase the distance.

11. Sideways kicking with the inner foot. Stand sideways to the wall, and kick the ball with the inner border of the foot furthest from the wall. Repeat twenty times on each foot, and increase your distance gradually.

12. Shuttle runs. Mark out a run of about thirty paces. Sprint as hard as you can between the markers, touch the floor and turn back, timing yourself for ten sprints consecutively between the markers. Rest for fifteen seconds, then repeat the sprints. Make sure you turn alternately to each side at the markers. Start with five sprints, with fifteen second intervals between each set of ten, and gradually building up to twelve sets.

13. Backwards figures-of-eight. Run as fast as you can backwards, in figures-of-eight. Start with large loops, then make them as small as you can. Do three sets of ten figures, and gradually build up to ten sets.

14. Bench jumps. Stand with your feet on either side of a bench. Jump up bringing your heels together above the bench, landing with your feet on each side of the bench, as you began. Start with five consecutive jumps, building up to three sets of ten (see illustration, p. 118).

15. Skip. Start by skipping with your feet together. Then skip on alternate feet. Progress to skipping on alternate feet, moving forwards, backwards and in circles. Starting with one minute build up to five minutes of consecutive skipping, for each kind, or as much as you can manage.

Complications

'HIDDEN' LIGAMENT DAMAGE

Immediately after the injury, it may not be possible to assess accurately the full extent of the damage. If the ankle is very swollen and painful, it will not be possible to test the various movements of the joint. Therefore ligament damage will be difficult to gauge. Serious ligament tears may only be discovered when you start to use the ankle again, and find that it remains painful, or functionally limited, long after it has had enough time to heal. A complete tear of the lateral ligament will give a feeling of continuing looseness in the joint, with pain, and a tendency to give way sideways. X-rays will show an abnormal amount of sideways tilt in the talus when the foot is held, usually by a doctor, forced into inversion.

A tear of the tibiofibular ligament, the band which binds the tibia and fibula together over the top of the ankle joint, will cause painful insta-

47

bility when you put pressure through your foot and ankle, for instance in jumping or sprinting. The pain is often worse when the foot is pulled upwards, into dorsiflexion. X-rays taken with the foot held firmly in dorsiflexion will show an abnormal separation between the tibia and fibula. If the ligament tear caused a lot of bleeding, new bone may form in the damaged area between the tibia and fibula, and this too will be visible on X-ray.

Given that it may not be possible to go through the various diagnostic tests immediately after an ankle injury, you must refer back to your doctor, if your ankle continues to trouble you, after the initial pain and swelling have subsided. Your doctor may refer you to an orthopaedic specialist for tests and treatment. Major ligament tears may need to be repaired surgically. The exact method of treating the damage will depend on the surgeon or specialist who diagnoses the problem.

'HIDDEN' BONE DAMAGE

Fractures caused by severe ankle injury may be missed at the initial examination. A spiral crack may extend up the length of the fibula, but it may not be noticeable at the lower end, if X-rays are only taken of the ankle joint itself. Bruising, and perhaps swelling, up the side of the leg indicate the extent of the injury. Your doctor or specialist will probably order check-X-rays, if you are continuing to have pain in the leg. If the bone is cracked, you will have to avoid stressing it, for instance by running or jumping, until it has healed. This usually takes three to six weeks. Unless the fracture is displaced, the specialist will probably think it unnecessary to immobilize the leg in plaster.

OSTEOCHONDRAL FRACTURES

The bone surfaces within the ankle joint may also suffer 'hidden' damage, which only becomes apparent after the immediate stages of the injury. The cartilage, the normal covering of any bone in a moving joint, may be cracked by the impact of injury. In a very severe injury, a fragment may be broken from the cartilage surface, or the bone underneath it. In the ankle, the talus is often damaged in this way on its upper, outer edge within the joint. The inner side of the fibular malleolus may also be affected. The damage usually becomes apparent when you find that you have continuing pain, perhaps with slight swelling, and a feeling of 'clicking' or 'locking' in the joint. Once diagnosed, the condition usually needs a surgical operation to remove any fragments of bone, and to treat the damaged cartilage.

48

EXOSTOSIS

A severe injury may cause irritation over the edge of a bone, causing the bone to produce a little outgrowth of extra bone. This is called an exostosis. In the ankle, this happens most often over the top of the front of the talus, and over the front and back edges of the tibia. Usually the cause is a severe direct injury, forcing the foot into extreme plantarflexion or dorsiflexion. The same movements done repetitively may also cause an exostosis to form. Once the new bone has formed, you will feel pain over it whenever you repeat the movement which caused it. For instance, an exostosis on the front of the tibia, caused by forced dorsiflexion, will give pain whenever the talus is pushed up against the tibia, for instance when you squat or jump down with your foot flat on the ground.

The exostosis will be visible on X-ray. If it causes enough pain to interfere with your activities, it is usually necessary to have the outgrowth removed surgically.

OSTEOARTHRITIS (OSTEOARTHROSIS)

One long-term result of severe damage to the ankle may be the development of osteoarthritis. This may occur when you are in your fifties or older (rarely earlier). It may appear many years after any direct ankle injury. Once arthritis has set in, the bones in the joint may show changes on X-ray, losing their normal smooth outline. Arthritis may occur without causing pain. Equally, it can cause pain, and intermittent swelling, which is usually worse if you have stressed the ankle, for instance by long-distance running, or when the joint is warm, perhaps in bed at night. If you do have pain, and the diagnosis is certain, you should look after the joint, as far as possible: avoid being overweight; avoid exercising to the extent of bringing on the pain; keep the joint as mobile as possible with free exercises, working your feet while sitting or lying down; avoid excessive weight-bearing exercise, such as long-distance running, but keep fit through sports like swimming or cycling, which put less load on the ankle.

If your pain and disability become severe, you should seek specialist help through your doctor. If treatment fails to bring relief, you may have to be referred to an orthopaedic surgeon for an operation to ease the pain, possibly by fixing the ankle so that you cannot move it and irritate the joint surfaces.

The Shin

Bones and joints

The shin-bone (tibia) is the main weight-bearing bone of the lower leg. It transmits the impact forces upwards when you are standing, walking, running or jumping. Its upper end forms the lower part of the knee-joint; its lower end is the top part of the ankle-joint. The inner side of the tibia lies just below the skin. You can feel it clearly defined as a hard band extending from the inner ankle to your knee. The fibula is a much finer bone, on the outer side of the leg, and it does not transmit much loading directly between the body and the ground. The name means 'buckle', and the bone serves mainly as a lever for muscle attachments. It also acts as a mobile surface dissipating some of the forces transmitted through the leg, by bending slightly at its finest point, just above the ankle, when your leg muscles work to propel you forwards or backwards. If you jump down from a height, the shock-absorbing movement of the fibula is enhanced by a sideways separation between the lower ends of the tibia and fibula, which is controlled by the strong ligament which lies between the two bones. At its upper end, the fibula moves less, being tightly bound to the tibia by an encircling ligament. It plays a part in the function of the knee. You cannot move either end of the fibula at will, as the bone only moves in conjunction with your knee and ankle. You can feel the fibula clearly at its top end, and even more so at its lower end, on the outside of the ankle. However, it is difficult to feel the bone moving.

Muscles and tendons

Tendons which move the knee are attached to the upper ends of the tibia and fibula. You can feel the hamstring tendons as hard cords on either side of the back of the knee, when it is bent; the adductors, which pull the thigh-bone inwards, are attached to the inner side of the upper tibia; the patellar tendon, the end of the quadriceps muscle which straightens the knee, is attached to the tibial tuberosity, or bump of bone at the top of the tibia, just below the knee.

The muscles and tendons in the lower leg, below the knee, move the ankle and foot. On the front of the leg, on the outer side of the tibia, are

50

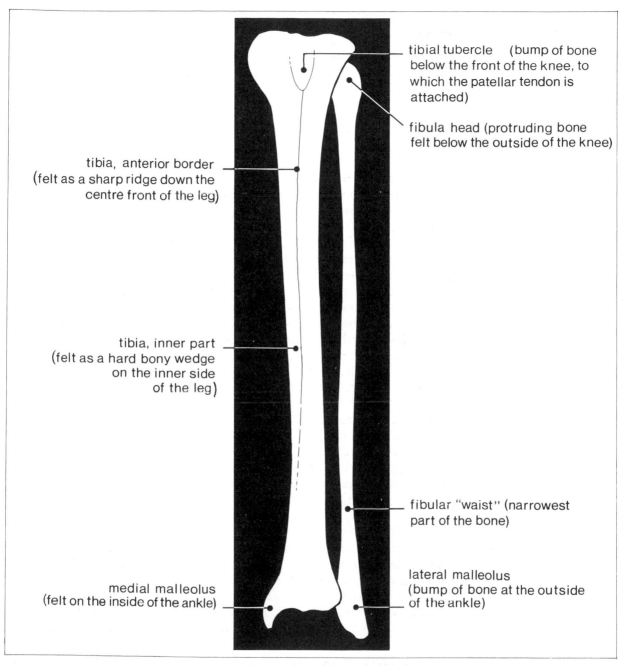

tibial tubercle (bump of bone below the front of the knee, to which the patellar tendon is attached)

fibula head (protruding bone felt below the outside of the knee)

tibia, anterior border (felt as a sharp ridge down the centre front of the leg)

tibia, inner part (felt as a hard bony wedge on the inner side of the leg)

fibular "waist" (narrowest part of the bone)

medial malleolus (felt on the inside of the ankle)

lateral malleolus (bump of bone at the outside of the ankle)

Shin structure, left leg from in front.

51

the muscles which pull the toes and ankle upwards. If you move your foot up and down, you can feel and see the anterior tibial muscles working. If you keep your ankle still, but pull your toes upwards, you can feel and see a similar movement, but less distinctly, as these muscles lie underneath the ankle movers in the shin. When you turn your foot outwards, you can see the muscles contracting down the outside of the leg, and their tendons stand out behind the fibula, winding forward round the lateral malleolus to their anchor points in the foot. The muscles which turn the foot inwards lie behind the tibia, and their tendons wind behind the medial malleolus into the foot. This part of the leg is fleshier, and the tendons less distinct than on the outer side. When you turn your foot inwards, you will notice that a large tendon on the front of the ankle contracts, especially if your foot is pulled upwards. Many of the foot movements involve co-ordinated action between different groups of tendons.

Where they lie close to the ankle, all the lower leg tendons have to change direction to some extent. Where this happens, they are protected by an enclosing sac of synovial fluid, similar to the fluid which lubricates your joints, to ensure free movement. The tendons are tethered close to the ankle by retaining bands, under which they are allowed free play by their self-contained lubrication.

SHIN PAIN

Pain which develops gradually in the leg may be due to an overuse injury, or it may have a less obvious, sometimes sinister, cause. Circulatory problems can mimic the pain of 'shin soreness'. A back problem may cause referred pain, tingling or numbness in the leg, without necessarily creating back pain. Very rarely, fortunately, a bone tumour can be the cause of shin pain.

Accurate diagnosis depends on the correct investigations into, and proper interpretation of, the history and nature of the pain. To help your doctor, try to keep an exact record of your pain: how it started, when it comes on, what makes it worse, and what relieves it.

In sport, the shin can be subjected to a variety of overuse and traumatic injuries. It contains bones, muscles and tendons, and joint structures, all of which may be damaged by misuse or abuse.

Ankle tendon injuries

The ankle tendons can be damaged when you have a severe ankle sprain. However, during the time in which the joint structures heal and are rehabilitated, the tendon strains usually cure themselves naturally, without needing specific treatment. It is relatively rare to suffer sudden damage to the ankle tendons as an isolated injury, without ankle damage. The tendons are more prone to overuse injuries, gradually increasing pain due to excessive use, faulty mechanics, or a change in the way you use your foot and ankle during sport.

TENDON STRAINS

When the tendons around the ankle are strained, you feel pain when you use the affected tendon. For instance, you will feel pain over the large cord on top of the ankle (tibialis anterior tendon) when you draw your foot up hard against a resistance, and the tendon may feel sore to touch. Planting your heel down hard, as in bowling in cricket, will also cause pain. If the outer ankle tendons (peronei) are affected, you will feel pain when you evert the foot, drawing its outer border up sideways. The strained tendons may feel tight when put on the stretch, but they will probably not feel particularly painful.

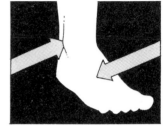

Tendon strains can last for some time, and it is advisable to refer to your doctor for specialist help. You must try to work out the cause of the problem, and avoid any activities which bring on, or aggravate, the pain. Meanwhile, you should gently stretch the affected tendon passively, and you should do alternative training for fitness, such as swimming. If the tendon is sore to touch, and painful on simple foot and ankle movements, it will not stand up to sport. You must not 'try it out' before it has eased out, and regained flexibility.

TENOSYNOVITIS

The enclosing lubricating sheaths around the tendons close to the ankle become inflamed, causing pain when the tendon works, and a feeling of 'grating' or 'crackling' over the affected tendon. Stretching the tendon is also painful. The problem may be caused by friction, for instance if the tongue of your shoe rubs over the tendons on the top of the foot. Restriction may lead to abnormal mechanics, for instance if you tie your shoe-laces too tightly. Or excessive use of the tendon, for instance if you have a particular style of foot movement during long-distance running, can bring on the problem. It is fairly common to have both a tendon strain and tenosynovitis together.

Rest from pain-causing activities is vital to curing the problem. Your doctor may provide, or refer you for, specialist treatment. However, if you try to continue your sport, and you have pain, the condition will not

53

clear up. If you rest, it usually resolves within two weeks. You should try to identify the cause of the problem, to avoid repetition. Check your shoes for faults or signs of excessive wear. If your sports shoes are unevenly worn down, it may be advisable for you to have a biomechanical assessment from a podiatrist. If your foot movements are awkward, you may have caused the tendon problem by placing uneven stresses on the tendon. Orthotic insoles may correct this type of imbalance. Swimming is a possible alternative exercise, while you rest from your own sport, provided you do not feel tendon pain during it. Otherwise, it is best not to do any specific foot or ankle exercises until the inflammation in the tendon sheath has completely subsided, and the 'crackling' feeling has disappeared.

Outer leg pain

TRAUMATIC FRACTURE OF THE FIBULA

If you suffer a severe ankle sprain, you are quite likely to damage the fibula at the same time, as the bone is so fine. This may not be apparent at the time of the injury, as the worst of the pain is usually felt over the ankle ligaments, and the crack may be too fine to be obvious on X-ray, or it may be higher on the bone than an ankle X-ray would show. If you can see bruising extending up the outer side of the leg after spraining your ankle, and if the fibula is sore to touch, you should not do any sport which stresses your leg until the pain has subsided, as you risk creating further damage in the bone.

The fibula can also be fractured in a crush injury, for instance if you are riding a horse which falls and traps your leg underneath its weight. A direct blow, perhaps with a hockey stick, or a kick, can crack the bone.

Provided the damage is not severe, and the bone has not separated or deformed, the specialists do not normally immobilize the fibula in a plaster cast. The bone usually heals within four to six weeks, if you avoid stressing it.

STRESS FRACTURE OF THE FIBULA

The fibula is particularly vulnerable to stress fracture, because of its structure and function. The fracture may occur in any part of the bone's length, but it happens most often about five to eight centimetres above the tip of the lateral malleolus, at the 'waist' of the bone, its finest part, where it allows the greatest degree of movement during leg movements.

The cause of the stress fracture is repetitive muscle pull, beyond the limits of the bone's normal strength. The fracture is always associated with a change and increase in activity. This may be an increase of distance or speed in running; a change of running or playing surface; or an over-enthusiastic return to sport after a lay-off. Long-distance runners in constant training are not normally prone to stress fractures. But if they rest for any time, and then resume training where they left off, they become vulnerable to the problem. Beginners are especially likely to suffer stress fractures, if they over-extend themselves trying to run a set mileage every day, instead of building up their running in gradual easy stages.

In a repetitive activity like running, your leg muscles exert a strong pull against the bones to which they are attached. While your leg muscles pull your foot forwards and backwards, and to a certain extent sideways, to achieve propulsion, they also exert a sideways pressure between the tibia and fibula. The fibula, as a non-weight-bearing bone, is continually bent towards and away from the tibia. It takes only a little extra stress to bend the fibula too much, causing it to crack. Muscle tightness can be a factor, increasing the muscle pull, and altering the angle of the pull. Compressive forces, such as those caused by running on hard surfaces, are not thought to play much part in causing stress fractures.

In the first instance, the stress fracture causes only slight pain in the fibula, starting with an ache, and gradually getting worse, if you try to continue your sport. Diagnosis is difficult, as the fracture will not show on X-ray at first. Sometimes it does not show up until the bone is healing, when a small cloud of new bone can be seen round the damaged part. A bone scan will confirm whether there is a stress fracture, but it is rarely worth going to the trouble of having this done in the case of the fibula. If you are aware of having increased or changed a programme involving repetitive training, and you have pain and tenderness directly over the bone, you can assume that you have a stress fracture.

You must allow the bone to heal by avoiding stressing it with any repetitive, pain-causing activities. Otherwise, you risk shattering the bone completely. Healing usually takes four to six weeks. During this time, you can safely swim, cycle, and do any type of exercise which does not cause pain directly over the bone. When the fibula no longer feels sore, you can try running, starting with a half to one mile only. If you want to build up running mileage, you should progress gradually, adding no more than a quarter to half a mile at a time, and allowing rest days between runs. If at any time you feel the pain recurring, rest for a few days, then start running again on a reduced distance. The fibula may ache slightly after sport, or sometimes simply because the weather is damp.

This is not significant, provided that the ache subsides quickly, and does not get noticeably worse. To avoid any recurrence of the stress fracture, you must remember never to make any sudden increase in sport involving repetitive leg movements.

Two complications may arise with fibular stress fractures: if you have a crack high on the bone, it may affect the nerve which winds round the top end of the bone, causing tingling or numbness in your lower leg. Secondly, in some cases, the bone does not heal readily, so that the pain and tenderness persist for months. In either case, you should refer back to your doctor: you may need to be referred to an orthopaedic specialist for help and cure.

THE PERONEI

The peroneal muscles turn your foot outwards under the ankle. They are very rarely strained or torn on their own. If this happens, you feel pain when you pull your foot up sideways against a resistance, and there is soreness over the fleshy part of the outside of the leg. The problem is usually quickly resolved by daily ice applications over the painful area, and rest from sport until the pain subsides.

It is unfortunately more common for these muscles to be damaged in conjunction with the fibula, the fine bone to which they are attached. Following a severe ankle sprain, you may develop pain along the outer leg, over the peronei. The muscles will probably be partly torn, but the chances are that the main pain is due to a crack in the fibula (see p. 54). If you have developed pain over the peroneal muscles without having an identifiable injury, but following an increase in your sporting activities, it is likely that the muscles have gone into protective spasm to protect a stress fracture in the fibula. If the bone is painful when you press it, treat the problem as a stress fracture, and rest from any pain-causing activities, until your specialist feels you are safe to start doing sport again, and the pain has completely subsided.

RECURRENT TENDON PAIN ON THE OUTSIDE OF THE ANKLE

One condition peculiar to the ankle is recurrent pain and 'weakness' affecting the tendons on the outside of the ankle (peronei), which turn the foot outwards. Usually this comes on after a severe twisting strain at the ankle. Some time after your apparent recovery from the injury, you find that you have continuing pain over the outer tendons, and a sensation of 'snapping'. What has happened is that the retaining band over the tendons has torn, due to the original injury, so that the tendons play over the lateral malleolus, instead of being held in their groove behind the bone.

You can see and feel this happening if you turn your foot inwards and outwards.

The only cure for this problem is surgery to repair the retaining band, and replace the tendons in their groove. Recovery after the operation takes about eight weeks, starting with simple foot and ankle movements, and gradually progressing to normal sport, under the guidance of your surgeon.

THE HEAD OF THE FIBULA

The joint between the upper end of the fibula and the tibia can be damaged by a direct blow onto the head of the fibula, or following a severe knee injury. You feel pain just over the bump of the fibular head, just below the outside of the knee. The pain is usually on the front of the bone. The injury affects the ligaments which bind the fibula to the tibia. In a severe injury, the head of the fibula may be dislocated, and you can see it protruding out of its normal line. In this case, your specialist will probably manipulate it back into place, and then immobilize your leg for a time in plaster. If a chronic weakness develops, and the fibula keeps dislocating during exercise, it may be necessary for you to have the joint repaired surgically. More minor injuries to the tibiofibular ligament may cause pain during knee movements, and your doctor may cure this with an injection. Injury to the tibiofibular joint is relatively rare, but it can be a complication after more serious injuries around the knee.

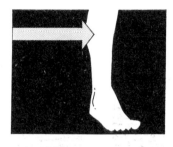

Muscle and tendon injuries around the shin-bone

'SHIN SORENESS' AND 'SHIN SPLINTS'

These are vague expressions, capable of multiple interpretations. They generally describe pain over the front and sides of the leg, especially the lower inner side. The pain may be just a nagging ache, usually associated with running. It will have started gradually, but developed into a notice-able pain over a space of time. It is often difficult to remember how the pain started, as it comes on insidiously. It is usually caused by running, or even walking, unaccustomed long distances, but it is sometimes triggered by an accident such as a kick or direct blow to the leg, developing after the initial bruising and pain have subsided.

ANTERIOR TIBIAL MUSCLE STRAIN

The muscles on the front, outer part of the leg can be strained, or partly

torn, by a sudden awkward movement. You may trip while running forward, so that your toes are caught downwards, and some of the muscle fibres will tear because the anterior tibials are taut and over-stretched. The muscles may be strained by overuse, if your ankle has had to work hard during particular forms of exercise. You may have been running or jumping on awkward surfaces, or trying to push off your toes harder, or landing more heavily on your heel and pulling your toes up hard, during running. The strained muscles feel sore if you press them. They hurt if you contract them against a resistance: pull your toes towards you at the ankle, and resist the upward movement by pressing down against your toes with your other foot.

Self-help measures

- Apply ice over the painful area (p. 15), at least once a day, to stimulate the circulation, reduce any swelling, and so avoid the development of a compartment syndrome.
- Stretch the affected muscles. Sit with your leg straight: press your toes on the injured leg downwards with the other foot or pull down with your hand, until you feel a pull over the injured muscles. Hold to ten, then gently let go.

- Kneel down, with the top of your foot flat on the floor. Gently sit back on your heels, until you feel the pulling sensation. Hold to ten. Do the stretching exercises only within the limits of pain. Do not force the movements, especially not by bouncing. Do not do the kneeling stretch if it hurts your knees. Try to stretch the muscles at least six times, three times a day.
- Rest from any pain-causing activities, until you can stretch the muscles fully, and they no longer feel sore to touch.

Specific complications

If the anterior tibial muscle strain is very close to the central ridge of the shin-bone, the bone covering (periosteum), to which the muscles are attached, may be damaged. The bony ridge will feel sore to touch, and the problem will take longer to clear up.

A more serious complication can be a stress fracture of the shin-bone in its upper central part, caused by excessive pull on the bone from the anterior tibial muscles. The stress fracture may give rise to protective spasm in the muscles, making you think that you have simply strained the muscles, when in fact the muscle pain is a secondary reaction to a more serious problem. Therefore, if your pain does not subside with a reasonable amount of rest and care, you should refer back to your doctor with an accurate account of what has happened.

58

ANTERIOR TIBIAL COMPARTMENT SYNDROME

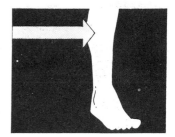

The pain of this condition is felt in the bulky muscles on the upper outer part of the shin. It usually comes on during hard exercise involving running, especially if you have recently increased your sporting activities. For instance, you may play several matches in quick succession at the start of the squash season, or you may change your running training from steady-state, relatively slow pace to fast interval training just before the track season. Changing your sports shoes may alter the mechanics of your leg muscles. The condition may be set up by a direct blow to the muscles, causing swelling and bruising inside them.

The pain usually starts gradually, but it may come on quickly. It is due to over-expansion of the anterior tibial muscles within their containing sheath. The sheath is a relatively inelastic binding holding the muscle bulk. The muscles may tend to swell due to injury, or simply overuse. Each time you use the muscles, they then swell further, and create extra pressure in the sheath. Therefore you feel pain on exercising, but it eases quickly when you stop, and the muscle swelling goes down.

If the condition develops to a severe stage, the leg muscles may be damaged and broken down, due to the reduction in their blood supply. Your doctor will probably refer you to an orthopaedic specialist. Pressure studies may be done, to gauge the exact changes in your leg muscles before, during and after exercise. If the studies show abnormal pressure changes, the usual cure for the condition is a relatively small operation to cut open the restricting fascia, and so relieve the pressure on your muscles.

Self-help measures

• Control the swelling, as soon as you feel the pain come on. Apply ice over the muscles (p. 15), and, if possible, elevate your legs, by sitting with your feet up above the level of your hips.
• Rest from any activities which bring on the pain.
• Try to identify the cause of the problem. Check whether you have changed your sporting activities, or increased the amount you do, so that you can avoid repeating the mistake in the future.
• Check your foot and leg movements. If you feel that faulty mechanics may have contributed to the condition, refer to a podiatrist for a bio-mechanical assessment. If necessary, your podiatrist will fit you with customized orthotic supports.
• Strengthen your feet. If your feet do not function efficiently, you should strengthen the small muscles which control your arches. The simplest exercise is to press your toes down into the floor, keeping your

59

heel on the ground, and not allowing the toes to curl; count to three, then relax. This can be done barefoot or in shoes, sitting or standing, and should be repeated about six times, every hour of the day.

• Strengthen the inner shin muscles. This is the opposite muscle group to the anterior tibials. The anterior muscles draw your foot up and out; their opposing counterparts pull the foot down and in.

Specific exercises:

1. Sit with your legs straight out in front of you; turn your feet inwards, pressing the inner arches against each other, and hold for a count of three; then gently relax. Do this as often as possible each day: you can do it easily if you sit at a desk at work, for instance.

2. Walk about on your toes, barefoot, placing one foot in front of the other, so that your feet turn in at each step. Start with twenty paces twice daily, building up to a hundred paces at a time.

3. Do the specific exercises for both feet (see pp. 31–34). The compartment syndrome normally affects both legs at the same time, but even if, exceptionally, only one leg is affected, it is worth improving the muscle work in both legs equally.

Specific complications

As compartment syndrome pain only comes on when the muscles are swollen enough to create an oppressive restriction within their sheaths, you normally only feel this pain when you have been running or walking for long enough to bring on the muscle swelling. This identifies the condition, and differentiates it from a muscle strain or tear, which would give pain immediately whenever you contract or stretch the muscle. However, the compartment syndrome can be caused by a tear in the enclosed muscles, so the two problems can co-exist. The condition may also be present when you have other shin problems, such as a stress fracture. These complications need careful specialist diagnosis, and curing the various problems takes comparatively longer.

POSTERIOR TIBIAL MUSCLE STRAIN

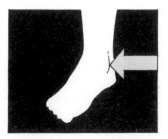

The muscles at the back of the shin, which lie under the bulkier calf muscles, pull your foot down and in, and curl your toes downwards. They may be injured in a severe ankle sprain, especially if the sprain forced your foot outwards, over-stretching the tendons, which lie behind the inner side of the shin-bone.

The tendons may be damaged by overuse strain. This is a common problem among runners, especially if you change your training in terms of distance or speed, or run on a particular camber, or change your running shoes. The condition is often linked to faulty foot mechanics. If you turn your foot inwards when you run, the tendons may become shortened, and therefore inefficient. If you tend to land on the inside of your heel and foot, turning your foot outwards and over-pronating at each footfall, you may be over-stretching the tendons. Worn soles or insoles in your sports shoes can exaggerate faults in foot movements, and so can trigger the tendon pain.

Usually, you feel the pain at the lower, inner edge of the shin, where the posterior tibial tendons lie close to the back of the shin-bone. Sometimes the injury is higher in the muscles, especially where they are attached to the strong ligament that lies between the tibia and the fibula: in this case, you will feel the pain as very deep under the calf, whenever you stress the muscles. As they have so many functions in your foot and leg movements, the muscles can cause pain even when you walk, once they are strained. The pain when walking may be aggravated by the shoes you wear, or by walking on uneven ground. The damaged part of the tendons or muscles will feel sore to touch if you press it hard, and you will feel pain in the same place when you push your toes and foot down and in against a resistance. A specialist can judge exactly which muscle or tendon is damaged by checking precisely which movements cause pain.

Self-help measures
- Ice the painful area (p. 15).
- Support the leg with your foot above the level of your hip, if there is any swelling. Bandage the leg from toes to knee, using cotton wool padding with a crepe bandage, or a stocking bandage, to contain the swelling. Keep your weight off the leg, and refer to your doctor or a casualty department, in case you need X-rays and specialist care.
- After the initial injury, and for the overuse strain, control pain and any swelling by applying ice, or doing contrast baths over the painful area (p. 15). Wear a supporting bandage, and try to rest with your leg supported whenever you sit down.
- Rest from any pain-causing sports, and substitute swimming or cycling, or any pain-free activities, to keep fit.
- Stretch the injured tendons. Stand with your injured leg behind the other, with your feet about 60 centimetres apart. Turn your toes, on your injured leg, inwards, towards the other leg. Keeping your feet flat on the floor, and your back leg straight, lean forward, bending the forward knee, until you feel a pulling sensation on the inner side of your injured leg. Hold to ten, then gently relax. You should feel the stretch directly over the injured muscles or tendons. If you cannot feel this, try turning your toes in different directions to alter the angle at which you are

61

stretching. Repeat the stretch about six times, two or three times a day.
• Identify the cause of the problem. Try to work out whether your pain coincided with any change in your training and sporting activities, so that you can avoid repeating the cause.
• Check your shoes. If the soles or insoles of your sports shoes are worn, invest in new ones. If you have worn down the soles unevenly on each foot, you should refer to a podiatrist for specialist analysis of your foot movements. If you cannot obtain specialist help, you can experiment with ready-made arch supports, or you could try cutting shapes of chiropodist's felt to provide support under your feet (p. 30).
• Strengthen your foot muscles, if it seems likely that your problem is related to faulty foot mechanics. Whenever you can during each day, press your toes down into the ground, without allowing them to curl, count to three, then gently relax. Do this when your foot is on the ground, barefoot or in shoes, sitting or standing, and try to repeat the exercise about five times every hour.
• Strengthen the anterior tibial muscles, the opposite muscle group. Sit on a high chair or table, with a weight resting on your foot, or strapped over the top of your foot. Keeping your knee at right angles, and your lower leg still, pull your foot up at the ankle, and turn it slightly outwards, lifting its outside edge. Hold for a count of five, then relax. Do the exercise ten times, two or three times daily. Start with a very light weight, perhaps one kilogramme, and increase the weight by a little every second day.
• When you re-start your normal sport, make sure you warm-up thoroughly, including stretching the posterior tibial tendons. Start with a little, and gradually increase the amount. Be prepared to rest again, and refer back to your doctor, if the pain recurs.

POSTERIOR TIBIAL COMPARTMENT SYNDROME

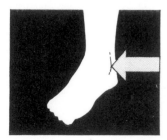

This is like the anterior tibial compartment syndrome (p. 59). The same condition of muscle swelling, tightness and consequent pain can occur within the sheath containing the tibial muscles on the back of the shin. You feel the pain behind the inner side of the shin-bone, mainly in its central and upper part, rather than close to the inner ankle. It comes on, typically, after a change or increase in sporting activities involving running or jumping, and it tends to recur, with increasing severity, each time you repeat the activities. The pain eases quickly when you stop exercising, especially if you apply ice to the painful area, and sit with your leg up. To find the cure, you must first define the cause, and correct this, if possible. You should rest from activities involving running and jumping for long enough to allow any continuing swelling to subside. If the problem becomes severe, it may be necessary for you to have an operation to decompress the tight muscle sheath.

Because the tibial tendons lie so close to the shin-bone, it is often difficult to distinguish between a posterior tibial tendon strain and a tibial stress fracture. The two problems often coincide, as the stress fracture is caused by excessive pull from the tendons against the bone, and tendon tightness and pain may be a protective spasm around the area of a fracture.

Injuries to the shin-bone

TRAUMA

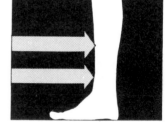

The shin is vulnerable to knocks, especially in field sports such as football and hockey, where tackles often result in kicks to the shin from a boot, or direct blows from a stick. In hurdling, you may catch your trail leg on the hurdle, hurting your shin. On the inner side of the front of the shin, the bone lies very close to the skin, without any protective muscle or fat covering. You can feel the hard edge of the bone for the whole length of the shin. There is no cushioning to absorb the shock of a blow. When the shin-bone is hit, bruising and possibly swelling form directly over the bone. If the blow is hard enough, the covering of the bone, called the periosteum, may be damaged, and the bruising may gather, like a kind of blister, between the bone and the periosteum. This is called a sub-periosteal haematoma. An extremely hard blow to the shin bone may damage the bone itself. In this case the bone feels very tender to touch, and bruising and swelling become visible over the damaged part.

First-aid in this kind of accident aims to control the internal bleeding over the bone. Ice must be applied immediately, preferably as a pack which can be held firmly over the shin (p. 15). Then you must apply a soft padding over the area, covered with a firm bandage extending from your foot to your knee. If the skin has been broken by the blow, you must wash it thoroughly with soap and water before applying the bandage over clean or sterile dressings. You must also check whether your anti-tetanus protection is up-to-date, and, if not, see your doctor or a casualty officer for a booster. Once the bandage has been applied, try to keep your weight off the leg, preferably supporting it up. You should see your doctor or attend a casualty department as quickly as possible, in case the bone needs X-raying.

You should keep the leg bandaged, with a dressing over the bruised area, for as long as you have pain and swelling. Once the initial discomfort has worn off, after two or three days, you will probably see a well-defined rounded area of swelling over the shin. Do not rub this. You should aim to stimulate the circulation around the bruised area by applying ice over and around it, at least twice a day. You can apply a heparinoid cream around the edges of the bruising, to help absorption of the extra fluid trapped under the skin. You should see the area of bruising and swelling reducing each day: if not, you must check back with your doctor for treatment. While you can see the visible signs of damage, you must not do any sport which involves running or jumping, and you must be extra careful to avoid hitting the shin again. When the visible bruising and swelling have disappeared, you can safely resume sport again, but if you can still feel tenderness over the bone, you must protect it with padding, if there is a risk of another direct blow to the area. It may take up to eight weeks for this kind of bone bruising to heal. If you try to resume sport too soon, one of the risks you take is of incurring a stress fracture.

STRESS FRACTURE

Tibial stress fractures are often confused with tendon or muscle strains. You may indeed be unlucky enough to suffer from both problems at the same time. The two problems may be directly related: muscles and tendons lying close to a bone, or attached to it, often tighten up in a protective spasm if the bone is damaged in any way; damage to the muscles or tendons may alter their angle of pull against the bone to which they are attached, and so cause a stress fracture in that bone.

Like any other bone, the tibia may suffer a stress fracture anywhere in its length. The fracture is a crack in the bone, caused by excessive strain against the bone from muscles or tendons pulling hard through their attachments to the bone. The fracture is always related to an increase or change in an activity involving repetitive movements. Runners and joggers are especially vulnerable to tibial stress fractures when they first start running on a daily basis; or they increase their mileage; or change training patterns, running surface, or sometimes even shoes. Compressive pounding forces are of little significance in causing stress fractures. The key factor is muscular pull against the bone. Your bones are only as strong as they need to be. If they are subjected to an increased strain, whether through increased activity, or an alteration in the angle at which the muscles pull against the bone, part of the bone structure may break down, forming the crack. The exact point at which this happens may be determined by your running style. If you turn your foot inwards as you run, you may overwork the posterior tibial tendons which lie close to the lower inner edge of the shin-bone. This is a common site of 'shin soreness' in runners, and the result may be a stress fracture in the lower part of the bone. The same problem may be caused by continual over-stretch of the posterior tibial tendons, if you tend to pronate your heel during running, landing on the inner edge of the heel. If you run pulling your foot up hard, as you have to when you run up a hill, you may suffer a stress fracture in the upper central part of the tibia, where the anterior tibial muscles are attached. If you run on camber, or round the bends of a running track, your leg muscles have to work at different angles on each leg, and this can have a bearing on where the stress fracture happens. Another factor which can alter the functioning of your leg muscles is a previous injury in some other part of the leg, which may make you unconsciously change your gait.

The cause

The cause of the stress fracture is always some change of routine, causing an increase in workload for which your bones and muscles are not prepared. What you feel at first may be little more than a mild ache which comes on after you have been exercising. If you keep running, the pain gradually gets worse, until your shin hurts when you walk, and even at rest in bed at night. The pain may ease with a few days' rest, tempting you to keep running, but then the pain gets progressively worse with each session.

Tibial stress fractures are especially difficult to diagnose. The signs of the crack are not dramatic. The bone feels sore to touch where it is damaged, and painful in the same region when you run. There may be some swelling and redness over the fracture. A child with a stress fracture may limp, without being able to pinpoint why. But the pain felt may seem no worse than the pain of a muscle or tendon strain. Circulatory problems may create similar shin pain. X-rays may fail to show up the bone damage of a stress fracture in its early stages. The crack will only show if the X-rays are angled in just the right direction, or if the crack is healing or widening. Bone scanning, a specialist investigation, is the only way to identify with certainty whether or not there is damage to the bone. If the scan is positive, and you know you have increased your activities involving repetitive leg movements, the diagnosis of a stress fracture can be confirmed.

If for some reason you cannot have a bone scan, diagnosis of the problem will depend on an analysis of the causative factors in your shin pain. If you have had a change in your training, or resumed running after a lay-off, and your shin pain is getting worse each time you run, with the bone becoming increasingly tender to touch, you must assume that you

65

have a stress fracture. The tibia is a weight-bearing bone, as your body-weight is transmitted directly through it each time you put your foot to the ground. If the fracture is transverse, eating horizontally into the strong outer struts of the bone, there is a real danger of the bone breaking completely, if you continue running. Most often, runners suffer from oblique, diagonally angled, stress fractures in the tibia, which carry less risk of total disruption to the bone. However, the exact diagnosis of the type of stress fracture is a matter for the specialists. If in doubt, the safest course is to fear the worst, and avoid the risk of disaster.

The cure

Rest is the only cure for a stress fracture. If a transverse fracture is diagnosed on X-ray or bone scan, the specialist may decide to immobilize your leg in a plaster cast, to minimize the risk of the bone shattering. Otherwise, it is rare to immobilize a stress fracture, partly because it is not necessary for the majority of oblique fractures, and partly because total immobilization tends to weaken the bone, creating the possibility of another fracture occurring when you resume sport. Rest simply means avoiding activities which cause pain. You should not run or jump, or even walk too far. However, you can safely keep fit with other sports which do not involve loading your legs with your full weight. Cycling, swimming, stretching and circuit exercises may all be suitable alternative fitness activities. The rest period must be for at least four weeks, or longer if necessary. Check X-rays or bone scans will show whether the crack is healing. If in doubt, continue your rest period for as long as the bone feels sore to touch.

Avoid recurrence

When you have recovered from the stress fracture, you must resume training cautiously, to avoid a repetition of the problem. If you suspect you have a bio-mechanical defect in your foot movements, it is worth referring to a podiatrist for specialist analysis. However, bio-mechanical correction will neither shorten the healing time of the fracture, nor make it less important to rebuild your training in carefully graded stages. Start running with a mile or less, wearing well-cushioned training shoes. It does not matter whether you run on pavements or grass, provided you do only short distances. Allowing rest days between runs, build up your mileage by no more than one mile per week for the first ten weeks. If you feel the shin pain returning during or after a run, do not run again until the pain has disappeared, and avoid increasing your running until you are sure there is no sign of the pain recurring. If you have no setbacks during the ten weeks, you can then build up your distance a little more quickly, and start to run more frequently, if you wish. Keep up a daily programme of stretching exercises, especially for the legs. To maintain overall fitness, continue swimming or cycling, at least through the first ten weeks of resuming running.

At no stage should you ever make a sudden change in the amount you do of any repetitive activity. Allow your body to adjust to any training changes. Avoid long-distance running when your leg muscles feel tired or fatigued. Do not try to run through the pain of an injury. If you have a rest period for illness or injury, resume your training very gradually, building up in easy stages. Never re-start a training programme where you left off. Trying to 'catch up' with a fitness schedule will only make you more vulnerable to a recurrence of the stress fracture, or some other debilitating injury.

PAIN ON THE TIBIAL TUBERCLE

The tibial tubercle is the prominent bump of bone, just below the front of the knee, to which the patellar tendon is attached. This tendon is the end part of the quadriceps muscle group, which forms the main bulk on the front of the thigh, and which acts to straighten the knee against gravity, or to control the movement of bending the knee in the direction of gravity. The tibial tubercle is a knob of bone which is only lightly connected to the tibia in childhood, but which gradually fuses onto the shaft of the main bone, completing the fusing process at about the age of sixteen.

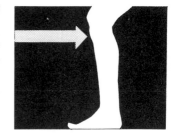

The patellar tendon pulls directly on the tibial tubercle when the quadriceps group is working. If the pull becomes excessive, the tendon can exert enough pressure to pull the knob of bone away from the tibia. This can happen as the result of a single overloaded effort which snaps the tubercle off the bone. Weight lifters lifting very heavy weights from the deep squat position are vulnerable to this injury. The tubercle can also be disrupted by cumulative stress. Long-distance runners can strain the patellar tendon and its attachment by increasing their mileage or speed. Hill running, especially downhill, stresses the tendon and the quadriceps group, because the muscles have to perform eccentrically under load. Direct pressure over the tubercle can also cause problems, for instance if you do too many knee-drops on a trampoline.

When the tendon attachment and the tibial tubercle are damaged, you feel pain localized over the bone whenever you work the quadriceps under load, for instance when you run, squat or kick. You feel soreness over the bone if you press it, or try to kneel on it. Stretching the quadriceps may cause a feeling of stiffness in the patellar tendon, without necessarily causing pain over the tibial tubercle. It is fairly common,

67

especially among children, for both legs to suffer the injury at the same time.

In the adult, damage to the tibial tubercle caused by repetitive tendon pull is really a type of stress fracture. Like any other stress fracture, the damage is caused by an increase or change in your training routine. If you continue the causative activity despite the pain, you will aggravate the condition. Rest will cure the problem, provided you rest for long enough. You will then be safe to resume normal sports, provided you do so in easy stages, resting again at the first sign of pain recurrence. If the tibial tubercle is completely disrupted in an avulsion fracture, caused by a sudden overloading pull from the tendon, the only cure is surgical repair. You will not be able to move the knee at all, so the leg must be immobilized, and you must be transported to hospital immediately. The same treatment applies to the child's avulsion fracture.

OSGOOD-SCHLATTER'S DISEASE

Overuse injury to the tibial tubercle in childhood should be considered as a more serious problem than when it occurs in an adult. Tibial tubercle pain is classified as a growing problem, and has a special name: Osgood-Schlatter's disease. It is not a disease as such, but a specifically activity-related injury. It tends to happen to boys between the ages of eleven and sixteen, but it can happen to younger children. It often comes on if the child has been doing increasing running mileage, or cross-country running over muddy, awkward ground. Weight-training at too young an age is another common cause of the problem. Once the child has pain over the tibial tubercle, the problem tends to be persistent. The pain may be present every time the child runs, plays football, cycles or jumps. It will be eased by complete rest, but it may take up to two years to disappear. If the problem becomes severe, the child may need an operation to stabilize the tibial tubercle and relieve the pain. A severe case of Osgood-Schlatter's disease may have long-term consequences. The tibial tubercle is one of the growth points where two parts of a bone fuse together. If this is badly damaged during the growth phase, it may fail to fuse properly, perhaps leaving loose flakes of bone at the tendon attachment, and causing recurring pain in adult life during any sports involving knee movements.

Although complete rest from sport is necessary to cure Osgood-Schlatter's disease, specialists often allow the child to do sport within the limits of pain, if the problem is not severe, as it is likely to take such a long time to go away completely. The guideline is to avoid any activity which creates more than a tolerable level of discomfort. If pain persists after a particular activity, then the child must rest, and avoid that activity in future.

Applying ice over the knee can help to relieve any immediate discomfort (p. 15). Support bandages will not help in any practical way, but if the child feels more comfortable wearing one, there is no reason not to. Good shock-absorbing shoes can help reduce the tension of the pull from the patellar tendon on the tibial tubercle: well-cushioned insoles should be inserted into all the child's shoes, provided they are big enough. If the child has an obvious mechanical defect in his feet, such as flattened arches, he should be referred to a podiatrist, as foot mechanics have a direct bearing on abnormal stresses at the knee.

Specific exercises

Osgood-Schlatter's disease is unfortunately a common problem among children, especially as more children are taking up training patterns which are geared to fully developed adult bodies. When the problem occurs, the child should be encouraged to take up a diversity of sports, and avoid concentrating on a single activity which might cause pain. Recreational rather than competitive sports are recommended, to avoid overtaxing the child's growing frame. The following exercises are recommended.

1. The child must maintain good muscle power around the knee, and full mobility in the joint and its muscles. Whenever there is pain round the knee, the natural tendency is to keep the knee slightly bent to relieve it. This must be counteracted by maintaining strength in the inner range of the quadriceps function. The child should practise straightening the knee hard, holding it tensed for a count of three, then gently relaxing. This exercise should be repeated two or three times, every hour of the day. It can be done sitting down or standing up, so it should not be difficult to incorporate into a daily routine.

2. Quadriceps flexibility can be maintained by stretching the group passively: the child lies face down and pulls his foot gently towards his seat with his hand, until the limit of the stretch is reached. The position is held for a count of ten, then gently let go. This exercise should be done six to ten times, twice a day, and before and after any exercise.

The Calf Muscles and Achilles Tendon

Gastrocnemius and soleus form the main bulk of the calf musculature. Gastrocnemius forms the bulky part of your calf, and extends from just above the back of the knee to your heel. If you stand on your toes and watch the back of your leg in a mirror, you can see the two parts of gastrocnemius standing out, and you can see where they unite to form the Achilles tendon, below the fleshy part of your upper calf. Soleus lies under gastrocnemius, and is attached to the back of your leg bones. It 'feeds in' to the Achilles tendon, to be attached to your heel. You can see soleus as the fleshy part of your leg on either side of your Achilles tendon.

The Achilles tendon itself is extremely thick and strong. It is attached to the middle of the back of your heel, and is separated from the upper part of the bone by a bursa, a small sac of fluid, which allows friction-free movement.

FUNCTIONS

Gastrocnemius and soleus contract to pull your heel back and up, when you point your toes down, or stand on your toes. They create the spring movement when you walk, run, jump and hop. Sprinters have shortened, powerful calf muscles, whereas oarsmen lengthen their calves through the fixed position of their feet in the boat. Gastrocnemius also helps to bend the knee against strong resistance, for instance if you do hamstring curls with heavy weights in weight-training. If your hamstrings are weakened, for instance through repeated injury, your gastrocnemius may gain strength to compensate, and help to bend your knee. Soleus does not affect the knee, but it is more active as a postural muscle, helping to control your leg over your ankle, against the influence of gravity.

CALF PAIN

Gradual, or unexplained pain in your calf can be caused by a circulatory

70

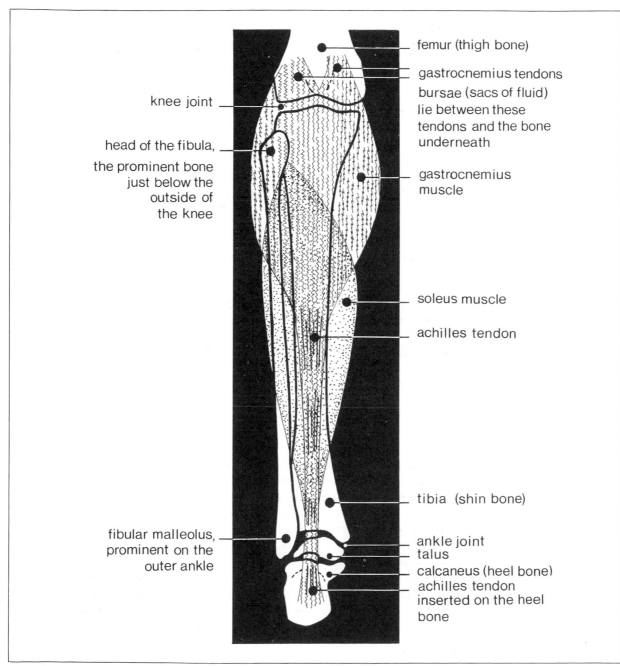

femur (thigh bone)

gastrocnemius tendons

bursae (sacs of fluid) lie between these tendons and the bone underneath

gastrocnemius muscle

knee joint

head of the fibula, the prominent bone just below the outside of the knee

soleus muscle

achilles tendon

tibia (shin bone)

fibular malleolus, prominent on the outer ankle

ankle joint
talus
calcaneus (heel bone)
achilles tendon inserted on the heel bone

Calf structure, left leg.

71

problem, like intermittent claudication, a condition of deficiency in your arteries; or thrombosis, blood clots in the veins; or by a back problem, giving referred symptoms into your leg (p. 207). You must record when and how the pain started, and any other symptoms, such as episodes of calf cramp, or even apparently unrelated problems, to help your doctor make an accurate diagnosis.

Varicose veins

This complaint is a common circulatory complication in the calf. Your veins are tubes which carry blood back to the heart. Unlike your arteries, they contain no muscle of their own, but operate under pressure from active muscles outside them. The blood in the veins is squeezed, and moves forwards. Back-flow is prevented by a system of valves. The blood in your lower leg is just starting its return journey to the heart, so it has to travel the length of your leg and trunk, usually against the influence of gravity. The calf muscles play a vital part in initiating the flow of blood upward in the veins.

Normally, two sets of veins take the blood back to the heart. The superficial veins lie close to the skin, and blood is pumped through them at relatively low pressure. The deeper veins operate at a much higher pressure. The two sets are linked by connecting veins, but protected by a system of valves. If the valves become faulty, there may be back-flow from the deep into the superficial veins, which are then subjected to higher pressure flow than normal. The superficial veins may then become swollen and engorged, standing out and looking 'knotted' under your skin.

Varicose veins can be hereditary, or they may be due to long periods standing still, for instance, if you have to stand up at work all day every day. Exercise is important to prevent them, and it can help in the early stages of the complaint. The more you use your calf muscles, the more efficiently the 'muscle pump' works to create blood flow in your leg veins. Stretching and strengthening exercises will help improve the calf muscle pump. If the varicose veins do not cause pain, there is no real need to have treatment for them, unless you are very worried about their appearance.

However, if the veins become very engorged, they will be painful, and they may burst. At this stage, exercise may aggravate the condition, and you will feel that the veins are more painful if you work the calf muscles. You should refer to your doctor for treatment, which may consist of injections or an operation. Meanwhile, you should protect your veins by wearing a soft stocking bandage stretching from your toes to your knee, to help the venous blood flow upwards; avoid standing still for long

72

periods, and try to keep your legs moving; do not wear socks with tight garters; do not sit with your legs crossed; when you rest, try to support your foot up, to help your blood to drain towards your heart; if you have to travel in an aeroplane, wear a double layer of stocking bandage, keep your feet up, if possible, and move around as much as possible.

Once your varicose veins have been treated, there is usually no reason why you should not return to all your normal sporting activities, provided your specialist has no objection.

Calf injuries

ACHILLES TENDON, AT ITS INSERTION ONTO THE HEEL-BONE

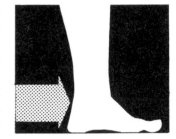

The tendon can be strained, or suffer a minor tear, at or close to its point of insertion on the heel. Or the bursa between the tendon and the upper part of the bone may become inflamed. The condition may be complicated by small bony outgrowths (spurs) forming on the heel-bone. The spur sometimes becomes detached, forming a focal point of pain.

The pain usually comes on gradually, but it can be sudden. You feel it on tiptoeing or running, and the tendon feels tender over the heel when you press on it. The cause is usually excessive use of the calf in extreme ranges of movement, as, for instance, when you run fast up a steep hill. Rough, protruding linings in your shoes can also be a cause, producing bruising and tenderness over the heel.

Specialist treatment may consist of an injection, or physiotherapy treatment. Your doctor may have X-rays taken, to make sure that there is no damage to the heel-bone, or spur formation. It may be necessary to line the backs of your shoes with felt or padding, to create a smooth surface. Sorbothane heel pads may help to reduce shock absorption, so easing the strain on the tendon. This injury is slow to heal, so you must rest it.

ACHILLES TENDON, JUST ABOVE THE HEEL-BONE

The tendon may become sore, thickened, and tender to touch at any point up to about five centimetres above the top of the heel-bone. Some of its fibres may be torn or degenerated, while the tendon's covering becomes thickened. The tendon feels stiff first thing in the morning, and on starting exercise. When you stand on your toes barefoot, the tendon hurts at first, but then eases. However, it remains very sore to touch.

The cause is almost invariably friction from shoes with high backs, or

73

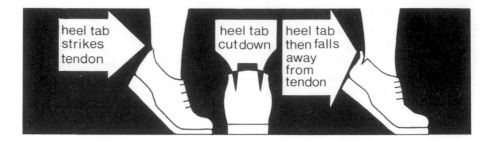

heel-tabs. The first priority is to remove the cause: cut down the heel-tabs with two vertical slits on either side of where the tendon lies, to the level of the back of your ankle, usually about five centimetres above the upper edge of the sole. If there is no spasm causing pain higher up where the tendon joins the calf muscle, you can safely resume running and sports, provided you warm-up and warm-down thoroughly. You will normally find that the tendon feels stiff at first, but then becomes less painful as it is eased out by movement. If the pain recurs during sport, and gets worse, you should re-check your shoes. There may be a rough edge rubbing the tendon, or you may have worn down the insoles, lowering the heel in the shoe, and so reproducing friction over the tendon. The tendon may remain thickened and sore to touch for months, possibly years, but provided you feel no pain during exercise, it is safe for you to continue your sport.

ACHILLES TENDON RUPTURE

This may happen at any level in the tendon. A sudden severe pain occurs, which often feels like a violent blow to the calf. Swelling and bruising may appear, and the two broken ends of the tendon often leave a visible gap. Usually, you fall at the moment of injury, and walking is then too painful to try.

The cause can be a blow to the muscle or tendon when they are tensed. More often, the injury is caused by strenuous activity involving the calf, such as sprinting or playing squash. The injury may occur at the beginning of the activity, when the muscles are 'cold' and tight, or towards the end, when they are fatigued.

At the moment of injury, it may not be clear whether the tendon is completely torn. One test for this is to lie on your stomach, and have someone squeeze the calf muscle bulk gently: if the tendon is partly intact, the foot will move to point downwards, but if the tear is complete, the foot will remain still.

74

This injury requires specialist treatment, which may consist of surgery, to stitch the two tendon ends together, or immobilization in a plaster cast, allowing the tendon to heal naturally. After surgery, you can usually resume sport within three to four months. If your leg is immobilized, the plaster will be on for eight to twelve weeks, so, after rehabilitation, you will probably resume sport about six months after the injury.

PARTIAL RUPTURE

Strenuous exercise involving the calf, especially if the muscles are cold, tight or fatigued, can cause a partial tear anywhere within the muscle bulk or tendon. If the injury is severe, it may feel like a blow to the calf, and swelling and bruising may appear. The point of injury will feel tender to touch, and walking will be painful. However, you will still be able to point your toes down, using the calf muscles, and squeezing the calf above the level of injury will produce the same movement.

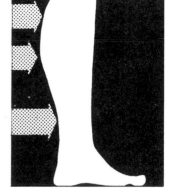

A severe partial rupture may take nearly as long to recover as a total rupture. A milder injury may improve markedly within a couple of days, and may recover within three weeks. There is usually no need to immobilize the leg in this injury, as early movement, within the limits of pain, will promote healing.

GASTROCNEMIUS TENDON INJURY

One or both of the gastrocnemius tendons may be damaged where they attach to the thigh-bone. Usually there is a small focal spot of pain, tender to touch, and the same pain can be felt if you use the calf muscles with effort, for instance sprinting up stairs. The damage may be a tear in the tendon, or inflammation in a bursa under the tendon. The injury may be sudden, on over-stretching, but more often it occurs gradually, during or after activities in which the knee is bent against strong resistance.

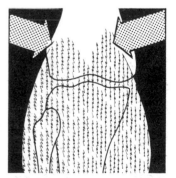

This injury is slow to heal: specialist help might consist of injection, or physiotherapy treatment.

Self-help measures for the calf and Achilles tendon

- First-aid for the sudden, traumatic tear in your calf muscles consists of applying ice (p. 15) over the painful area. Try to support your leg up, rather than keeping your foot down, to prevent any swelling from tracking down into your foot. Rest your leg on a cushion, not a hard surface. Do not try to walk on the injured leg. Use crutches, or lean on a

Calf and Achilles

friend and hop, if you have to move around. As quickly as possible, you should be taken to the local casualty department or your doctor, in case the injury needs to be repaired surgically.

• If you do not need specialist treatment, or when you are on the recovery phase after surgery or immobilization in plaster, you may need to continue applying ice to your calf, if soreness and swelling persist.

• As soon as the initial pain of the injury subsides, or as quickly as your specialist allows, you should start regaining flexibility in your injured calf. After a severe injury, this will mean simply trying to put your heel down to the ground, without forcing the movement or causing increasing pain. As soon as you can do this, you should start doing the passive stretching exercises for the calf. Try to do about six stretching exercises every hour, if possible.

• If you can take weight through your leg, but have difficulty walking normally, you should wear heeled shoes, or put thick pads under your heels. Try to walk normally, and avoid limping.

• Once you can put your injured leg flat to the ground, you should start doing strengthening exercises, avoiding any movements which hurt, but gradually building up the number of exercises you do. Start and finish any strengthening session with passive stretching for the calf.

• Alternative fitness training at this stage can consist of swimming, perhaps cycling (pedalling through your heel) and circuit exercises which do not stress your calf.

• If you regain good flexibility in your injured calf, and are able to build up strengthening exercises without setbacks, you should progress to the dynamic strengthening exercises, always maintaining stretching exercises before and after a session. When you have progressed to the most demanding of these exercises, you can safely resume your sport.

• To prevent a recurrence of your calf injury, you must maintain good flexibility in the muscles, so a daily session of calf stretching is advisable, and you should always do calf stretching in your warm-up and warm-down routines. If you have had cramp in your calves, perhaps at night, you should drink plenty of water, complemented by moderate salt on your food. If the cramp persists, you should consult your doctor. If you wear high-heeled shoes during the day, you must take extra care about stretching your calves before you start exercising in flat shoes. If your calves feel tight, you should not do sport until they are loosened by stretching, as they will be vulnerable to re-injury. As a preventive measure, you should trim down the heel-tabs on your sports shoes, even if you have not had a friction problem from them (p. 73). If the tabs are high, they may cause a reaction in the Achilles tendon, leading to spasm where the tendon joins the calf muscles: this tightness can cause a tear.

76

Calf exercises

STRETCHING EXERCISES

1. Single calf stretch. Place one leg behind the other, with feet parallel, and back heel flat on the ground. Bend the forward knee, until you feel a 'pull' on the calf of the hind leg. Hold this position to ten, then slowly release. Repeat with the other leg back.

2. Two-leg calf stretch. Lean forwards against a wall or support. Move your legs backwards, keeping your heels flat, until you feel the pull on both calves. Hold to ten.

3. Single or double-leg calf stretch, sitting. (Do not try this exercises if you cannot reach your toes easily.) Sit on the floor, with your legs straight out in front of you; or one leg forward, the other tucked out of the way sideways. Reach down to hold one or both feet in your hands, keeping your knees straight, and pulling your toes towards you with your hands. Hold to ten.

4. Soleus stretch. Standing with your heels flat on the ground, bend both knees, letting your ankles bend as far as they can while your heels stay flat. Hold to ten.

5. 'Extra' calf stretch. Stand with your toes on the edge of a step, or place a block, about five centimetres high, under your toes. Lean forward over your toes, letting your heels drop down, if you are on a step, and hold for ten.

Start with a few at a time, and build up gradually to three sets of ten for each exercise.

1. Standing with your feet together, go up and down on your toes.

2. Standing on one leg, go up and down on your toes, then repeat on the other leg.

3. Stand on one leg; bend your knee, keeping your heel flat on the floor; straighten your knee, going up onto your toes; then bend your knee again to repeat the movement in a continuous rhythm. Repeat on the other leg.

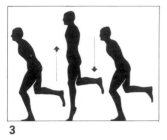

3

4. Stand on a step, with your heels dropped over the edge; go up and down on your toes.

5. Repeat (4), one leg at a time.

6. Sit with your legs straight out in front of you on the floor; loop a belt round under the soles of your feet, holding the free ends in your hands. Push your toes down against the belt, pulling the belt with your hands to resist the movement.

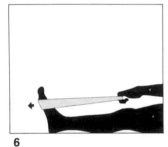

6

7. Repeat (6), on each leg in turn.

8. When exercises (1) to (5) become easy, use weights to make them more difficult. Either hold the weights in your hands, or strap them to your wrists.

9. Leg extension or leg press weights machine. If you have access to weight-training equipment, you can use the leg extension exerciser for your calves, by pressing your feet up and down against the weights, when your knees are fully extended. Use both legs together, then each leg in turn. Start with light weights, then gradually increase the resistance. (See photograph on p. 117.)

DYNAMIC, FUNCTIONAL EXERCISES

1. Walk around, pushing yourself right up onto your toes. (Start with twenty steps, increasing to one hundred.)

2. Standing jumps: without bending your knees, spring upwards from your toes, letting your knees bend slightly on landing. (Ten jumps up to thirty times.)

3. Hop on each foot in turn, first on the spot, then forwards and backwards. (Ten sets, up to fifty.)

4. Skip with a rope, first with feet together, then alternating feet, on your toes. (Twenty sets, up to 500.)

5. Sprint forwards for twenty metres, jogging back to the start. (Three times, building up to twenty.)

6. Sprint backwards for ten paces, jogging to return to the start. (Three times, up to twenty.)

7. Shuttle runs: sprint forwards for twenty paces, bend to touch the ground, turn, sprint back to touch the ground at your starting point or a different point, sprint forwards again, in a continuous routine. (Five times, up to twenty.)

8. Run as hard as you can up stairs, jog or walk down. (10–20 stairs, three up to ten times.)

9. Sprint up stairs, two at a time.

10. Sprint up a hill, jog or walk down. (Fifty to one hundred metres, three up to ten times.)

Complication

Spasm is felt in the calf muscles, over a stress fracture. If you have had an injury to your calf, but the pain persists despite rehabilitation and care, one possibility is that the calf pain was secondary to the more serious problem of a stress fracture in the underlying leg bones. The calf muscles go into protective spasm when their underlying bone is damaged: the outer part of gastrocnemius, for instance, protects a fracture in the upper part of the fibula (p. 54), while soleus may react to a stress fracture at the back of the tibia (p. 64). If you know you have built up your sporting activities suddenly, or following a lay-off, and you feel tenderness when you press over your leg bones, you should rest completely from any painful activities, and ask your doctor for specialist advice.

The Knee

Bones

The knee-joint is a compound joint, made up of three bones: the thigh-bone (femur), shin-bone (tibia) and the knee-cap (patella). The main part of the knee, through which your body-weight is transmitted, is formed between the lower end of the thigh-bone and the uppermost part of the shin-bone. The end of the thigh-bone consists of two rounded knuckles, called condyles, which form an enlarged bony area at the end of the bone. The condyles are roughly shaped to conform with the flat, elliptical surfaces on top of the shin bone. The part of the thigh-bone enclosed within the joint is greater than the receiving surface of the shin-bone. There is a natural gap between the two bones, which is filled with fluid. Therefore, although the joint surfaces of the two bones are matched, they are not perfectly congruent.

The knee-cap and the thigh-bone form a separate, but functionally connected, joint within the knee-joint complex. The knee-cap is a loose bone, formed in the lower end of the quadriceps muscle group. It serves as a kind of pulley between the bulky thigh muscles and their narrow tendon, which runs from the pointed end of the knee-cap to the tibial tubercle at the top of the shin-bone. The undersurface of the knee-cap is shaped to conform to the surfaces of the thigh-bone condyles over which the knee-cap runs during knee movements. There is a fluid-filled gap between the knee-cap and the thigh-bone, so the two bones do not fit perfectly together. This joint, the patello-femoral joint, does not transmit direct loading between your trunk and your feet, but it automatically takes part in any movements at the knee.

The bone surfaces involved in the two joints at the knee are all covered with cartilage, a special type of bone covering which occurs only in bone ends which meet to form moving joints. This type of cartilage, which is a functional part of the bone structure, is quite distinct from the more familiar 'knee cartilages', or menisci, which are soft buffering pads lying on the two joint surfaces on top of the shin-bone.

Soft tissues

The internal cartilages, or menisci, are attached to the top of the shin-bone by special ligaments which bind the edges of the bone and the

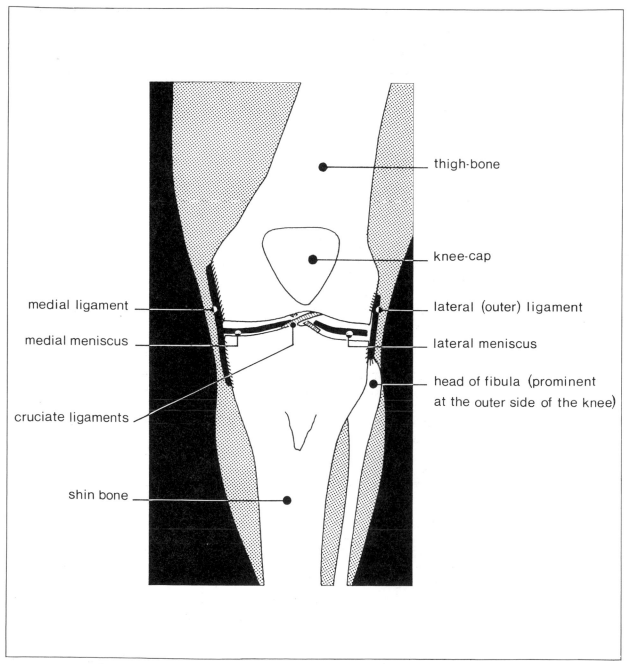

thigh-bone

knee-cap

medial ligament

lateral (outer) ligament

medial meniscus

lateral meniscus

head of fibula (prominent
at the outer side of the knee)

cruciate ligaments

shin bone

Knee structure, left knee from the front.

81

cartilages together. The outer cartilage (lateral meniscus) is otherwise free-lying, but the inner (medial) cartilage is integrally attached to the inner, or medial, knee ligament. The medial ligament is the strongest of the ligaments protecting the outside of the knee-joint, and it forms a band stretching some fifteen centimetres along the inner side of the knee, from the thigh-bone to the shin-bone. On the other side of the knee, the outer, or lateral, ligament is a smaller protective band linking the outside of the thigh-bone with the top of the fibula, on the knob of the fibular head which you can feel at the outside of the knee. The back of the knee is protected by weaker ligaments which cross the back of the joint, but these do not have the same stabilizing strength as the medial and lateral ligaments. Inside the knee, two strong ligaments hold the joint together internally. They bind the centre of the thigh-bone to the shin-bone. Because they cross each other in the middle of the joint, these ligaments are called cruciates, or cross-shaped.

All the external ligaments of the knee are specially thickened parts of the joint capsule, the covering which encloses the whole joint. Because the knee-joint is both extensive and complex in structure, the capsule is not the simple covering sack that it is in other joints of the body. It does not enclose the knee-cap at all. As in all other moving joints, the capsule is lined with synovial membrane, which produces the lubricating fluid promoting free motion between the moving parts. When the knee is straight, the synovial membrane extends to about five centimetres above the top of the knee-cap. Within the capsule, the synovial membrane lines the knee-joint, below the knee-cap at the front, and around the whole extent of the sides and back of the joint. Above the knee-cap, the synovial membrane forms its own pouch, and has no joint capsule covering.

Although the knee capsule is attached to the sides of the knee-cap, the patello-femoral joint has no ligaments as such to limit movement. The patellar tendon, which joins the knee-cap to the shin-bone, is often called the patellar ligament, but it is functionally a tendon, as it forms the end part of a muscle group which you can actively contract, by straightening your knee. The patellar tendon is the only tendon on the front of the knee. Many more tendons are attached at either side of the lower part of the knee. On the outer side of the knee lies a strong band called the iliotibial tract, which links the outer hip muscles with the top of the shin-bone, and which stands out as a firm long band when you straighten your knee hard.

FUNCTIONS

The knee is not simply a hinge-joint: you bend and straighten it, but you

82

can also turn it slightly in a twisting movement, when the knee is bent. This rotatory movement automatically accompanies the bending and straightening movements. As you bend your knee, the shin-bone turns inwards slightly relative to the thigh-bone. As you straighten, the shin-bone rotates outwards. You can only rotate the knee actively and voluntarily when the knee is bent. For instance, when you are sitting down, you can turn your feet inwards and outwards without lifting your heels off the floor, and this movement is achieved through rotation at the knee.

When you bend your knee against gravity or a resistance, the muscles at the back of the knee contract to perform the movement. The hamstrings do the main work of bending the knee, but the gastrocnemius tendons help, especially if the movement takes place against a strong resistance. When you straighten your knee in the direction of gravity, for instance while you are lying on your stomach, the hamstrings pay out to control the movement. The quadriceps muscles on the front of the thigh straighten your knee against gravity or a resistance, but they also act to control the movement, when the knee bends in the direction of gravity's influence. If you bend your knees to squat down from standing, the quadriceps group lengthens out to allow the movement to happen; as you straighten your knees to stand up again, the quadriceps group contracts to effect the movement. The knee's rotatory movements are achieved actively by the muscles at the sides of the knees. The outer hamstring tendon turns your foot outwards from the knee, while the inner hamstrings turn it inwards. The patello-femoral joint moves whenever you create movement in your knee, by bending, straightening or twisting it. The only way you can move the patello-femoral joint independently of the rest of the knee is by contracting the quadriceps muscles when the knee is straight. Then you will see the knee-cap being pulled upwards along its grooves on the joint surface of the thigh-bone.

The structure of the knee-joint has two effects. Firstly, the knee is a very stable joint, by virtue of its strong binding ligaments and the protective effect of the muscles which control the joint's movements. Secondly, the joint has quite a wide freedom of movement, because the bones are not closely bound within their own configuration. The knee is one of the three major joints in the leg which transmit loading forces between one's body and the ground. Its stability helps to keep us upright on our feet when we are standing, walking, hopping or jumping. In conjunction with the ankle and the hip, the knee helps to absorb shock, when we land on our feet from any kind of height. It allows us to kneel, crouch and squat. It also allows us to perform complex leg movements: we can dance the Charleston and the Twist; we can kick; we can sit on a horse side-saddle or straight; and we can balance on skis.

KNEE PAIN

This can arise from various causes. The knee can be affected by a spontaneous inflammatory arthritis. Or it can be one of many joints involved in a multiple inflammatory arthritis. Pain referred from the hip or back may be felt as a simple knee pain. Problems in the thigh-bone may cause knee pain. In older age, the knee, like the hip, may be affected by osteoarthritis, or wear-and-tear degeneration. In children, unexplained knee pain can be a sign of a very serious hip condition, the slipped epiphysis (p. 170). To help your doctor differentiate between a medical condition, and the pain of an overuse injury, you should keep an account of how the pain started; what you were doing when it started, and whether it gets worse with any particular activity, or for no apparent reason; whether your knee hurts at night, or when you are sitting at rest; and whether there is anything you can do to relieve the pain.

KNEE SWELLING

Joint swelling is an important symptom in knee conditions. Because of the complex and extensive synovial lining in the knee, the joint may distend alarmingly, with swelling right round the joint, reaching about seven centimetres above the knee onto the front of the thigh. However, it can also be more subtle. You may only see a small pocket of swelling, perhaps on one or the other side of the joint; or there may be just a slight puffiness on the front of the joint, on either side of the knee-cap. Swelling may occur at the back of the joint, without any visible signs of it at the front.

Joint swelling always indicates inflammation. As in the ankle, knee swelling can be caused by gravity bringing the fluid down from some higher tissues: the swelling may track down from the hip joint or some part of the thigh muscles. However, unlike the situation in the ankle, if you have persistent swelling in the knee, which delineates the joint's shape, it is unlikely to be gravitational swelling, and it is very likely to mean that there is something wrong inside your knee.

If the swelling has appeared for no obvious reason, it may indicate that you have an inflammatory or degenerative condition. Your doctor will probably arrange blood tests and X-rays, to decide whether this is so. If the swelling occurs as the result of an injury to the knee, and you are aware of having wrenched, hit, or fallen on the joint, it is likely that you have damaged one or more of the knee's internal structures, with irritation or damage to the synovial lining. The swelling may come on at the moment of injury, or some hours afterwards: it is useful if you can remember when the swelling appears, as this can give an indication as to how much damage has been done.

Self-help first-aid for the swollen knee

• Apply ice, preferably by the wet-towel method (p. 15), enclosing the whole joint in the ice-towel.
• Support the joint, with a double stocking bandage, or a crepe bandage wound over cotton wool padding. The bandaging must reach from about ten centimetres below the knee to the same distance above it, at least. If the swelling is severe, wrap the leg in cotton wool from your ankle to the top of your thigh, and encase the whole leg in one or two crepe bandages to apply even pressure.
• You should keep off the injured leg. Hop, if you have to, or use crutches, or, preferably, arrange to be carried, if you have to move about.
• You must refer straight away to your doctor or a casualty officer. If your knee is badly swollen, your medical specialist may decide to remove the excess fluid by siphoning it off through a sterile needle. He is very likely to do so if he suspects that there is blood in the joint, although the extra fluid may be either blood-stained or clear synovial fluid. Blood trapped inside the joint for any length of time can create damage to the joint surfaces, so it is important for any swelling in the knee to be reduced as quickly as possible.
• As knee swelling indicates that there is internal damage, it may be necessary for you to have an orthopaedic opinion on the nature of the damage, either immediately after the injury, or if the swelling and pain fail to subside with care and treatment. As long as you have swelling in your knee, you must continue to apply ice once or twice a day as a routine, and you must keep wearing a knee support, perhaps a simple one like a doubled stocking bandage. Remove the bandage at night, if it becomes uncomfortable, but otherwise try to wear a support all the time. If your knee injury is very severe, the specialist may apply a plaster of Paris cast to immobilize it. The cast extends from just above your ankle to below your groin. It protects the joint from damaging movements, while it allows you to do the straight-leg exercises (p. 112) to maintain your thigh muscles. You must start these exercises almost immediately, unless your specialist tells you not to, for some specific reason.
• Avoid bending the knee. If you try to bend your knee while it is swollen and painful, the swelling is likely to increase. You can damage the knee even more, if you try to do squatting movements over it. Keep your knee straight, and support your leg on a cushion or stool whenever you sit down. Move your knee only within the limits of pain.

85

● Maintain your knee muscles. The muscles around the knee waste very quickly after an injury. They lose power, partly because of inhibition due to pain, and partly through inactivity, as you avoid moving the painful joint. The quadriceps muscles on the front of the thigh can lose up to three centimetres of their girth within a day or two of a knee injury. The innermost part of the group, vastus medialis, can become totally inhibited within six hours of the injury.

● To maintain muscle tone, do static contractions to straighten the knee. This will not create further damage, and will help prevent the otherwise inevitable loss of muscle function. Sit with your leg straight in front of you; press your knee downwards to straighten it hard, pulling your toes back to you from your ankle. Hold for a count of three, then gently relax. Repeat this exercise at least six times every hour. You can do it while sitting or standing. The more you practise the exercise, the more protection you are giving your knee within its recovery process. By maintaining good quadriceps tone, you will speed up your rehabilitation, and you will avoid the secondary problems associated with weakness in the knee's protective muscles.

Knee injuries

The knee is very prone to injury, because of its mobility and the variety of stresses we subject it to. The most common type of traumatic injury to the knee is the twisting or wrenching injury. This happens most frequently when your knee is bent, while carrying your body-weight, and you twist awkwardly or unexpectedly. Skiers and footballers are most susceptible to this type of injury, but it can happen to you while walking or running, if you trip and catch your foot, or fall while turning. Any of the knee's structures may be damaged in this type of injury. The full extent of the damage may be impossible to assess immediately after the injury, and may only become evident when the knee subsequently fails to recover its full function.

The knee is also vulnerable to overuse injuries: gradual pains brought on by an activity, which progressively get worse, if you continue the activity. These are the injuries which must be distinguished from the other, more serious, medical conditions which can cause similar pain.

Pain at the front of the knee

PATELLAR TENDON STRAIN

The patellar tendon is very short, extending only between the pointed lower end of the knee-cap and the tibial tubercle, the prominent bump of bone at the top of the shin-bone. However, it acts as the concentrating point for the pull exerted by the quadriceps muscle group during knee movements, so it is an extremely powerful tendon. The tendon works hard whenever the knee bends and straightens under load. It works hardest when knee movements involve a full bend under your body weight and gravity, for instance if you do a full squat exercise in weight-lifting, or when you take off from one leg in high jumping or long jumping. The tendon also generates a strong pull when you go up and down stairs, when you run on hilly ground, and when you kick a football.

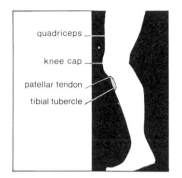

Because the tendon plays such an important part in all movements at the knee, it may be strained simply by overwork. This type of overuse strain is usually due to a repetitive activity, such as long-distance running, or extended sessions of hill-running, hopping and bounding, kicking, or squatting exercises. An overuse strain is more likely to occur if the tendon is working inefficiently, because it is fatigued through overwork, or tight due to cold or previous excessive exercise. Faulty or altered mechanics can contribute to overuse strains of the tendon. Normally, the patellar tendon forms a perpendicular line, passing straight down from the point of the knee-cap to the top of the shin-bone. However, the tendon may deviate from the vertical, either because of the particular development of the leg bones during growth, or because of habitual faulty posture or movement, or as a result of a knee injury. Bad shoes can also contribute to changing the tendon's angle of pull. This is especially true if children and adolescents wear shoes with too little support underfoot, or high-heels, during their growth years.

The tendon may also be subject to sudden injury. It works at a mechanical disadvantage when it has to move the knee from the fully bent position under load, and it is particularly vulnerable to strain in this situation. If a weight-lifter overbalances in the deep squat position, or if he is struggling to lift too heavy a weight, the patellar tendon is one of the knee structures which may give under the stress. Blocking the knee movement while the patellar tendon is exerting the tension to create the movement can also result in sudden tearing in the tendon. This happens when a kick is blocked in football, or if you catch your foot while running or jumping forward.

What happens

When the patellar tendon is strained, a few of its many fibres may be torn. This causes pain when you use the tendon, but it does not necessarily stop the tendon from working through its normal range of movement. As a result of a strain, or partial tear, the tendon may become thickened, and tight, because of scar tissue forming in the torn fibres. This limits the tendon's function, and the tendon becomes more painful on movement. The thickening and limitation may result in the tendon becoming bound down by adhesions, which act like glue in sticking the tendon to the tissues around it. Through this vicious circle of pain and limitation, a minor strain may result in major functional damage. This pattern may occur, whether the original strain came on gradually, or as a sudden injury.

The tendon may tear completely, causing immediate functional disability. When the tendon tears right through, the whole of the quadriceps muscle group on the front of the thigh is incapacitated, as its lower attachment point is destroyed. The knee-cap rides upwards over the thigh, as it is no longer held tethered over the front of the knee-joint. There is of course severe pain, and it is impossible to take weight through the leg. A normal patellar tendon can only tear completely if a sudden enormous force is applied to it. However, it may give way under less pressure, if it has been previously weakened by repeated strains which have made its centre degenerate. Steroid injection into the centre of the tendon can result in severe weakening of the fibres. Following inexpert injections to 'cure' a strain, the tendon may tear under minimal pressure, for instance if you squat down, or if you try to climb onto a higher step.

Treatment

Specialist treatment may consist of an injection administered by a medical expert, or various forms of physiotherapy treatment.

• You must avoid any activities which cause pain over the tendon, as they would inevitably aggravate the damage already done. You will probably be unable to run on hilly ground, squat, hop on the injured leg, jump off it, or swim breaststroke. However, you may find that you can run on soft ground, do half-squats, and swim crawl, without pain. You can safely continue any painless forms of exercise.

• Stretch the tendon. Passively stretching the quadriceps muscle group, within the limits of pain, gradually restores flexibility, and prevents it from tightening up and forming adhesions (p. 133). Repeat the stretching exercise at least ten times, three times a day. You should also stretch the tendon before and after any exercise session you do.

- Apply ice over the tendon, if it is very sore (p. 15). While you apply the ice, if you use the wet-towel method, you should do some tendon stretching. One easy way to do this is to kneel on the ice-towel, on a soft but firm surface, and sit back gently on your heel, holding the tendon on the stretch.
- Maintain the quadriceps muscles. To avoid secondary knee problems, and weakening in the joint's stability, you should do static quadriceps contractions (p. 112) at frequent intervals during each day. You should not do the exercises too many times at once, as you risk further strain to the patellar tendon. If the tendon does get sore, reduce the amount you do, but make sure that you do one or two static quadriceps contractions at least three times daily, in conjunction with the stretching exercise.
- Strengthen the quadriceps. If you have access to a leg press machine, you should start to use it as soon as your specialist allows, or as soon as the injured patellar tendon feels less sore to touch, and pain-free on the stretching and static strengthening exercises. Only use the leg press from a slight bend (about thirty degrees) to the fully straightened position. Start with very light weights, working on a routine of three sets of ten, increasing the weights by one or two steps in each session, but no more. As your legs get stronger, gradually increase the amount of bend from which the movement starts. Once you have increased the weights resistance by six steps from the original weight, and you can press from a ninety degree bend, you should reduce the weight loading again, and repeat the process on the injured leg only, increasing resistance and range of movement in the same easy stages.
- Knee bending exercises. If you do not have access to a leg press machine, an alternative is to practise knee bending movements, as soon as the injured tendon is pain-free. Start by standing up straight, bending your knees to about thirty degrees (quarter squat), then straightening them again and locking them into the straight position. Repeat in a routine of three sets of ten, two or three times daily. Gradually, over the space of a week or two, increase the amount you bend your knees, until you are bending them just beyond ninety degrees (half-squat). Once you can half-squat on both knees, repeat the progression on the injured leg only.

If at any stage the strengthening exercises aggravate the injured tendon, rest the tendon for a few days, keeping up the static exercises only, and then resume the strengthening work with lower weights resistance or less range of movement.
- Once you can half-squat on the injured leg, you should be capable of resuming your normal activities. However, do not over-stress the tendon at first. Allow it to adjust in easy stages. If you run, start with short

distances, and gradually build up, in terms of speed, mileage and hills. If you play football, practise kicking the ball on your own, a little at a time, for two or three sessions before trying to play a practice game.

PATELLAR TENDON RUPTURE

When the patellar tendon tears completely, you must refer for specialist treatment as a casualty. The tendon will have to be repaired surgically, as quickly as possible after the accident. You will not be able to put weight through your leg, and you should be transported to hospital, keeping the leg as still as possible.

To make the leg comfortable, the knee can be immobilized in an inflatable splint (p. 10), but the most comfortable form of bandage is probably a cotton wool and crepe bandage support. Wrap the knee in cotton wool from a large roll, extending the support from just above the ankle to just below the hip, then cover the cotton wool with a wide crepe bandage binding. This provides a firm, but not constricting, support.

Recovery after the surgical repair will be dictated by the specialist who has performed the operation. The sequence follows the programme outlined for rehabilitation for a patellar tendon strain. Flexibility must be regained, then the tendon is gradually strengthened with specific exercises. The final phase of rehabilitation comprises active exercises such as running, squatting and hopping. Progression through the rehabilitation phases is inevitably slower than the recovery from a simple strain, but the sequence must be adhered to, as shortcuts will lead to setbacks.

Complication: Sinding-Larsen-Johannson Syndrome

Osteochondritis, a form of degeneration in a bone's growth point, can occur in the lower part of the knee-cap, where the patellar tendon attaches to the bone. This complication is called Sinding-Larsen-Johannson syndrome, and it causes severe pain when the tendon is stressed during activity, as well as soreness if you press over the point of the knee-cap, or if you try to kneel on it. It can occur in one or both knees, according to the activity which caused it. The condition may clear, if the knees are rested for long enough from any kind of aggravating activity, but this may take up to six months. If the condition is very severe and persistent, a surgical operation may be needed, either to 'clean up' the degenerated parts of the patellar tendon, or to help the disrupted bone at the lower edge of the knee-cap to heal. After the operation, rehabilitation to full recovery follows the same pattern as the programme following a cartilage removal operation.

The joint between the knee-cap and the thigh-bone is a common site of pain in sportsmen. The joint is not directly load-bearing, but it takes part in all the movements of the knee-joint proper. The knee-cap is a free bone, formed in the lower end of the quadriceps muscles. Its joint surface is V-shaped, and corresponds to a V-shaped groove on the lower end of the thigh-bone. Therefore it has its own guiding track on the thigh-bone, although it has no ligaments directly binding it down. When the knee moves, the knee-cap glides up and down along its track, under the influence of the shortening and lengthening activity of the quadriceps group, which is either contracting or paying out in all knee movements.

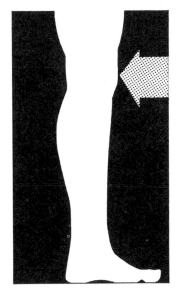

What you feel

Knee-cap pain is felt over the front of the knee only. It generally starts as an ache, but it can be severe. It is worst when you walk or run up and down slopes or stairs, but you may feel it walking on level ground. Squatting and kneeling are painful. The knee becomes stiff if it is held in one position too long. It aches if you sit down for extended periods, and gives a sharp pain as you stand up from sitting (this is called the 'Cinema sign'). The pain may affect one or both knees, and it may be intermittent. Usually, it is difficult to define a cause for the pain, although it occasionally occurs suddenly, as the result of a particular activity or injury. The knee may swell a little around the knee-cap.

What happens

Pain from the knee-cap joint is caused by damage or degeneration in the cartilage covering the bones where they move against each other. In children and adolescents the most common condition affecting the joint cartilage in the knee-cap is chondromalacia, which is a term defining the particular type of changes occurring in the cartilage. In older people the joint may be affected by osteoarthritis, or wear-and-tear degeneration. In all cases, the pain pattern is the same, whatever the exact nature of the cartilage damage is, and the factor triggering the pain is friction between the back of the knee-cap and the front of the thigh-bone.

Why it happens

In the normal way, the knee-cap is guided along its track by the co-ordinated pull of the quadriceps muscles acting together. However, the three largest parts of the quadriceps group lie over the top and the outer side of the knee-cap. Only one small part, called vastus medialis, lies on the inner side of the knee-cap (see p. 126). Vastus medialis is therefore the only force directing the knee-cap inwards during its movements, while

91

the other parts of the quadriceps pull the knee-cap upwards and out-wards. Although vastus medialis acts whenever the knee-cap moves, it works hardest when the knee is fully straightened. The knee can only be fully straightened and 'locked out' actively if vastus medialis is working efficiently. If vastus medialis stops working effectively and harmoniously with the other parts of the quadriceps, you will not be able to straighten out your knee fully. More importantly, your knee-cap will no longer move straight within its groove during knee movements, but will tend to be pulled upwards and outwards instead. This is the main cause of the friction between the cartilage coverings of the moving bones.

As a primary condition, knee-cap pain due to this type of friction can occur at any time that vastus medialis becomes weakened, or the other parts of quadriceps become relatively stronger. This imbalance happens if you do any activity which involves bending the knee more than you straighten it. Cycling, canoeing, hurdling and fencing are sports in which one or both knees work mainly in the bent position. In other sports, excessive knee bending may happen by chance. In rowing and sculling, your knees should be straight at the end of each stroke, but if your stretcher is not properly adjusted, your legs may be blocked from reaching the fully straight position. In trampolining, you normally work your legs through a full range of movement, but this can be undermined if you do an excessive session of 'knee drops'. If you run fast, your knees straighten as you push off, but on a slow jog, especially on hilly ground, your knees tend to remain bent.

As a secondary condition, knee-cap pain often follows knee injury, whether or not the knee-cap was involved directly in the injury. A direct blow onto the knee-cap, or a twisting injury which damages the knee's ligaments or internal structures, may equally bring on knee-cap pain. The pain is due to the same mechanics which cause primary knee-cap pain. When the knee is hurt, you tend to hold it slightly bent, as this almost invariably eases the pain. If the knee is badly hurt, the muscles behind it go into a protective spasm to hold it slightly bent, as a natural way of easing the pain. If the knee is held in this position, vastus medialis will waste rapidly, and become inhibited within about six hours. The rest of the quadriceps will also waste, but more slowly, within one or two days. In this way the imbalance is created, and it is difficult to correct. Because vastus medialis wastes more quickly than the rest of the quadriceps, it is slower to recover function, and it is particularly important to re-educate vastus medialis intensively, before you actively re-strengthen the rest of the quadriceps.

You can check whether your pain is due to a problem in the joint between the knee-cap and the thigh-bone, and whether you have a quadriceps imbalance with weakness in vastus medialis, by applying the following tests:

• Sit facing a mirror, on the floor, with your legs straight out in front of you. Straighten both knees hard, pulling your feet back towards you at the ankle. Your heels should be lifted off the floor by the movement. If the heel lift is uneven, it is likely that vastus medialis is weak, failing to straighten the knee to its fullest extent, into hyperextension.

• Sit on the floor, with your legs straight, and ask a helper to straighten your knee as much as possible, by pressing down over the thigh just above the knee, and lifting your heel upwards from the floor as far as it will go. In the normal way, your knee should extend passively in this way to some degrees beyond a straight line between the thigh-bone and the leg-bones. While your helper is holding your foot up, actively try to straighten the knee hard, tightening up your quadriceps muscles. Still holding the muscles tensed as hard as you can, tell your helper to let go of your foot. If vastus medialis is strong, you will maintain your knee in its fully extended position. If the muscle is weak, you will see and feel your heel drop slightly, as you fail to keep your knee fully straight.

• Sit on the floor, with your legs straight and relaxed. Press down with your hands onto your knee-cap, and push the bone against the thigh-bone underneath it. If you press the bones together in a circular movement, you will feel 'grating' sensations at certain points in the movement, probably accompanied by pain.

• Sit with your legs straight and relaxed. With your hands, press your knee-cap sideways, so that its outer part lies clear of the thigh-bone. Then feel the underside of the knee-cap. If the cartilage is damaged, the bone will feel tender when you touch it. By pushing the knee-cap to left and right, you can feel most of the edges of the bone, although you will probably be unable to reach into the centre of the underside of the bone.

• Sit on the floor with your legs straight in front of you. Place your hand over the upper edge of the knee-cap, and press the bone downwards towards your feet. Then try to tense the quadriceps, but keep the pressure on the knee-cap, so that you stop it moving as the muscles try to pull it upwards. Repeat the test, but this time pressing the knee-cap downwards and out to one side of the knee before you tense the quadriceps. Repeat again, but pressing the knee-cap towards the other side of the knee. If you have any damage to the cartilage in the knee-cap joint, you will feel pain when movement of the knee-cap is blocked in one or more of these positions. This test is known as 'Clarke's Sign'.

Treatment for knee-cap pain

Specialist treatment is directed at correcting the quadriceps imbalance which gives rise to the pain, in the first instance. Physiotherapy treatment may consist of electrical stimulation (faradism) to re-educate vastus medialis, complemented by self-help exercises. If the muscle imbalance is linked to faulty foot mechanics, specially constructed foot supports, or orthotics, may be prescribed by a podiatrist to help the associated problem. If the knee-cap pain is severe, it may be necessary to refer to an orthopaedic specialist. The simplest operation to help the condition is the 'lateral release' operation, which is a small cut into the outer parts of the quadriceps muscles, designed to inhibit them and relieve pressure on the knee-cap, and so allow vastus medialis to function more effectively. If you have severe pain, or if you are in doubt about the exact diagnosis of your problem, you must refer to your doctor.

Self-help measures for knee-cap pain

• When vastus medialis loses its co-ordination with the rest of the quadriceps group, the problem is not just that the muscle loses its power. More importantly, the message pathway between your brain and the muscle is disrupted. This communication is called proprioception, and has to be re-trained. Some exercises help with this retraining:

Proprioceptive quadriceps contraction. Sit on the floor with your legs straight in front of you. Put your fingers over the small bulge of vastus medialis which lies just above the knee, on the inner side of the thigh. Tighten your thigh muscles to straighten the knee, for a count of five. If vastus medialis is weak, you will feel the muscle tightening and then involuntarily relaxing under your fingers. Each time you do the exercise, try to maintain the tension in the muscle, so that it feels rock solid when it contracts. Repeat the exercise ten times, three times daily.

Static quadriceps contraction, and static quadriceps contraction with heel support (p. 112). Do these exercises ten times, three or four times each day.

• Straighten your knees routinely during your everyday activities. If you have to sit down for long periods, either stand up to straighten out your knees, or stretch your knees straight from the sitting position, locking them out hard to tighten the quadriceps muscles.

• Avoid any activities which involve bending the knee, and avoid any sports which cause pain during or after play. If you can run without pain, keep on flat ground, not hills. Swim crawl rather than breaststroke. Avoid cycling, hopping and kneeling. Check your sports shoes for excessive wear, and replace them if necessary.

• Avoid recurrence of the problem. When you can straighten out your knee effectively, so that vastus medialis is working efficiently, you will find that your pain has subsided. You will then be safe to resume your normal sports. However, you must take care to maintain good function in vastus medialis, by incorporating some static quadriceps bracing exercises into your training, and into your daily life, and by balancing out any activities which bend your knees with a session of the straightening exercises. If you cycle, take care to stand up in your pedals whenever you go up hills. Raise your bicycle saddle so that your knee is virtually straight on the downward push. If you row, make sure that your stretcher is adjusted so that you get your knees straight at the end of each stroke. If you do weight training, make sure that you lock your knees straight at the end of power clean or squatting movements. If you run, either try to sprint off straightened knees, or, when you jog, straighten your knee consciously on heel strike.

Complications

If you manage to correct quadriceps imbalance at the knees by re-training vastus medialis, but you find that you still have pain, with or without swelling, over the front of the knee, you must suspect that there is some other problem, apart from a simple knee-cap problem. If you have suffered a direct blow to the knee-cap, you may have a crack in the bone. A child or adolescent may have osteochondritis affecting the knee-cap: this means that the growth points of the bone have been damaged, and it may result in loose chips of bone becoming detached from the knee-cap to lie in the joint, causing 'clicking', swelling and pain. The fat pads which lie on either side of the lower end of the knee-cap and the patellar tendon are also tissues which can be damaged or inflamed, causing continuing pain at the front of the knee. To differentiate between the possible causes of continuing pain in this area, it is essential that you refer to your doctor for specialist investigations, and perhaps referral to an appropriate expert.

'HOUSEMAID'S KNEE' (PREPATELLAR BURSITIS)

The front of the knee-cap is protected by a fluid-filled pouch, or bursa, which lies between the bone and its covering skin. When the bursa is inflamed, it swells up, forming a large egg-like protrusion over the knee-cap. The condition is called 'housemaid's knee', identified in women who had to kneel down constantly to scrub floors and so were particularly prone to suffer from it. They damaged the bursa as a cumulative effect from the repeated pressure on the front of the knee. The bursa

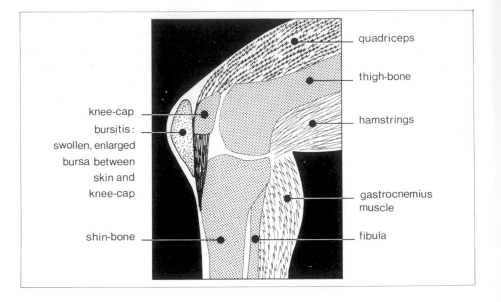

quadriceps

thigh-bone

knee-cap

hamstrings

bursitis:
swollen, enlarged
bursa between
skin and
knee-cap

gastrocnemius
muscle

shin-bone

fibula

can easily be damaged by a single hard blow on the knee-cap, for instance if someone kicks your knee, or if you fall onto your knees from a height. The bursa may also swell because of a medical inflammatory condition. Your doctor will be able to differentiate between the various possible causes of the bursitis, if you can give him an accurate account of exactly when and how it first occurred.

Although the bursa may become large and unsightly, it is not necessarily very painful or functionally disabling. It hurts when you press it, and possibly when you stretch the skin on the front of the knee, by bending your knee fully, or squatting down. If it does become painful enough to interfere with your normal activities, it will need specialist treatment. Your doctor may drain off the extra fluid in the bursa, although the swelling may recur after this is done. Otherwise, the bursa may be removed completely by surgery to eliminate the problem and the possibility of recurrence. After surgery, the knee is usually kept immobilized in a plaster, to prevent a secondary bursa from forming in place of the original one. About four weeks after the operation, the surgeon normally allows rehabilitation to start, following removal of the plaster.

Self-help measures in mild bursitis
• To help protect the bursa, and prevent the inflammation from getting worse, you should wear a protective pad over the knee, perhaps consisting of layers of cotton wool or gauze, covered by a stocking bandage.

96

- Avoid direct pressure over the knee: do not kneel on it, for instance. If the swelling is warm and/or reddened, do not aggravate it by bending the knee and stretching the bursa. However, if it is not noticeably inflamed, you should maintain mobility in the knee by stretching your quadriceps muscles: stand on your uninjured leg, and bend the other knee, holding your ankle in your hand; gently pull your ankle behind you towards your seat, keeping your hip forward, and bending your knee as far as you can; hold to a count of ten, then gently let go, Repeat this stretching exercise about six times, at least twice a day, and more often if possible.
- Apply ice (p. 15) over the bursa, if it feels painful. Gently rubbing in some heparinoid cream twice a day may also help (p. 16).
- You are unlikely to reduce the swelling, once it has occurred, but if the bursitis can be controlled, you may avoid the more serious forms of medical treatment, and still be able to do your normal activities.

KNEE-CAP DISLOCATION

This is a problem which can occur at any age, but which often happens to children. If it starts in pre-teen years, it tends to be a continuing problem, with episodes which gradually get worse over the years. Girls are particularly vulnerable to the problem. When the dislocation is a continuing, chronic problem, the episodes tend to be relatively mild, so that the dislocation is hardly recognizable as such. However, in the older sportsman especially, the dislocation can be severe, with the knee-cap remaining out of alignment until it is manipulated back into place.

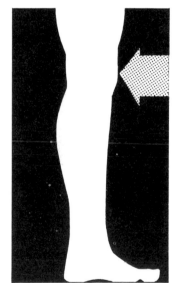

What you feel

In mild recurring cases, how you feel the dislocation is sometimes difficult to define. You may be running along, or running upstairs, when you feel a sudden pain, as though something in your knee goes out of place, and the knee then gives way completely, so that you fall down. If you straighten your knee out, you may feel a click, and the knee may feel all right again. After this, the knee usually swells up, and feels painful over the front of the joint. The symptoms are very similar to those of a cartilage tear, so you must tell your doctor in detail what happened to your knee, so that he can distinguish the factors. He will probably test your knee-cap by having you sit with your legs over the end of a couch, and your injured knee supported and held straight. He will gently push your knee-cap towards the outer side of the knee, and then gradually let your knee bend. At a certain angle, your knee-cap will feel as though it is going to dislocate again, and you will automatically try to protect it. Your reaction, although involuntary, is a good indication that your symptoms

97

have been caused by knee-cap dislocation. In a severe, acute episode of dislocation, there is no doubt about what has happened, as the knee-cap does not slip back into place, but remains lodged towards the outside of your knee. You may find that it rights itself, if you bend your hip up gently, and try to straighten your knee. On no account should you try, or allow anyone else to try, wrenching the knee back into place. You can wrap ice towels round the joint, to reduce the swelling and pain, and you should be taken straight to hospital, keeping the knee absolutely still, if the knee-cap has remained stuck.

What has happened

In this form of dislocation the knee-cap has slipped, or been pulled out, sideways, under the influence of the contracting quadriceps muscle group. In repetitive cases, this usually happens at a certain angle of knee bend, and can be associated with: weakness in the inner part of the quadriceps group, vastus medialis; or previous injury causing tears in the tissues holding the inner side of the knee-cap; or by a sharp angulation between the line of pull of the quadriceps muscles and the pull of the patellar tendon. The angle of pull between these two lines of force, known as the 'Q angle', is made greater than the accepted normal if your tibial tubercles are situated to the outer side rather than the centre of the

The 'Q' angle.

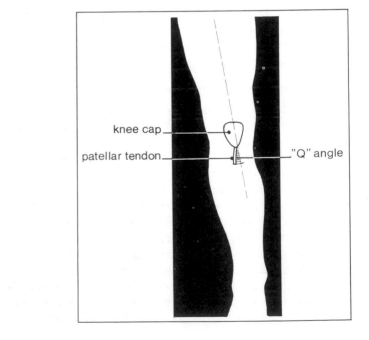

top of your shin-bones; if you are knock-kneed; if your feet tend to roll inwards and pronate, bending your knees inwards; and if, in women, your hips are set quite wide apart.

As the knee-cap acts as a free pulley between the patellar tendon and the quadriceps muscles, a large angle between the two makes the bone deviate from its normal pathway on the end of the thigh-bone. These mechanical factors may cause persistent minor dislocations of the knee-cap, and they may contribute to the more serious kind of accident, which is usually triggered by some external factor forcing the knee inwards while bending it. The goalkeeper in hockey may suffer this injury while kicking a hard ball away from the goal. Your knee is forced into a similar position if you are shaping up to kick a football and an opponent kicks your foot back. Or your foot may slide when you are running and turning fast for a low ball in squash or tennis.

Specialist treatment

Specialist care will aim to correct the mechanical defects which contribute to, and are caused by, the knee-cap dislocation. You will be set a programme of exercises to strengthen the inner part of the quadriceps. If your foot mechanics have contributed to the weakness in your knee, a podiatrist will make up special orthotic foot-supports for you. If the dislocation problem is severe, you may be referred to an orthopaedic surgeon for an operation which would aim to strengthen the knee-cap from its inner side, and perhaps correct the 'Q-angle' at the knee. In the worst of cases, the surgeon may recommend removing the knee-cap to eliminate the problem.

Self-help measures for knee-cap dislocation

- If your knee is swollen and painful, you must apply ice to it, once or twice a day (p. 15), and wrap the joint in a stocking bandage or similar support to contain the swelling.
- You must practise straightening the knee out hard, holding it straight for a count of three, at least five times, every hour of the day, to try to increase power in the vastus medialis.
- Twice a day, you should try to do the regime of straight-leg exercises (p. 112). Do not try to force your knee to bend. Avoid any activities which hurt it. Once the swelling and pain have abated, you can start doing the exercises which help bend the knee, following the regime for recovery from cartilage problems (p. 113).
- You may find that you recover from a knee-cap dislocation episode well enough to be able to do most activities, but one particularly demanding exercise or sport will re-create the problem. In this case, you must

decide whether that activity is important enough to warrant complex surgery and an extended recovery period, or whether you are better off accepting a slight limitation on your normal range of activities.

Complications

Knee-cap dislocation is often followed by knee-cap pain (p. 91). This can be minimized by following the procedures for coping with knee-cap problems, but in the long-term, arthritis may develop in the joint between the knee-cap and the thigh-bone. If this causes severe pain and disability, you must refer to your doctor, with a view to receiving specialist treatment.

One complication which may occur at the moment of a severe knee-cap dislocation, but not become apparent until afterwards, is fracture of the knee-cap. If there is a possibility that this might have happened, your doctor will order check X-rays, showing the knee-cap from different angles, to reveal the suspected crack or break.

Pain on the inner side of the knee

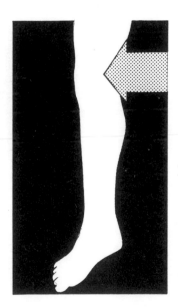

MEDIAL LIGAMENT STRAIN

The ligament which protects the inner side of the knee can be injured by a twisting strain on the knee, especially if the knee is bent at the time. Your foot may slip while you are running forward, turning your leg outwards, and stressing the inner side of the knee. Similarly, a tackle in football can force your foot sideways as you are bringing your leg forward to kick the ball, so that the inner knee is over-stressed. If you fall sideways with your foot held in a ski-boot, the medial ligament is one of the structures at the knee that may be damaged. The ligament may also be damaged by overuse strains. Breaststroke swimmers with a forceful leg kick are especially prone to medial ligament strains, as the knee is twisted slightly with each stroke.

What happens

The ligament may be only slightly damaged, with over-stretched fibres, or a small tear in some of its fibres. However, a severe injury may cause more serious tearing in the ligament, and may even break it completely. If the ligament is strained at its attachments, to the side of the shin-bone or the thigh-bone, it may pull away a flake of the bone as it tears.

If the injury is traumatic, you feel a sudden pain over the inner side of the knee, as the joint is twisted. This may be momentary, or it may be severe enough to prevent you from moving the knee. You may see some swelling over the torn part of the ligament. If swelling is visible over the whole joint, it is likely that you have damaged some of the internal structures in the knee, as well as the ligament at the side of the joint. The torn ligament feels tender to touch. The knee may feel 'loose' on its inner side, as though it has opened up abnormally, allowing an uncomfortable amount of sideways movement in the leg. If the ligament is completely torn, you may see the abnormal gap in the joint, if a specialist tests the damage by gently pushing the leg away sideways from the knee.

An overuse strain to the medial ligament causes only slight pain at first, but this gradually gets worse if you continue with the activity that caused the strain. Initially you only feel the pain during the damaging activity, but as the pain increases, you may begin to feel it during normal activities when you move the knee in certain directions. As the knee rotates slightly when it moves, stressing its ligaments to a small extent, if the damage to the medial ligament is allowed to become severe, the knee may hurt when you walk, or when you are sitting down at rest.

Self-help measures for medial ligament strain

- First-aid for a traumatic strain consists of ice applications to ease the pain, and reduce any swelling that has come up (p. 15).
- A double stocking bandage or similar support (p. 11) will help to control any swelling, and make the knee more comfortable. If the knee is very painful, it may be necessary to apply an inflatable splint to support it.
- Try not to walk on the injured leg, if it is very painful. Use crutches, or simply hop, if you have to move around.
- Do not try to force the knee to bend, if this causes pain. Keep your leg straight. To minimize the muscle wasting which will inevitably follow the injury, you must start practising straightening your knee hard, even immediately after injuring it. You may not be able to straighten your knee fully, but the effort of tightening the thigh muscles and holding the contraction for a count of three, at regular intervals, will help prevent quadriceps wasting.
- You must refer to your doctor, or a hospital casualty department, as quickly as possible after the injury. The damage must be assessed by a specialist. If, for instance, the medial ligament has been completely torn, an orthopaedic surgeon may think it advisable to repair the ligament surgically.

• If you have gradually increasing pain in the knee ligament, as an overuse injury, you should refer to your doctor, firstly so that he can assess the nature of the problem, and rule out any possible medical complications, and secondly in case he feels any specialist treatment, such as an injection, might help. The pain from a severe overuse strain can last for a long time. It is fairly common for the medial ligament to continue causing pain for up to a year after the symptoms first developed into noticeable pain. Therefore it is important for you to accept your doctor's guidance, to avoid such long-lasting problems, and to allow the ligament to heal as quickly as possible.

Phasing your recovery

Unless your doctor advises you not to exercise at all for some specific reason, you should start doing exercises with the knee straight immediately after injuring the joint. You should try to do a selection of straight-leg exercises (p. 112) at least twice a day, for about half-an-hour at a time. Throughout each day, you should practise straightening out your knee hard for a count of three, at least three times, every hour.

When the initial soreness and any swelling have subsided, you can start gently bending the knee, using bending exercises (p. 113). Do not force the knee to bend. Revert to straight-leg exercises only, if the mobilizing exercises aggravate the knee. While you are at the stage of doing non-weight-bearing exercises only, you can safely swim crawl, and do any exercises in the swimming pool which do not cause pain.

Once you can bend the knee comfortably past the right-angle, you can start to do weight-bearing, knee bending exercises (p. 116), and you can begin to run a little. Provided you suffer no setbacks, you should then be able to progress gradually into the more difficult functional exercises, including kicking a ball; hopping; squatting; and running and turning at speed. You should not try to go back to full participation in your sport, until you are confident that you have regained full power and movement in your knee.

Complications

A common problem which develops after a medial ligament strain at the knee is secondary knee-cap pain (p. 91). This is very likely to develop if you have failed to do enough straight-leg static quadriceps exercises before resuming normal activities.

If there is continuing pain in the area of the ligament, despite a properly graduated rehabilitation programme, it may be due to the formation of calcified flakes where the ligament was torn away from its bone attachment. This tends to be especially common where the ligament is attached to the thigh-bone, and the condition is known as Pellegrini-Stieda's disease. It may be necessary for a specialist to inject the area of calcification, or to remove the flakes surgically, but often the problem is cured by correct exercises to strengthen the knee muscles.

Sometimes continuing pain in the knee is due to more serious damage which was missed at the time of injury. In children and teenagers, a crack in the epiphysis (growth point) of the shin-bone or the thigh-bone may be caused by a twisting injury to the knee, and the subsequent pain may mimic the pain of a torn medial ligament. More commonly, the injury damages not only the medial ligament, but the medial cartilage which is attached to it. If the injury is severe enough, the cruciate ligaments in the centre of the knee may be damaged at the same time. Therefore, if you have continuing pain after twisting your knee, especially if the knee tends to swell up, you must refer back to your doctor for further assessment. Investigations such as X-rays, arthrograms (X-rays taken with dye injected into the knee), and arthroscopy (in which a surgeon looks into the knee through a small 'periscope'), will show accurately which structures in the knee are damaged, and whether specialist treatment is needed.

Pain on the outer side of the knee

LATERAL LIGAMENT STRAIN

The lateral ligament can be damaged by twisting strains at the knee. Sometimes it is injured together with the medial ligament. If it is injured alone, it is usually because the knee was forced outwards when it was bent. Footballers and rugby players are particularly prone to this type of injury, especially when they fall, and another player falls onto the inner side of the outstretched leg.

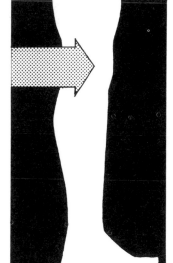

The lateral ligament is less vulnerable to overuse injury than the medial ligament. Like the medial ligament, if it is injured traumatically, other knee structures are often damaged with the ligament. Therefore it is important to obtain an accurate assessment of the injury, immediately if possible, or subsequently if there is continuing pain and disability.

Self-help follows the same pattern as for a medial ligament strain. You must progress through a defined programme to re-strengthen the knee muscles, gradually regain full movement in the joint, and finally regain the ability to use the knee functionally.

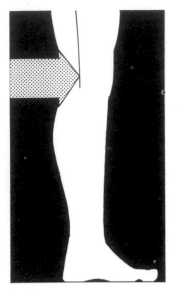

The iliotibial tract is a strong band, extending down the outer side of the thigh to the top of the outer edge of the shin-bone. The tract links the largest of your seat muscles (gluteus maximus) to the outer part of the knee, so it plays a part in a complex range of movements, whenever you extend your hip backwards and/or straighten your knee. You can see the tract standing out as a hard, taut band just above the outer side of the knee, if you straighten your knee as hard as you can. In a muscular person, you can see almost the full extent of the tract delineated at the side of the thigh, separating the fleshy quadriceps on the front of the thigh from the hamstrings behind it, when the knee is held straight.

Near the knee, the iliotibial tract passes over the outer edge of the thigh-bone. Bursae, or small sacs of fluid, lie between the tract and the bone to provide friction-free movement in the normal way. A change in your normal movement pattern, perhaps through running on a different surface, or because you have had to walk or run some distance downhill, can create friction between the tract and its underlying tissues. The inner side of the tract may become inflamed, or the friction may cause the natural bursae to become inflamed cysts. The injury is almost invariably an overuse injury, associated with sports involving repetitive knee movements, such as long-distance running and cross-country ski-ing.

What you feel

The pain may come on suddenly, but usually it is gradual: you notice a slight ache at first, which gradually increases. Typically, the pain, once it has started, comes on at a particular moment during your sport, for instance after about ten minutes' running, and this happens each time you run. You may then find that, although the pain remains constant, you can carry on running without it getting worse. The pain may even ease towards the end of a long run. Sometimes, however, the pain becomes so severe that you have to stop your sport. In this case, you may even feel it when you walk. More often, you only feel this injury when you are doing the causative activity, so you may find that you are still able to do other sports, like hockey or squash, although you are unable to do any training runs at even pace.

When you press your finger over the inflamed part of the iliotibial tract, you may feel a tender spot, although you may find you can only feel it when the knee is at a certain angle. If you put your finger over the painful area, with your knee bent to a right angle, and then straighten the knee while you press the side of the joint, you will probably feel the pain of the injury when the knee is at an angle of about thirty degrees from straight. You may also feel a 'snapping' sensation, as the inflamed part of the tract jumps over the prominent part of the edge of the thigh-bone.

What you should do

As this is generally an overuse injury, you must check with your doctor, in case there is a medical cause underlying the pain you feel. You may need to have investigations, such as X-rays, bone scans or blood tests, or your doctor may find it appropriate to refer you to a specialist, whether rheumatological, orthopaedic or paramedical, for treatment.

If the pain is diagnosed as a mechanical strain, you should try to identify its cause. If you are aware of having changed your sporting activities, or of having taken up an unaccustomed new activity, you should take care to avoid repeating the mistake in future. If the triggering factor is not obvious, you must try to analyse your movement patterns when you feel the pain. For instance, are your legs working symmetrically, or is one leg more splayed out than the other during sport? If you run, your foot movements may have a bearing on the problem, so you should check your sports shoes for signs of uneven or abnormal wear. If there is any indication that your foot biomechanics may be at fault, you should refer to a podiatrist for help.

Self-help measures for iliotibial tract friction syndrome

- Apply ice over the inflamed area, if it is very sore (p. 15).
- Do not continue doing any sport which increases the pain. Substitute pain-free activities, if necessary: perhaps swimming, cycling or squash.
- Strengthen the knee, choosing two or three straight-leg and bent-knee exercises to do as a session twice a day (p. 112, p. 113).
- Stretch the outer thigh: sit on the floor with your injured knee bent, and the foot of that leg on the floor beside the outer side of your other knee, so that your legs are crossed. Keeping your foot on the floor, gently push your injured knee over across the other leg until you feel a 'pulling' sensation along your seat and down the outside of your thigh. Hold the position for a count of ten, then gently let go.

The stretching exercises can also be done lying on your back or standing up: you pull the injured knee across the other leg, or towards the opposite shoulder, and hold the stretch for ten seconds. You should stretch the thigh as often as possible, but at least three times, three times daily.

Complications

If the problem does not clear up, despite resting from your sport, and having treatment or following the self-help measures described, you must refer back to your doctor. If a large inflamed cyst has formed under the iliotibial tract, it may be necessary to have it removed surgically.

POPLITEUS STRAIN

Injury to the popliteus tendon can cause pain at the side of the knee which is very similar to the pain from iliotibial tract inflammation. Popliteus is a small muscle lying at the back of the knee, and its tendon winds round the side of the joint to be attached to the side of the 'knuckle' of the thigh-bone. Besides acting to help bend the knee, popliteus rotates the shin-bone inwards relative to the thigh-bone, and it acts as an important stabilizing force in all knee movements.

The muscle can be overstrained in the same way as friction can be caused between the iliotibial tract and its underlying structures. A slight change in the pattern of movement at your knee during a repetitive activity like long-distance running can strain the tendon fibres, or cause inflammation in the protective fluid-filled covering over the tendon where it lies inside the knee itself, at the side of the joint.

What you feel

You feel pain at the side of the knee during the causative activity. Two features make pain from the popliteus different from iliotibial tract friction pain. Firstly, you may feel the pain during full-range knee movements, especially squatting. Secondly, because popliteus is further from the skin surface than the iliotibial tract, you have to press harder over the damaged part to find the tender spot. If the tendon is damaged where it is attached to the thigh-bone, you may be able to feel the spot if you bend your knee up, rest your foot on your other knee, and let the knee relax sideways. Then you may be able to feel the sore tendon by pressing over the thigh-bone 'knuckle', just in front of the taut band of the knee's lateral ligament, about four centimetres from the knee-cap.

What you should do

This involves much the same factors of care as in coping with the iliotibial tract friction syndrome. You must rest from any painful activities, analyse the possible cause of the problem, do alternative forms of exercise, and do specific exercises to strengthen the knee. You will probably find that activities which involve twisting the knee cause pain in a popliteus strain, so you will probably have to avoid sports like squash until the problem has cleared. You should also avoid squatting, sitting on your haunches, and sitting cross-legged, as all these movements are likely to cause pain, and so aggravate the damage to the tendon.

Popliteus is attached to the internal knee cartilage at the back of the knee, so any severe strain involving popliteus is likely to damage the cartilage as well. If you have a lot of pain from a so-called 'popliteus strain', and especially if you notice swelling in your knee, you must refer back to your doctor for further checks on the joint.

Pain at the back of the knee

POPLITEAL BURSITIS

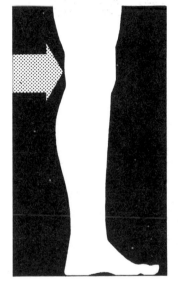

There are many bursae, or fluid-filled sacs for friction-free movement, at the back of the knee. They lie between moving structures, especially between tendons and the tissues over or under them. The largest of the bursae at the back of the knee lie between the gastrocnemius and hamstring tendons at the inner side; between the hamstring tendon and the outer knee ligament, on the knee's outer side; and between the popliteus tendon and the outer knee ligament.

Any of these bursae may become inflamed and swollen. If an inflamed bursa becomes very enlarged, it may push sideways into the space at the back of the knee called the popliteal fossa. You will then be able to see a defined, soft swelling protruding at the back of the knee. It need not necessarily be very painful, but by taking up space it may limit full movement at the knee. You should refer to the doctor for an assessment of the swelling, as this type of swelling can be disease-related. If it does prove to be simply a bursitis caused by friction, perhaps because you have changed your style in distance running, or changed boats in rowing, it may not be necessary to have any treatment for the swelling. However, if it does cause a lot of problems, you should refer back to your doctor. It may be possible to have the excess fluid drained off, or aspirated, although it is quite common for the swelling to recur after this has been done. The definitive cure is to have the swollen sac removed surgically by an orthopaedic surgeon. After surgery, your knee is usually kept held still in plaster for some weeks, after which you have to re-strengthen the muscles, and then regain full movement. While your leg is in plaster, you should do the straight-leg exercises (p. 112) unless your surgeon forbids them, for any reason. If you do not have surgery for the bursitis, you must take care to maintain strength around the knee, and especially to keep the knee as mobile as possible: you must stretch your quadriceps muscles (p. 133) and your hamstrings (p. 144), at least six times every day, preferably more often if possible.

These include gastrocnemius tendon strains (p. 75) and hamstring tendon strains (p. 139) as well as tears to the knee joint covering or its internal cartilages.

Damage inside the knee

Any of the knee's internal tissues can be damaged by a severe injury, but the cartilages (menisci) and the cruciate ligaments are those most commonly harmed in sportsmen.

CARTILAGE TEARS

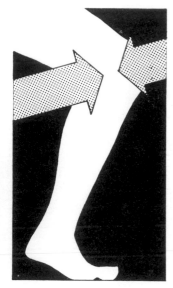

The knee's soft-tissue cartilages can be damaged by pressure from the bones of the joint when an abnormal force twists the bones against each other unusually. In the normal way, the cartilages move slightly, backwards and forwards, during knee movements, following the pattern of bending and straightening with the slight rotation that accompanies normal knee movement. In this way, the cartilages act as buffers throughout the whole movement, although the joint surface of the thigh-bone is bigger than the receiving surface on the shin-bone. However, with abnormal pressure, the cartilages may be jammed between the two bones: if the bones then twist on each other and apply a shearing stress on the cartilage, the tissue splits.

What happens

The most common cause is an abnormal twist in your knee while your weight is on the leg. You may catch your foot and twist as you fall; your foot may be trapped in a ski-boot as you fall forward; you may be pushed sideways by a tackle as you run forward in rugby; you may over-balance while lunging in fencing or squash. In each case, your knee is bent at the moment of injury. A sudden stress with the knee bent, even when you are not standing on the leg, can be enough to tear the cartilage. This may happen if you miss a kick in football, or try to sit back on your haunches with a forced bouncing movement when your feet are stretched out sideways beside your seat. Cartilage tears can also be caused by a sudden over-stress when your knee is straight, for instance if you miss a drop-kick in rugby.

What you feel

This injury gives instant pain, to the extent that you may not be able to move the knee at all, let alone take weight through your leg. Immediate swelling will inhibit movement further, although the swelling may not appear until some hours later, in which case the knee will feel weak rather than stiff in the first instance. Visible swelling may extend right round the knee, making the joint look bloated, or it may be only a small patch, barely visible over the line of the joint. At the moment of injury, it is impossible to tell, from the outside, exactly how much damage has been done. First-aid for the swollen knee must be applied (p. 85).

The only external sign that you might have torn a cartilage is the so-called 'locked' knee. You may feel, at the moment of injury, that your knee is stuck in one position: if you shake it gently, it frees itself, often with a clicking noise. More often, the knee is too painful to move immediately, and this 'locking' feeling only becomes evident when the knee has recovered enough for you to be moving it and using it more or less normally. Then you may find that the knee locks in a certain position, so that you cannot bend or straighten it, unless you twist your foot to free it. This type of locking indicates that the torn part of the cartilage is blocking movement in the joint by jamming itself between the shin-bone and the thigh-bone.

What you should do

Once you have applied first-aid measures (p. 85), and made the knee comfortable, you must be taken for specialist help as quickly as possible. The sooner an accurate assessment of the extent of the damage is done, the better off you will be in the long-term. The locked joint is a good indication that cartilage damage has happened, but it is not a definitive sign, as there are other types of knee damage that can cause a similar feeling that the knee has 'stuck', although the precise mechanism will not be the same. If you are taken to a casualty department in a hospital, your knee will probably be X-rayed, to see whether there is any bone damage. You may also have arthrograms done, in which dye is injected into your knee, so that soft-tissue damage shows up on X-ray. You may even be admitted to hospital so that an orthopaedic surgeon can perform arthroscopy, looking into your knee with a small 'periscope', while you are under general anaesthetic.

Specialist treatment

Once a specialist has diagnosed a cartilage tear in the knee, there are two possible courses of action. Either the torn part of the cartilage must be removed surgically, or the problem must be treated with rehabilitation only. The one certainty is that the torn cartilage will not heal, or mend itself, naturally. If the specialist decides on immediate surgery, it is because he deems that the torn cartilage will create functional problems in the knee. If only part of the cartilage has to be removed, a kind of substitute cartilage will eventually grow from the remaining part, so that the knee regains its buffering tissue, although the replacement will not be as strong as the original tissue.

The cartilage removal operation is called a meniscectomy. There are two chief methods of removing a knee cartilage surgically nowadays. The surgeon may be able to remove the damaged part through the arthroscope, so that he does not have to make a scar through the skin, and leaves only a few tiny holes in the surface of the skin. This makes the recovery process much quicker. However, depending on the exact extent of the damage, it may not be possible to do the whole operation through the arthroscope, so the surgeon may choose to operate through the more traditional incision through the skin. In this case, the trauma from the operation is more severe, and there will be disturbance to the skin sensation where the scar has cut through the sensation nerves, creating functional disability.

Recovery from both types of surgery follows the same pattern. Firstly, it is important to control any swelling, by ice applications, and by wearing a stocking bandage. Knee exercises must start straight away, but keeping the knee straight, to avoid stressing the joint harmfully and increasing the swelling (p. 112). As the knee becomes more comfortable, and the swelling goes down, your surgeon will allow you to progress to exercises which bend the knee, but without your weight on it (p. 113), while you maintain a daily routine of straight-leg exercises. Once you can bend your knee beyond a right angle, you are ready to start running, on soft surfaces such as grass, and you should start simple weight-bearing exercises to bend the knee, like half-squats, without twisting the joint (p. 116). The final phase of recovery includes exercises which stress the knee in different situations. If there are no setbacks at this stage, the knee is fully recovered from the injury and the operation.

Recovery from the surgery can take a varying time, according to individual circumstances. It is possible to be back to full sporting activities within two weeks of removal of the cartilage through the arthroscope. More commonly, full recovery takes about three months, or anything up to six months, if there are any complications during rehabilitation. It is advisable to work through the process of rehabilitation in its graduated stages. Any sudden increase of swelling or pain is a sign that you have done too much exercise, or exercise that your knee was not ready for, so you should revert to straight-leg exercises until the knee is less painful and swollen. If you work gradually through the phases of rehabilitation suggested, you minimize the risk of over-stressing the knee before it is strong enough to cope. You should remember that, even though the discomfort after arthroscopy is only slight, the knee has still suffered a lot of trauma, firstly when it was injured, and secondly through the surgical intrusion. You must not allow the absence of pain to make you over-confident: you must make sure that the knee is strong and stable, firstly in straightening, and secondly bending under load. Only then will you be safe to play demanding sports, like squash, football or rugby again. Otherwise the risk of re-injury is high.

Recovery without surgery

If a specialist decides not to remove the torn cartilage, after diagnosing the tear, it is because he believes that the damage is slight, and the knee can recover functionally without any need for surgery. Your leg may be immobilized in plaster, to protect the knee, if the injury was severe; or you may simply be given a supporting bandage to control the swelling.

In either case, you must start straight-leg exercises immediately, to maintain knee stability. You progress to gentle mobilizing exercises to bend the knee as soon as your specialist allows, when the knee is no longer acutely painful and swollen. The third phase of recovery is to strengthen the leg working the knee through a full range of movement, and finally you progress to free active exercises, which test the knee through functional movements. It is possible to regain muscle power and good movement within ten days of injury, but full recovery to the stage of resuming sport is likely to take about three months at least. As with recovery from surgery, you must watch for signs that you are overdoing your exercises, and revert to straight-leg exercises and ice applications if your knee swells up again and becomes painful. If, as you progress into the final phase of rehabilitation exercises, or even after you have resumed your normal sport, the knee shows signs of 'catching' or 'locking', you must refer back to your doctor, with a view to having another specialist orthopaedic opinion. The torn cartilage, in this case, is causing functional problems. Each episode in which it blocks your knee movement, and causes swelling and pain, is increasing the danger of damage being done to the joint surfaces in your knee. Therefore there is little alternative but to remove the torn part surgically, if you want to continue doing sport. After surgery, you have to progress through the graduated phases of rehabilitation again, but the process will be quicker if you have done the specific knee exercises intensively before the operation.

Straight-leg exercises (Static quadriceps regime)

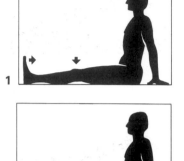

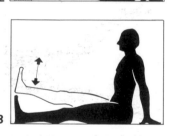

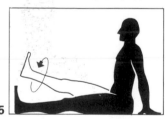

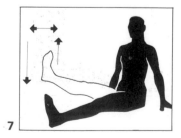

1. Knee-bracing. Sit on the floor with your legs straight in front of you. Straighten your knee as hard as you can, pressing it down into the floor, and pulling your foot back towards you from the ankle at the same time. Hold the knee straight for a count of five, then relax completely. (Ten times, three times a day.)

You can practise knee-bracing standing or sitting, so you should incorporate the exercise into your everyday activities, for instance straightening your knee out at intervals when you are sitting down for long periods.

2. Knee-bracing with heel support. Sit with your legs straight out in front of you, on the floor. Place a support (rolled towel or block, about five centimetres high) under your heel. Press your knee down, tightening your thigh muscles, and pulling your toes back towards you from the ankle. Hold to five, then relax, and repeat ten times, at least twice a day.

3. Straight-leg-raise. Sit with your legs straight. Keeping your knee locked straight, lift your leg straight up in the air, lower to just above the floor, then lift again, in rapid succession, ten times over. Try to build up to thirty lifts in one go.

4. Sitting with your legs straight, and a weight over your ankle, lift your leg straight up in the air, then slowly lower. Start with no more than one kilogramme, and gradually increase the weight, but make sure you keep your knee locked straight as you lift. Start with five lifts, and build up gradually to three sets of ten.

5. Hip-circling. Sit with your legs straight. Keeping your knee locked straight, lift your leg up in the air, and describe rapid circles in the air with your foot, starting with five and building up to three sets of ten. Then add weights over your ankle.

6. Alphabet. Sitting with your legs straight, lift up your leg, keeping your knee straight, and 'write' the alphabet in the air, without stopping. Add weights when the sequence becomes easy.

7. Sit with your legs straight. Lift your leg straight up, keeping your knee locked straight, swing your foot out to the side, slowly return to centre, then slowly lower. Do five on each leg, building up to three sets of ten, and then add weights over your ankles.

8. Hip abduction. Lie on your side, with your injured leg uppermost. Keeping your knee straight, lift your leg up sideways, hold for a count of three, then slowly lower. Start with five, building up to three sets of ten, and then add weights.

9. Prone leg-raising. Lie on your stomach. Keeping your knee straight, lift your leg a little way backwards, hold to a count of three, then slowly lower. Do five on each leg, building up to three sets of ten, and then add weights.

10. Lie on your stomach. Keeping your knee locked straight, lift one leg a little way backwards, take it slowly out sideways, back to centre, then slowly lower. Do five on each leg, building to three sets of ten, then adding weights.

Mobilizing exercises to bend the knee

1. Sit on a table or high chair, with your injured leg straight in front of you, supported on your other leg. Very gently let your uninjured leg bend, until you reach the limit of movement in your injured knee. Hold this position for a count of five, then straighten both knees again. (Ten times.)

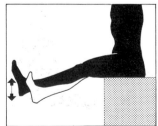

2. Sitting on a table or high chair, with your injured leg supported straight by your good leg. Gently let your knees bend to the limit, then rock them backwards and forwards twenty times at this point. (Repeat ten times.)

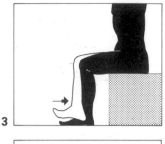

3. Sit on a table or high chair, with your legs relaxed, and your uninjured leg resting on top of your injured one. Gently press downwards with your good leg, so that your injured knee bends to its limit, and rock your legs a little so that you feel your knee gradually bending further. (Ten times.)

4. Lie on your stomach, with the heel of your good leg resting on the front of the shin on your injured leg. Push back with your good leg to bend your knees, pressing your heels towards your seat with a rhythmical bouncing movement. (Repeat ten times.)

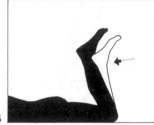

5. Lying on your back, bend your injured knee onto your chest. With your hands over the top of your shin, gently pull your knee towards your chest in a bouncing movement, so that you feel your knee gradually bending further. (Ten times.)

6. Lying on your stomach, bend your injured knee. With your hand, pull your foot towards your seat, and hold the knee still for a count of ten when you reach the limit of the knee-bend. Gently relax, then repeat five times.

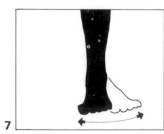

7. Sit in a chair, with your injured knee bent as far as it will go, keeping your foot on the floor. Keeping your heel on the ground, turn your toes inwards then outwards six times, twisting the knee slightly. Then try to bend your knee a little further back. Repeat the process three times.

8. Standing on your good leg, rest your injured knee on a chair (with a pillow for comfort) as though you were kneeling on it. Gently rock your seat back to your heel, to bend your knee. (Ten times.)

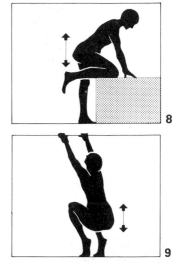

9. Holding onto a bar or support at shoulder height with both hands, gently bend your knees in a bouncing movement until you are squatting down as far as your knee will bend. Straighten your legs, then repeat the squatting movement five times. (If possible, do this in front of a mirror, so that you do not 'cheat' by taking your weight on your good knee).

10. On an exercise bicycle, set the saddle to a level just below the point at which you can turn the pedal fully with your injured knee. With no resistance, push the pedal round as far as you can with your injured knee, then push down to return to the starting position, helping the momentum with your good leg if necessary. Keep pushing the pedal rhythmically backwards and forwards until you can make a full turn. Pedal normally with both feet for a minute, then lower the saddle by three centimetres and repeat the process.

The exercise bicycle, which you can use to strengthen and mobilize your knees, and for general training.

115

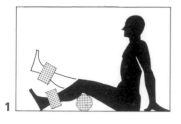

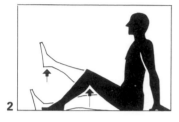

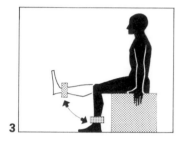

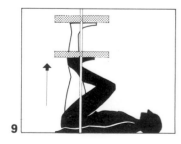

Strengthening exercises

These are all strengthening exercises with knee movement. Build up to achieve three sets of ten, for each of the twelve exercises.

1. Inner range work for vastus medialis. Sit with your legs in front of you, with a cushion or rolled towel under your knee, and a weight over your ankle. Straighten up your knee hard, then slowly lower. Repeat each set on the other leg.

2. Knee bend to straight-leg raise. Sit with your legs straight out in front of you. Bend one knee, keeping your heel on the floor, then straighten up your leg to lift your foot in the air. Slowly lower, keeping your knee straight. (One set on each leg in turn.) Add in weights.

3. Knee extensions. Sit on a chair or high table, with a weight over your foot or ankle, and your knee bent to ninety degrees. Straighten your knee, locking it out hard, then slowly lower. (One set on each leg in turn.)

4. Leg press. Sit in the leg press weights machine, with the seat adjusted so that you bend the knees as far as you can. Straighten your knees out hard, then slowly return to the knees-bent position. (See photo opposite.)

5. Squats. Stand, keeping your back as straight as possible. Slowly bend your knees to just beyond a right angle, then push up straight, locking out your knees in full extension. Add in weights, either held in your hands or over your shoulders.

6. Stand-ups. Sit on a low chair or stool, with your feet parallel, and your hands folded across your chest. Stand up straight, then bend your knees in fairly quick succession, to touch the chair lightly with your seat at each repetition. Do not sit down fully until the end of the set. Add weights, held in outstretched hands.

7. Stand-ups. As 6, but on one leg at a time for each set.

8. Step-ups. Stand in front of a bench (or double stairs), about sixty centimetres high. Step up onto the bench, straightening your knees fully, then down, in quick succession. Alternate your leading leg on each set of the exercise. Add in weights, held in your hands.

9. Supine Leg Press. Lie under the leg press machine, making sure that the whole of your lower back is in contact with the floor. Press your knees to straighten them fully, hold, then slowly lower. (Start with light weights, and build up.) Your lower back should stay in contact with the floor throughout the movement.

116

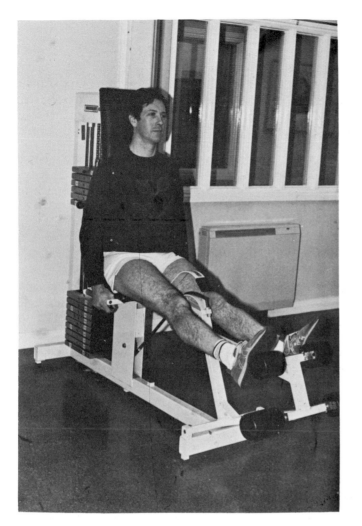

The leg press machine.

10. One-leg squat. Balance on one leg. Bend your knee to a right angle or just beyond, slowly, then push upwards to straighten your knee fully. (One set on each leg in turn.)

11. Rowing exerciser. Sit in the rowing machine, making sure you can bend and straighten your knees fully. When exercising, push your knees straight hard, then slowly bend them.

12. Static bicycle. Adjust the saddle height so that your leg is almost straight, with your foot's sole on the pedal, on the downward sweep of the pedal. Set the resistance to a moderate tension, and pedal at constant speed for ten minutes. Increase the resistance, then the exercise time.

117

Dynamic exercises

1. Alternate leg thrusts. Crouch on the floor with your legs straight out behind you, your weight resting on your hands. Bend one knee up to your chest, then kick that leg straight out behind you, while you bend the other knee up to your chest. Repeat the movement in quick succession. Start with twenty movements (ten on each leg), build up to fifty.

2. Squat thrusts. As (1), but bend and kick back both knees together. Start with ten, build to three sets of ten.

3. Burpees. Bend and kick back your knees as for the squat thrust, with your weight on your hands, but jump upwards after bending your knees up to your chest, then spring down to kick your legs back again.

4. Squat jumps. Stand with one foot slightly in front of the other. Jump down, to touch your hands to the floor; spring up, changing feet in the air as you jump, so that you land with the 'hind' foot forward. Repeat in quick succession, starting with six, building up to three sets of ten.

5. Bench jumps. Stand over a bench, with your feet on either side of it. Jump up to touch your heels together in the air over the bench, landing on either side of the bench. Six in rapid succession, building up to three sets of ten.

6. Medicine ball lift. Stand with a medicine ball (or similar large weight) in your hands. Keeping your back straight, squat down to touch the floor with the weight, then straighten your legs rapidly, reaching upwards to hold the weight above your head. Six, building up to three sets of ten, in rapid succession.

118

7. Medicine ball throw. As (6), but throw the medicine ball upwards as you straighten your knees, and let your knees give as you catch the ball, keeping your back straight. (Make sure you have plenty of space for this one!)

8. Hop. Hop forwards and backwards, springing up as high as you can, on each leg in turn. Start with ten hops, build up to fifty. Progress to hopping up steps on each leg.

9. Stair run. Run up steps as fast as you can, first one at a time, then two at a time. Start with twenty steps, build up to fifty. (Jog down.)

10. Shuttle runs. Mark out a distance, starting with thirty metres, building up to one hundred metres. Sprint this distance, touch the ground and sprint back, repeating the sequence, touching the ground at each end of the course, five times, building up to ten times.

11. Kicking. Stand in front of a wall, starting ten metres away, progressing to about thirty metres. Kick a light ball against the wall in quick succession. Progress to kicking a heavier ball. One set of twenty kicks on each leg in turn.

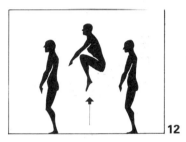

12. Chest jumps. From standing, jump up, trying to bring your knees right up to your chest. Repeat rapidly six times, building up to twenty times.

CRUCIATE LIGAMENT TEARS

The cruciate ligaments are two strong bands which bind the shin-bone to the thigh-bone, across the centre of the knee. It takes a strong force to damage them: they can be torn in a severe twisting injury, for instance in a blocked kick or a sliding fall in a tackle during football; or by excessive pressure forcing the knee to 'bend backwards' when it is straight, for instance if an opponent falls across your extended leg in rugby or hockey.

What happens

A major shearing force can tear both cruciates together, usually tearing one or both of the cartilages at the same time. A moderate injury may tear one of the cruciates completely, without damaging the second, and with or without accompanying cartilage damage. In a more minor injury, there may only be a part-tear to one of the cruciates. Which of the cruciates is damaged depends entirely on the nature and direction of the abnormal shearing force.

What you feel

The severe injury is extremely painful, and the knee usually swells up immediately. If both cruciates are torn, the knee feels completely floppy,

119

if you move it at all. It will in fact be capable of bending in the forward direction as far as it is normally able to bend back, having become totally flaccid, but pain will probably stop you from moving it enough to find this out. The more moderate injuries are as painful as the injuries causing cartilage tears, with much or little swelling, according to severity.

At the moment of injury, it is totally impossible to assess the extent of the internal damage through outward signs. The only certainty is that, if your knee has swollen painfully, some of its internal structures have been damaged. If you do not have an accurate diagnosis at the time of injury, it may only become apparent that the cruciate ligaments have been damaged much later when you have started doing sport again. Then you may find that in certain positions your knee feels loose and unstable. It may feel as though it is 'rolling' on itself, backwards or forward, usually giving a 'clunking' sound, with a sharp pain. This makes running and turning difficult: you may even find that you fall over when it happens, either because the knee has given way, or because the pain is so severe. This unstable feeling is an external indication that there is some damage to the cruciates. If your knee locks as well, then there is also likely to be cartilage damage.

What you should do

At the moment of injury, the knee should be made comfortable by applying the first-aid measures for the swollen knee (p. 85). It is essential to obtain a specialist opinion as quickly as possible. When you attend a hospital casualty department, you may be referred directly to the orthopaedic surgeon. For an accurate assessment of the damage, you will probably undergo investigations, such as X-rays, arthrograms and arthroscopy.

Specialist treatment

If the surgeon finds that both cruciate ligaments are completely torn, he will probably perform an immediate operation to try to repair the damage. If there is partial damage to one or both of the cruciates, the surgeon will choose whether to operate, or whether to allow the knee to recover enough for you to resume sport, and see whether there is any residual disability when you use the knee. Even though the cruciates will not repair themselves once they are torn, you can compensate for some degree of slackness in them by strengthening some of the knee's muscles to provide external stability. If, having done a careful rehabilitation programme, you find that your knee is still not strong enough to cope with your sport, you will probably have to face the choice between undergoing surgery to try to stabilize the joint, or giving up your normal sport. You may be able to do some sports but not others. For instance, your knee may be strong enough for cricket, but too unstable for football. Then, following your surgeon's guidance, you must weigh up carefully the advantages and disadvantages of having a surgical repair.

Whether the repair is done straight away, or after residual disability has shown up, there are various methods which the surgeon may choose to mend the damage. Some procedures involve mending the cruciates themselves, either by re-attaching a torn end to the bone from which it has snapped off, or by replacing the whole ligament with a synthetic substance. Other methods of stabilizing the knee involve tightening up the capsule and tissues around the joint, to compensate for the internal instability. Whichever method the surgeon chooses, rehabilitation is a slow process: full recovery may take up to a year. It is vital to follow the surgeon's rehabilitation programme to the letter, as recovery phases differ according to the particular operation done.

CRUCIATE TEAR INSTABILITY EXERCISES

Cruciate tears cause abnormal gliding movements between the thighbone and the shin-bone. The thigh-bone may slide forwards, backwards or sideways relative to the shin-bone. The direction of the abnormal movement depends on the exact injury to the cruciates, and whether any other structures in the knee have also been damaged. The instability may show when the knee is straight or bent, according to the injury. Usually you are only aware of it when your weight is on the leg, but you may also feel the unusual degree of movement when your knee is stressed, perhaps by the surgeon twisting it, or under load, if you do weights exercises.

If the specialist decides in favour of a stabilizing rehabilitation programme, rather than surgery, it is likely that the first phase of the programme will be intensive strengthening for the hamstrings. These muscles can help to control the gliding movements between the knee-bones, and conversely, if they are weak or over-stretched, they can contribute to abnormally free movement at the knee. If it is necessary to strengthen one side of the muscle group, your surgeon will advise you in detail. The most common pattern for this rehabilitation process is for the first phase of hamstring strengthening to last between four and six weeks; you then strengthen the quadriceps, but without straightening your knee fully; you progress to straightening the knee out again gradually, maintaining a consistent daily programme of hamstring exercises all the while; if you have suffered no setbacks up to this stage, you start doing more demanding free dynamic knee exercises, leading up to a gradual resumption of your sport. Many of the various surgical repair operations are followed by this pattern of rehabilitation. Often, the operated knee is immobilized in a plaster cast bent to an angle of ninety degrees, and the first phase of the knee exercises starts immediately, so that the leg muscles work, but only the hip moves, and the hamstrings are forced to tighten.

Strengthening exercises, with shortened hamstrings

1. Lie on your stomach with your knee bent at a right angle. Keeping your knee bent, lift your leg a little way backwards from the hip, twenty times in quick succession. Build up to fifty repetitions, then gradually add weights, resting at the lower end of the back of your thigh.

2. Lie on your stomach with your knee bent at a right angle. Keeping your knee bent, lift your leg a little way backwards, carry it out sideways, hold for a count of three, take it back to centre, and slowly lower. Build up to three sets of ten, then add in weights over your lower thigh.

3. Lie on your side with your injured leg uppermost, knee bent to a right angle. Lift your leg up sideways, keeping your knee bent, hold for a count of three, then slowly lower. Build up to three sets of ten, then add in weights, resting on your thigh, just above your knee.

4. Sit in a chair with your knee bent to a right angle. Lift your thigh up, keeping the knee bent, hold to a count of three, then slowly lower. Build up to thirty lifts in quick succession, then add in weights, resting just above your knee.

5. Stand on one leg, with your injured knee bent behind you to a right angle. Extend your bent leg behind you from the hip, keeping the knee bent. Hold for a count of three, then slowly take the leg back to neutral. Start with ten, build up to thirty.

Isometric hamstring strengthening exercises

1. Sit in a chair with your knee bent to a right angle, and your heel resting against the chair leg. Press your heel back against the chair leg, hold for a count of five, then relax completely. Repeat three times, building up to ten.

2. Sit in a chair with your foot on the floor, and the outside edge of your foot against a table leg. Press your foot against the table leg, without lifting your heel up, as though you were trying to turn your leg from the knee. Hold for five, then relax. Build up to ten repetitions.

3. Sit as in (2), but with the inside edge of your foot resting against the table leg. Press your foot against the table leg, so that your leg is trying to turn inwards. Hold to five, then relax. Build up to ten repetitions.

4. Arrange your chair so that the back of your heel rests against the chair leg, while the outside edge of your foot presses against a table leg or similar immovable object. Press your heel back, at the same time as you

press your foot sideways, holding for a count of five. Build up to ten repetitions.

5. As (4), but pressing the inside edge of your foot against the resistance. (Some of these exercises are illustrated on p. 146.)

Dynamic exercises

These exercises are for the hamstrings and quadriceps, gradually straightening the knee.

1. Lie on your stomach with a weight over your foot. Swiftly bend your knee, taking your heel towards your seat as far as you can, then slowly lower back until your foot is about fifteen centimetres from the ground, so that the knee does not straighten out. Build up to three sets of ten, then increase the weights resistance.

2. Stand on one leg, with your injured leg slightly bent, and a weight strapped to your ankle. Bend your injured knee up behind you, taking your foot towards your seat, then slowly lower back until the knee is slightly bent again (not fully straight). Build up to three sets of ten, increasing the weight.

3. Sit on a high chair, with a weight over your ankle. Straighten your knee until it is about thirty degrees from fully straight, hold for a count of three, then slowly lower. Build up to three sets of ten, then increase the weight.

4. Sit on a leg press machine, with your knees bent as far as you comfortably can hold them. Press the weights down, until your knees are about thirty degrees from being fully straight, then slowly bend back. Build up to three sets of ten, then increase the weight-loading.

5. When your specialist allows, you can do these exercises with increasing range through your knee, so that you are fully straightening the joint. At this stage, you can do the straight-leg exercises and dynamic strengthening work appropriate to the majority of knee injuries (p. 112, p. 118).

Functional dynamic exercises

Besides the general knee rehabilitation exercises (p. 118), you should do the following exercises for stabilizing co-ordination:

1. Stand on the wobble board (p. 44), on your injured leg. Slowly bend and straighten your knee, without losing your balance. Try to maintain your balance for up to fifteen minutes, building up gradually.

2. Run backwards for twenty paces as fast as you can, then jog forwards. Build up to one hundred paces, repeating the routine up to five times.

3. Set out ten skittles in a straight line at intervals along one hundred metres. Run backwards, weaving in and out of the skittles, turning at the

last and returning backwards to the starting-point. Start with one complete circuit, and build up to ten circuits.

4. Set out three skittles at intervals along a straight line. Hop backwards (on your injured leg) weaving in and out among the skittles. Start with three complete circuits, and build up to ten circuits.

5. On your injured leg, hop backwards onto a low step. Start with five continuous hops up and down, and build up to twenty. If you can, raise the height of the step when the exercise becomes easy.

COMPLICATIONS

Knee injuries causing internal damage may result in complications.

Loose bodies

Any particle floating freely inside the joint, which should not be there, is termed a loose body. Any torn or broken structure can become a loose body, so the particle may be a piece of cartilage which has broken away in a cartilage tear, or it may be a bone chip from a crack caused by a direct blow.

A small loose body may not be detected immediately after the injury, but it may cause problems later when you start to use the knee normally again. You may find that the knee tends to lock or swell up, without any recognizable reason. If this happens, you must refer back to your doctor, so that you can have more investigations. If a loose body is diagnosed as the cause of the problems, it will probably have to be removed surgically.

Osteoarthritis

If you have a severe knee injury, with internal damage, even when you are quite young, you are more likely to suffer from osteoarthritis in later life. Your vulnerability to this type of wear-and-tear arthritis is further increased if you suffer a series of knee injuries; if the joint remains distended with blood for any length of time, following an injury; if you use the joint too quickly after an injury; or if you try to return to active sport without regaining full power and mobility in the joint and its muscles.

In osteoarthritis, the bone surfaces within the joint are damaged. X-rays will show the signs of damage, and the bones will probably look closer together than normal. The signs of degeneration may affect one side of the knee only, or the whole joint may be affected. If the condition develops to a severe stage, the joint may look deformed from the outside, so that you can see that it has changed shape. You may find that you can no longer straighten it fully, or it looks as though your leg is curving

124

unusually inwards or outwards. Osteoarthritis does not usually set in before the age of about fifty, although it can occur much earlier, even in the thirties, if the knee has suffered badly from injuries.

Pain is not necessarily related to the degree of degeneration visible on X-ray. You can have quite severe degeneration, and no pain in the knee. In the beginning, pain from osteoarthritis tends to be slight. It is usually brought on by weight-bearing activities, like long-distance running. You may notice a slight pain, with some swelling, after a certain session of a particular activity, without having been aware of injuring your knee. If osteoarthritis is diagnosed as the cause of your pain, you will probably have to modify your activities, although you should be able to continue with some sport.

It is very important to protect your knee, by keeping it strong, especially through straight-leg exercises (p. 112), and by maintaining full flexibility in the joint. Stretching and mobilizing exercises should be a daily routine, once you know you have osteoarthritis. Excessive weight-loading or compressive activities will accelerate the degenerative changes in the joint. Your best guide to what is good or bad for you in terms of exercise is the amount of discomfort you feel. If, for instance, running ten miles brings on pain and swelling, whereas running five miles does not, then you should reduce your training mileage. If your knee pain is increasing, you must reduce all activities which involve running and jumping. As the condition becomes more severe, you will notice increasing pain during and after any aggravating activities, and you will also notice pain when the knee is warm, for instance in bed at night.

Trying to press on with sport at this stage will only make the condition much worse. You must be prepared to modify your exercise: cut out pain-causing weight-bearing activities, and substitute free exercise and swimming instead. The more mobility you can maintain in the knee, combined with stabilizing strength in the muscles protecting the joint, the less painful the knee will be. In the long term, good movement and strength will stop the arthritic condition from developing to the stage of severe pain and deformity. For detailed advice, of course, you must consult your doctor.

The Front-of-the-Thigh Muscles

STRUCTURE

The muscles which form the fleshy bulk covering the whole of the front of the thigh are the quadriceps group, consisting of four functionally linked muscles, and the sartorius, the longest muscle in the body. Sartorius extends from the prominent bone at the front of your pelvis (just below your waist), diagonally across your thigh, over the inner side of the knee, to be attached to the top of the inner side of the shin-bone. Rectus femoris, so named because it extends in a straight line between its attachment points, is the only one of the quadriceps group to be attached to the pelvis. It lies just below sartorius on the hip-bone, and passes directly down, over the top of the other quadriceps muscles, to the knee-cap. The other quadriceps muscles are closely attached to the thigh-bone, one extending over the inner side of the thigh (vastus medialis), and the others, vastus intermedius and vastus lateralis, spreading over the outer side.

The four quadriceps muscles join up at the knee-cap, which is a free-floating knob of bone actually formed within the muscle fibres, and they form a single tendon, the patellar tendon, which extends from the pointed end of the knee-cap to the tibial tubercle at the top of the front of the shin-bone.

When you tense up your thigh muscles by straightening your knee as hard as you can, the quadriceps muscles stand out clearly delineated. You can see the bulge of vastus medalis just above the inner side of your knee, while the limits of vastus lateralis at the outer side of the thigh are defined by the iliotibial tract, which forms a straight indentation down the side of the thigh, dividing vastus lateralis from the hamstrings at the back of the thigh. If you sit down and put your hand over the prominent bump at the front of your hip-bone, just below your waist, you can feel the top of sartorius tightening if you lift your leg up from the hip.

FUNCTIONS

The quadriceps group straightens the knee, against gravity or a resistance,

126

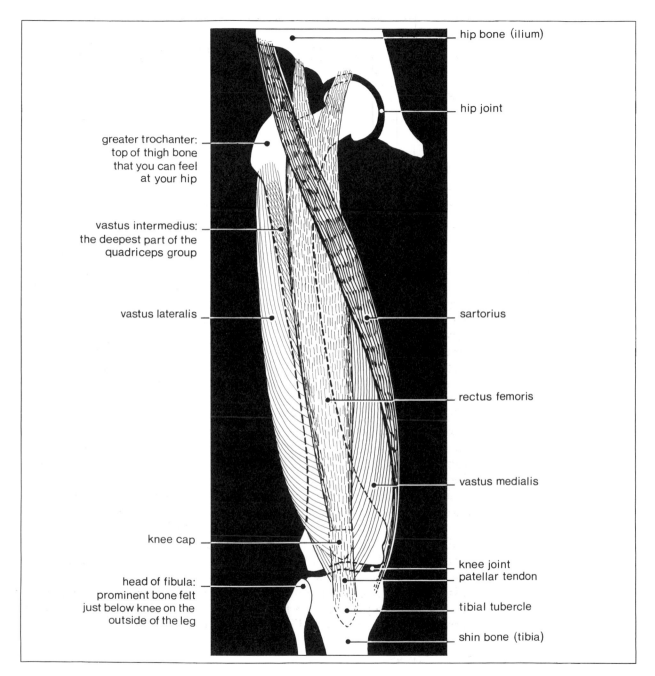

hip bone (ilium)

hip joint

greater trochanter:
top of thigh bone
that you can feel
at your hip

vastus intermedius:
the deepest part of the
quadriceps group

vastus lateralis

sartorius

rectus femoris

vastus medialis

knee cap

knee joint
patellar tendon

head of fibula:
prominent bone felt
just below knee on the
outside of the leg

tibial tubercle

shin bone (tibia)

Muscles on the front of the right thigh.

127

and also controls the opposite movement of bending the knee, when this is done in the direction of gravity. When you squat down from standing, your quadriceps muscles pay out, keeping the movement at the speed you choose, and preventing gravity from pushing you down. When you straighten up to stand up, your quadriceps muscles shorten to perform the movement. Rectus femoris and sartorius also help to bend the hip, when you bring the thigh forward, or when you bring your trunk forward, for instance when you sit up with your back straight from lying on your back.

Sartorius has quite complex functions, because of its extended diagonal line of pull, crossing two joints. Besides helping to turn the thigh-bone at the hip, it also pulls the leg inwards, towards the other leg. This makes it an important muscle for such movements as running uphill, or kicking a football with the inside of your boot.

Your thigh muscles are vital in any sport involving use of the legs. Your quadriceps muscles work hard when you run up a hill, but even harder when you run down it and they have to control your knee movements at speed. Propulsion in a modern rowing boat, where the seat moves up and down a slide, is achieved through quadriceps power as you push your legs straight while you pull the blade through the water. Footballers use the quadriceps muscles for running and kicking. In horse-riding, your rhythm during trotting is achieved by your quadriceps muscles straightening your thighs, to lift your seat off the saddle; sartorius helps to keep your knees fixed against the saddle. Cyclists develop exceptionally strong thigh muscles, as they work them hard both on the upward swing and on the downward thrust against the pedals.

The quadriceps also act as postural muscles, helping to stabilize you when you are standing upright against the influence of gravity. They feel relaxed when you are standing, so if you tense them to straighten the knees you can feel the difference. But the muscles are in fact active, just enough to prevent gravity from buckling your knees.

PAIN AT THE FRONT OF THE THIGH

A common cause of insidious pain in the thigh is referred pain, stemming from a back problem. If a certain level of the vertebrae is affected by strain damaging the spinal joints, the nerves supplying the front of the thigh can suffer. You may experience pain on the front of the thigh, or perhaps numbness or tingling, or a combination of these symptoms. You may also find that the muscles on the front of the thigh become weak. The symptoms will seem to come on for no reason, but in fact they will be related to posture and movements in your spine. You may not feel pain in your back, but usually you are aware of stiffness, which you may not at first associate with your leg symptoms.

A circulatory problem may cause sudden swelling and pain in the thigh, with no obvious cause. Similar, unexplained, symptoms may be caused by a bone tumour, a very serious condition. It tends to occur in young people rather than adults, and fortunately is very rare indeed. When it does happen, the tumour will usually show up on X-ray, so the diagnosis can be made fairly quickly.

Any gradually increasing pain, with or without swelling, must be referred to your doctor. You must keep an accurate record of when and how the problem started, to give your doctor a full account, so that he can make an accurate diagnosis.

Injuries to the muscles on the front of the thigh

INJURY FROM A DIRECT BLOW OR KICK

This is an injury which creates particular problems in the front of the thigh, so it has a special name – 'charley-horse'. If the quadriceps are contracting when they are hit, the muscles fibres may tear, with internal bruising and bleeding which may slowly increase. If the muscles are relaxed when the blow falls, there may be instant internal bruising, which may spread, slowly or rapidly, on the front of the thigh.

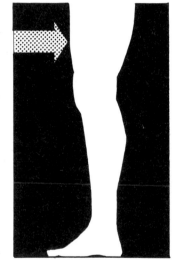

This injury may happen in a variety of different circumstances. In gymnastics, some competitors tend to slap their thighs repeatedly against the lower of the asymmetric bars; a footballer may be kicked in the thigh after he has fallen to the ground; a goalkeeper without protective padding may be hit by the ball or stick in lacrosse or hockey.

In the first instance, the injury may or may not be very painful, depending on its severity. But if not immediately, your thigh will become stiff and painful some hours after the injury. It will hurt when you try to straighten your leg, contracting the quadriceps, and it will be particularly painful if you bend your knee, putting the quadriceps on the stretch.

The danger of this injury is that, if there is extensive internal bleeding, and it is not correctly treated, the blood may solidify within the tissues, creating a functional loss which is difficult to put right. At worst, this may even lead to some bone formation within the quadriceps muscles. This is a danger in any quadriceps injury involving muscle fibre tearing and internal bleeding, but it is especially likely to happen when the internal inflammation has been caused by direct trauma.

Specialist treatment may include drugs to help prevent the blood from

129

going solid inside the quadriceps muscles. Your doctor may also have your leg X-rayed, in case the thigh-bone has been damaged in the injury. First-aid and self-help measures during recovery follow the same pattern as for the other types of injury to the thigh muscles.

COMPLETE TEAR IN THE THIGH MUSCLES

If the injury is severe enough, any of the thigh muscles can be completely torn, sometimes in conjunction with damage to the thigh-bone. When there is a complete tear without bone damage, sartorius and rectus femoris are the muscles most often damaged in this way, because they are both long, free-lying cords, not anchored to bone, except at either end.

The tear can happen through a direct blow onto the muscles when they are tense, but it usually occurs when the muscles are blocked suddenly while they are contracting. Footballers are especially vulnerable to this, when they are tackled as they try to take a kick. A high-jumper can slip on take-off, creating a shearing effect by over-stretching the muscles just when they are trying to shorten for propulsion.

When sartorius or rectus femoris are torn, you will see a visible 'gap' on the front of your thigh, with a bump above and below it, where the torn ends of the muscle have bunched up. The pain you feel at the moment of injury can vary from severe to surprisingly mild, depending on how you suffered the injury. However, if it does not hurt much at first, it will gradually become more painful and stiff over a few hours.

Specialist treatment may consist of surgery, to tie the two torn ends together. Or your doctor or casualty surgeon may decide not to operate, as it is possible to make a good functional recovery, returning to full sporting activity, even if the muscle remains torn. The muscle will not stitch itself together again without an operation, and you will always have the 'lumps' of the torn ends visible in your thigh, but functionally other muscles in the thigh can compensate for the loss of these more superficial ones.

First-aid in this injury follows the same pattern as for all thigh muscle injuries (p. 132), followed by the progressive phases of rehabilitation.

PARTIAL TEARS IN THE THIGH MUSCLES

Less severe traumatic injuries can cause partial tears in any part of the thigh muscles. Injury may be due to a sudden twist, over-stretch or over-contraction of the muscle, or inefficiency due to fatigue. Like the more severe injuries, the partial tear is sudden, and you feel the pain instantly when it happens.

The pain at the moment of injury may be mild or severe, according to the damage done. You may notice bruising and some swelling appearing, either immediately or later on. The damaged part of the muscles hurts if you press on it, and when the muscles contract or stretch. If there is bruising, it may not be directly over the painful area, as it will tend to spread out.

Sometimes swelling from a thigh muscle tear tracks down into the knee under the influence of gravity. It looks as though you have damaged your knee, when in fact the damage is considerably higher on your thigh, while your knee is perfectly all right.

Partial tears in the thigh usually mend well, if you follow an appropriate system of rehabilitation, so a specialist is unlikely to perform any kind of treatment, once he has checked that there is no underlying damage. However, these injuries can be slow to recover, and the rehabilitation process may spread over weeks if not months. This is especially the case in young sportsmen. Teenagers often suffer severe strains in both thighs from sudden activities over-stressing the muscles, like a sudden sprint up the rugby field, or rapid full-squat exercises when the muscles are cold. It is essential that full recovery is made in terms of flexibility, strength and painless movement, before the child is allowed back to sport, even though this may mean many weeks out of sport. Continuing in sport despite the pain inevitably prolongs the problem, and can cause complications.

OVERUSE STRAINS

A gradually increasing pain in the thigh muscles, related to a repetitive activity using the muscles, and only present when you do that activity, indicates that the muscles have been strained by overwork, either because you have simply overdone your sport, or because your muscles have become inefficient due to fatigue or cold.

The pain usually starts as an ache, not severe enough to stop you doing sport. If you continue, however, the ache develops into a noticeable pain, and you have increasing difficulty in performing. At this stage, the damaged muscle feels sore to touch, and hurts when you contract or stretch it, giving a 'tight' feeling.

This type of injury is usually associated with sports involving constant repetitive movements, such as long-distance running or cycling, but it can also be caused by training repetitions for other sports, for instance sets of hops and bounds for high jumping, sprint repetitions for pole vaulting, or quick squat-thrust exercises.

Treatment for overuse strains involves rest from causative and

131

aggravating activities; stretching exercises to regain full flexibility; and a gradual return to sport, taking care to build up in easy stages, and to warm-up and warm-down thoroughly every time. The important factor in curing overuse strains is making certain that the diagnosis is correct. The pain must be directly associated with a particular activity, and not present at other times. There have to be localized signs of muscle damage. You have to keep an accurate record of the pain, and give your doctor exact information. Your doctor has to decide whether you have a simple muscle strain; or whether your pain is due to a more subtle problem, such as muscle spasm over a stress fracture, or a bone tumour, or referred pain from a back problem.

Self-help measures for thigh muscle injuries

- First-aid for the acute injury consists of ice applications to reduce pain and limit internal bleeding (p. 15). If there is visible swelling, the whole thigh should be supported by a bandage, either of the tubular type, or a cotton wool binding covered with a large crepe bandage (p. 11).
- You can normally manage to walk with a thigh muscle injury, although you will probably limp because of the pain. If the pain is severe, it is best to avoid taking weight through the leg, so you should use crutches or be carried. You must see your doctor or the casualty officer at the local hospital for a full check on the extent of the injury.
- Within a day or two of the injury, as soon as your doctor allows, you should start gently stretching the injured thigh muscles, within the limits of pain (p. 133). If rectus femoris or sartorius are damaged, you may have to start stretching keeping your hip bent while you gently bend your knee to its limit. Gradually, you should try to straighten the hip a little more each time, until you can achieve the fully stretched position. Remember to hold the stretch absolutely still for a count of ten, and do not try to force the muscles through pain, but hold the position just where you feel a slight 'pull' over the injured muscles.
- If you have bruising or a localized patch of swelling in the thigh, you can safely apply heparinoid cream (p. 16) *around* the area, but on no account should you rub the cream into the painful muscles. This is especially important in the early stages of the injury. Heat of any kind should not be applied to the injury at first. Knowing when or if massage and heat are appropriate for a thigh muscle injury is a question of expertise, and so is best left to a qualified specialist practitioner. There is a strong risk of complications if you make a mistake in this.

• Once you can bend your knee beyond a right angle without pain, you should start doing thigh strengthening exercises (p. 116), but always starting and finishing your exercise sessions with stretching for the injured muscles. Build up the amount of strengthening work you do gradually, adding in weights only if you have no pain during the exercises. Avoid any exercises that cause pain. If your injured muscles become more painful as you progress, you must stop doing strengthening exercises, and revert to applying ice to the muscles to reduce the soreness, and gently stretching them within the limits of pain.

• When you have regained full flexibility in the thigh muscles, and you can do strengthening exercises without pain, you should progress to more demanding dynamic exercises (p. 118). These are the final stage of recovery, and lead up to your return to sport. Once you have resumed your normal activities, remember to do thigh stretching exercises as the first part of your warm-up, and do not try to work the muscles if at any stage they feel tight. Loosen them with stretching exercises, and rest from sport until they have become flexible again.

How long?

A mild strain, whether due to a sudden injury or a gradual overuse problem, may clear itself within ten days to two weeks. But a severe strain can linger for two to three months. Your guide to progress is firstly how much pain you feel when stretching the muscles, and secondly the pain you feel when you use the muscles. There is no short cut through the recovery process. If you try to return to sport too early, you will inevitably re-injure the muscles. If you try to speed up recovery by progressing too quickly, you may suffer further damage in the muscles, or complications.

Stretching exercises

1. Standing stretch. Stand on one leg. Bend the other knee up, holding your ankle behind you with your hand. Pull your heel towards your buttock, keeping your hip well forward, until you feel a 'pull' on the front of your thigh. Hold to ten, then repeat on the other leg.

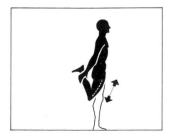

2. Prone lying stretch (for one leg, or both together). Lying on your stomach, bend one or both knees, holding your ankle(s) in your hand(s). Press your heel(s) towards your seat. Hold.

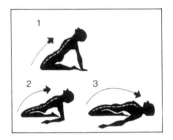

3. Kneeling stretch. Kneeling, with your knees and feet together, lean backwards as far as you can, pressing your hips forward. Hold. Rest on your hands (1), elbows (2), or shoulders (3), according to your flexibility.

4. Kneeling stretch for the quadriceps, excluding rectus femoris. Kneel, sitting back on your heels. Hold.

5. Standing stretch, especially for the inner side of the knee. (Do not do this exercise if you have any kind of knee problem.) Stand on one leg, bending the other behind you as in (1). Holding your ankle, take your foot gently towards the outside of your hip, keeping your hip forward and your knee bent. Feel the 'pull' on the front of the thigh and a little on the inner side of the knee. Hold, then repeat with the other leg.

Complications

If the initial damage from the injury is very severe, and not treated properly, the blood and fluid released from the torn muscles can form a clot, which gradually becomes solid. This may also happen if you rub the muscles after a mild injury. Bone can then form within the clotted fluid, causing pain and restricting movement. When this happens, you can feel the lump of bone, if you press the muscles, and it shows up clearly on X-ray. It may then be necessary to have the new bone removed surgically. However, your specialist may decide to let nature take its course: provided that you rest from sport, and only stretch the muscles very gently within pain limits, the condition can settle sufficiently to allow you to build up your activities again. If there is then no functional restriction for you, there is little point in undergoing an operation, even

134

though the new bone may remain visible on X-rays. The condition of bone forming in a muscle is called myositis ossificans.

Thigh muscle strains may involve other complications affecting the underlying thigh-bone. A stress fracture may cause spasm in the thigh muscles, making you think that you have simply suffered a muscle strain. If you have just increased your activities in a sport involving repetitive movements, like long-distance running, and if you first noticed your thigh pain after exercising rather than during it, you must suspect that you might have suffered a stress fracture in the thigh-bone, if you then have gradually increasing pain whenever you exercise. You must rest, as this is the only cure for a stress fracture, and you risk breaking the bone completely, if you try to carry on. Although the stress fracture will not show up on X-rays in the early stages, bone scans will show up the bone damage, so your specialist will probably arrange for this type of test for you, if there is any doubt about the real nature of your problem.

If you suffered a severe strain affecting the top of the thigh muscles, where rectus femoris or sartorius are attached to the pelvic bone, and your pain seems to persist despite a certain amount of recovery in terms of muscle flexibility and strength, you may have detached a chip, or even the whole bone from the muscles' attachment point. This is called an avulsion fracture, and it usually causes an ache, rather than severe pain, whenever you use the muscles. If there is a suspicion that this might have happened, your specialist will arrange for X-rays to be taken, which will show up the bone chip. He will then decide on appropriate treatment, which may consist of surgical removal of the chip, in a severe case, or an injection to relieve the inflammation in the area and allow painless movement.

The Hamstrings

There are three muscles forming the hamstring group, and they cover the whole of the back of the thigh. Two of the hamstrings, semitendinosus and semimembranosus, extend down the inner side of the back of the thigh, while the third, biceps femoris, lies on the outer side. All three start in more or less the same place, from the ischial tuberosity, or seat-bone. Biceps femoris and semitendinosus are joined together in a common tendon on the bone, but semimembranosus is attached separately, to the side of the attachment of the other hamstrings.

The three muscles form separate strands on the back of the thigh. Semitendinosus has a very long tendon, explaining its name, while semimembranosus is a fleshier muscle lying underneath semitendinosus. Biceps femoris spreads downwards, directed diagonally outwards to be attached by its tendon to the outer part of the knee and the top of the fibula, while the other two hamstrings are fixed onto the inner side of the knee, at the back of the top of the shin-bone.

If you put your hands under your seat while you are sitting relaxed in a chair, you can feel the hard bumps of your ischial tuberosities in the centre of your fleshy glutei, or seat muscles. Sitting with your knees bent, you can place your hands under the lower end of your thighs and feel the cords of the hamstring insertion tendons, just above the back of your knees. If you try to bend your knee against an immovable resistance, by pulling your heel back against the chair leg, the hamstrings contract isometrically, and you feel the tendons tighten up. While they are tense, you can feel most of the semitendinosus tendon, which extends about halfway up the inner side of the back of the thigh. The biceps femoris tendon is equally prominent on the outer side of the back of the knee, whereas semimembranosus is not so near the skin surface, although you can still feel it, just under the semitendinosus tendon at the inner side of the knee.

FUNCTIONS

All three hamstrings cross both the hip and the knee, and so act on both joints. When you are standing up or lying on your stomach, they help

136

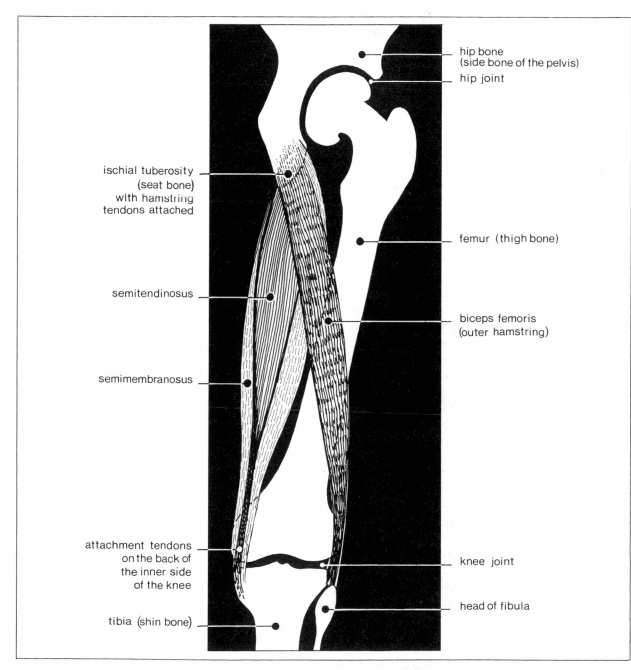

hip bone
(side bone of the pelvis)

hip joint

ischial tuberosity
(seat bone)
with hamstring
tendons attached

femur (thigh bone)

semitendinosus

biceps femoris
(outer hamstring)

semimembranosus

attachment tendons
on the back of
the inner side
of the knee

knee joint

head of fibula

tibia (shin bone)

Hamstrings, back of right thigh.

137

Hamstrings

your glutei (seat muscles) to take your leg backwards from the hip. If you bend forward at the hips while you are standing, your hamstrings and glutei work to straighten you up again. At the knee, the hamstrings bend the joint, working against gravity, and control the straightening movement in the direction of gravity. So if you lie on your stomach and bend your knee, your hamstrings contract and shorten to bring your heel towards your seat, and then pay out to control the movement as you straighten your leg out again.

In sport, the hamstrings play a complex part. Their name probably relates to the fact that they are relatively inelastic, as compared to other major muscles, because of their taut, cord-like tendons. If you have short hamstrings, you will have difficulty in touching your toes. You may be born with relatively short hamstrings, or the muscles may shorten as a result of injury, or in protective spasm to protect the knee following damage to the joint.

Any sport involving sprinting tests the hamstrings to the utmost. As you stretch your legs out in a full stride, the hamstrings on your forward leg are stretched. They contract as your foot lands on the ground and your other leg begins to be drawn upwards and forwards off the ground. Once the other leg has completed the arc, it has gone through a movement in which your knee has been fully bent, with your hip extended behind you, into a full stretch taking the leg forward to plant your foot on the ground. So your hamstrings have had to work from a full contraction in their inner range, where they are most bunched up, and least efficient, to paying out into a full stretch, to repeat the process on the next stride. The hamstrings are therefore under stress in both legs, at every pace during a sprint. A similar situation exists when you kick the ball in football, as you prepare for the kick by bending your knee and taking your hip backwards, and then your hamstrings have to pay out as your leg is suddenly extended to strike the ball. Karate kicking is another example of a movement which depends on full-range, efficient contraction balanced by relaxation and paying out in the hamstrings. The hamstrings may also play a part in less dynamic movements. In rowing, the blade is drawn through the water at each stroke by the extension effort of the muscles on the front of the thigh, which push the oarsman backwards on his sliding seat, co-ordinating a leverage system which simultaneously allows the arms and trunk to pull the end of the oar backwards. To prepare for the next stroke, the oarsman has to move forward on his sliding seat, and this is achieved mainly by the hamstrings contracting and shortening.

Posturally, your hamstrings help to stabilize you against gravity's influence. They harmonize and co-ordinate with the counterbalancing muscles on the front of the thigh. When you are standing up, any

138

movement which tends to bring your line of gravity forward, such as lifting your hand forward, initiates a contraction in the hamstrings, to prevent you from falling forward.

PAIN AT THE BACK OF THE THIGH

A very common cause of pain in this region is referred pain from a back problem (p. 207). The sciatic nerve passes down the back of the thigh, so pain relating to the sciatic nerve may be felt here. The pain may seem like the pain of a hamstring injury, in that you will feel it when the back of the thigh is stretched, for instance if you sit on the floor with your legs straight and lean forwards from the hips. But it will differ from simple muscular pain in that it will come on at odd times, for no apparent reason, for instance while you are sitting still. Muscle pain is generally only felt when you are using the muscle, either by contracting or stretching it. The other distinguishing features between sciatic and muscular pain are: noticeable pain and stiffness in your back, associated with your leg pain; leg pain directly related to certain back movements, and not to leg movements; pain extending down the back of the leg into the calf, without an obvious cause. Therefore, if there is doubt about the origin of pain in the back of your leg, and especially if you have noticed any other nerve-like symptoms, such as tingling or numbness, your specialist is very likely to check your back. The other complication that sometimes arises in sportsmen is that you can have both a referred pain and a localized muscle strain at the same time. Then both problems have to be treated, but the back problem is likely to be seen as the more serious.

Like pain at the front of the thigh, pain at the back of the thigh can be a symptom of more serious medical problems like a tumour or a circulatory condition. Your doctor will be helped in his initial diagnosis if you keep a careful record of your symptoms, including when your pain first occurred; what you were doing when it came on, and immediately before that; details of any visible swelling or bruising; and any factors that noticeably relieve or aggravate the pain and other symptoms.

Injuries to the hamstring muscles

ACUTE INJURY

An acute hamstring injury can happen in a variety of different ways, with the one common factor that there is a sudden pain in the muscles, which is directly related to a particular movement or incident.

139

Hamstrings

The hamstring muscles or their tendons may tear as the result of an over-stretch injury, for instance if you have to sprint suddenly when you are cold, or when your muscles are tightened because of a previous strain, or fatigue from training hard the previous day. Over-stretching may happen if your foot slips forward when your leg is straight in front of you, for instance as you land during hurdling. A direct blow to the hamstrings while they are contracting can tear the muscles. You may be hit by a hockey ball or a squash racket while you are running fast. Inefficient muscle function can also contribute to sudden tears in the hamstrings.

Normally, it is supposed that the hamstrings work at about sixty to seventy per cent of the contraction power of the opposing quadriceps, although in cyclists the hamstrings may be equal to the quadriceps in power. If the hamstrings are weakened because of previous strains, inappropriate training, or tightness, they will be prone to break down under the stress of exercise. This is a common cause of the sprinter's sudden hamstring tear in a race, and it can happen while the muscles are contracting or paying out, because they are not able to work fast enough to cope with the loading.

What you feel is a sudden pain in the hamstrings, which may be no more than a twinge, up to a searing pain. You may see bruising, immediately, or some time after the injury has happened, and the bruising, with perhaps swelling, will tend to track downwards towards the knee. If there is a severe tear, you may see a knot of tissue forming a bump on the thigh, especially if you work the hamstrings by trying to bend your knee. After the initial pain, the torn part feels sore to touch, and gives pain in the same area whenever you contract the hamstrings, either by extending your hip or bending your knee; and when you stretch the muscles, by keeping your leg straight and bending forwards at the hips.

A severe tear, involving a lot of muscle tissue, may need to be stitched together again by a specialist surgeon. However, if the tear is more minor, your doctor may decide that you need no more than a conventional rehabilitation programme, which you must follow completely, to regain full recovery before you try to do your sport again.

OVERUSE INJURY

A gradual pain in the hamstrings, directly related to a particular movement or activity, is usually termed a hamstring 'pull' or 'strain'. This injury happens for similar reasons to the acute tear. The muscles are tight, fatigued, or weakened, and are then strained by overwork. Over-training, especially if this involves repetitive movements, is a common cause of hamstring overuse strains. Track athletes frequently suffer from this injury when they do interval sprints in training, and the problem may start at the beginning of their session, if they have failed to warm-up properly and their muscles are still cold, or towards the end of the workout, when they are tired. Sometimes a slight change in the angle at which the muscles have to work can bring on the problem. This can happen to distance runners who change their running shoes, or their running surface, especially if they run on camber. An oarsman who changes the angle at which his foot is set may find that the alteration causes strain over the hamstring insertion tendons on one or the other side of the back of the knee.

By definition, the overuse strain starts with only a very slight pain, which gradually gets worse, as you continue with the activity which caused the problem. You begin to notice the pain whenever you do your sport, and it then turns from a nuisance into a limiting factor. You may not be able to find a sore spot if you press the muscles, although you will know exactly where in the muscles you are feeling the pain. If someone presses against your foot, resisting your knee bending movement while you are lying on your stomach, you will probably feel the familiar pain in one part of the movement. If there is no pain when you bend the knee against resistance, it will probably occur when you lie on your stomach and extend your hip against someone resisting the movement by pressing down against your leg. Occasionally, the pain is only evident when you work the hamstrings against resistance in their least efficient range, lying on your stomach with your knee held bent to a right angle, and extending your leg backwards at the hip.

The problem with overuse injuries to the hamstrings is that they tend to recur. Even if they do not develop to the stage of an acute tear, they limit your ability to run, sprint, hop, and stretch your leg out. Specialist treatment may include injections, and various forms of physiotherapy. But the most important factor in recovery is regaining full flexibility in the muscles, and efficient function. If you try to resume your sport before you have completed the whole recovery process, you are making a recurrence of the problems inevitable. You may be unlucky enough to suffer repeated strains to the hamstrings, despite careful rehabilitation. In this case, a specialist surgeon may operate, possibly to remove scar tissue from the muscles, or to release the covering sheath enclosing the muscles, if the sheath is causing constriction.

Self-help measures for hamstring injuries

- First-aid for an acute hamstring strain or tear consists of ice applications, to reduce the pain and limit internal bleeding (p. 15). If the thigh swells up, it will be more comfortable if it is supported in a bandage, either the tubular type, or a cotton wool covering held by a large crepe bandage (p. 11).

- If the pain from a sudden injury is very severe, it is best not to walk on the leg, so you should be carried, if possible, or use crutches. You must see your doctor or casualty officer at the local hospital as quickly as possible, to decide on how much damage has been done, and whether specialist treatment, such as surgery, is necessary.

- Stretching exercises should start as soon as possible after the injury. If you are under specialist care, this will be as soon as your specialist allows. In a moderate strain, you should be able to start the stretching exercises within a day or two after the injury. For the gradual, overuse type of strain, you should start stretching the muscles as soon as you are aware of the injury. You must not work the muscles, by contracting them consciously, or trying to continue with your sport, at this stage. The stretching exercises are the only specific exercises you can do safely, and you must remember not to force the stretch, but hold the positions only within the limits of pain.

- If the injury has caused bruising and swelling, you should continue the ice applications, once or twice a day, until these signs disappear. You can apply heparinoid cream (p. 16) around the painful area, but do not rub the cream in, and do not apply pressure into the sore areas of the muscles.

- As you regain flexibility in the hamstrings, so that you can stretch them comfortably, you should start to work on strengthening the muscles. The safest way is to start with isometric strengthening exercises (p. 145), provided that you do not suffer from high blood pressure. Using only exercises which do not cause pain over the injury, you should do two or three isometric contractions at a time, and then stretch the muscles carefully, so that they do not tighten and shorten. You will probably find that you can only work in certain parts of the hamstrings' total range at first. For instance, you may be able to contract the muscles without pain when your knee is almost straight, but the same tension with the knee bent will cause pain. Gradually, you should be able to alter the range, until you can contract the muscles isometrically in any part of their range without pain.

- When you are able to contract the hamstrings isometrically in most positions of the knee, you should start doing the dynamic strengthening exercises (p. 147), using weight-resistance as soon as possible. The exercises should not cause pain over the injury. You must maintain a daily routine of stretching exercises for the hamstrings, as well as stretching before and after any session of strengthening exercises. If you feel your hamstrings stiffening up as the result of the strengthening exercises, you must reduce your workload, and if necessary revert to doing stretching exercises only, until the muscles feel loosened again.

• When you are able to do quite a number of the strengthening exercises without pain, while still maintaining flexibility in the hamstrings, you should start doing the more testing 'functional' exercises (p. 148). These aim to increase the co-ordination between your hamstrings and the other major muscle groups in your leg. Remember that your hamstrings are supposed to work at roughly sixty per cent of the power of the opposing muscle group, the quadriceps, and in certain sports they need to be, and usually are, more powerful than this. If the hamstrings are weakened by injury, and you do not regain full strength and co-ordinated power in them, they are much more likely to break down again if you stress them in sporting activities.

• While you are working at increasing the flexibility and power in your hamstrings, you should do other forms of exercise for fitness, and avoid any types of exercise that cause pain. Swimming will probably be the most suitable exercise for this purpose.

• Once you can do the most demanding of the functional exercises, you can safely resume your normal sport. But you must remember to maintain good flexibility in the hamstrings, making sure they are loosened by stretching before you stress them, and avoiding stressing them if at any time they tighten up noticeably.

How long?

Hamstring injuries can take a long time to clear, relatively, and they are notorious for recurring, if you try to resume sport too soon after an original injury. In general, the overuse, insidious strains take much longer to recover than sudden strains. Although the pain of the overuse injury may be much milder, it is extremely important to make a full functional recovery before stressing the muscles again.

Your progress through the rehabilitation scheme will be guided by your specialist, and will be dictated by pain. Increasing pain is your signal that you are doing too much, so you must slow down your exercises, and if necessary revert to stretching exercises only. If you have any setbacks during recovery, you must build up your exercises very gradually after having scaled them down.

A mild hamstring injury may recover within ten days to two weeks, but a more severe problem can last for over three months.

143

Hamstring exercises

1. Sitting stretch. Sit on the floor with your legs straight out in front of you. Reach forward to hold your feet or ankles with your hands, bending at the hips and keeping your back as straight as possible, your head up. Hold to a count of ten.

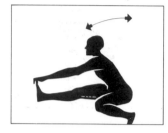

2. Hurdle stretch. Sit on the floor with one leg straight in front of you, the other tucked out of the way sideways. Lean forward from your hips over the straight leg, with back straight and head up. Hold to ten, then repeat with the other leg.

3. Upward stretch. Sit on the floor with one leg tucked sideways (hurdle position). Holding the foot of the other leg, straighten it upwards until you feel a 'pull' on the back of the thigh. Hold to ten, then repeat with the other leg.

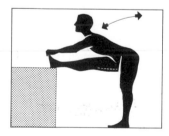

4. Standing stretch. Stand on one leg, place the other straight in front of you on a support (fence or chair). Reach forward from the hips to hold your foot or ankle, keeping your back straight, head up. Hold, then repeat on the other leg.

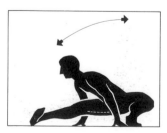

5. Crouching stretch. Bend one knee, balancing with your hand if necessary. Stretch your other leg straight out at right angles to the bent knee, with your foot pointing upwards. Lean forward over the straight leg from the hips, keeping your head up. Hold, then repeat on the other leg.

144

6. Crouching stretch for the inner hamstrings. Crouch down on one leg (as 5), with the other leg straight out sideways and your foot at an angle of forty-five degrees with the ground. Lean over the straight leg, feeling the pull over the inner hamstrings, on the inside of the back of the thigh. Hold, repeat on the other leg.

7. Standing stretch. Stand with your legs straight, feet a few centimetres apart. Lean forward and down from the hips to hold your ankles, keeping your back straight. Hold to ten.

Alternatively, stand with your feet crossed, close together. Keep the front knee pressed straight against the back knee, and bend forward from the hips. Hold, then repeat, changing leg positions.

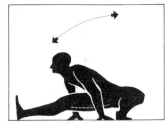

8. Contract-relax stretch. Sit on the floor with your legs straight in front of you. Lean forward as far as you can from the hips, keeping your back straight, head up. Press your legs and heels into the floor hard for a count of five. Relax for a count of three, then gently try to lean forward a little further, for a count of ten.

ISOMETRIC STRENGTHENING EXERCISES

Isometric exercises work by increasing muscle tension without creating joint movement. Do about three of these exercises at a time, starting with those which hold your knee only slightly bent. Do the exercises about three times daily, at first, and gradually build up to doing more exercises, more often. Take care to relax completely between each exercise, and stretch out your hamstrings frequently, to avoid cramp.

1. Lying on your stomach, with a fixed resistance about twenty centimetres above your heel, bend your knee to press your heel against the resistance, hold to a count of five, then relax completely. (You may be able to use heavy furniture for the resistance, or fix a strong band to press against.)

2. Sitting on the floor with your legs straight in front of you. Bend your knees slightly, then press your heel down into the floor, keeping your knee slightly bent. Hold to five, then relax.

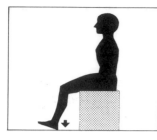

3. Sitting in a chair, with your knee bent to an angle of about forty-five degrees, press your heel down into the floor, without altering your knee position, hold to five, then relax.

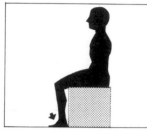

4. Sitting in a chair, with your hip and knee bent to right angles, and your heel resting against the chair leg, press your heel back against the chair leg, holding the position for a count of five, then relax.

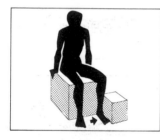

5. Sit in a chair, with your hip and knee bent at right angles, and a fixed resistance, such as a wall or a heavy piece of furniture, along the outer side of your foot. Keeping your knee still, press your foot against the resistance, as if you were trying to turn it outwards. Hold to five, then relax. If you put your hand over the outer hamstring tendon, just above the back of your knee, you will feel it tighten up as you do this, increasing in tension, although there is no apparent joint movement.

6. Sit forward in your chair, so that your knee is bent to a more acute angle. Press your heel back against the chair leg, keeping your knee still. Hold to five, then relax.

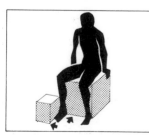

7. Sit forward in your chair, with your heel against the chair leg, and your foot against a fixed resistance resting along its outer side. Press your heel backwards, while turning your foot outwards against the resistance. Hold to five, then relax.

146

8. Lying on your stomach, bend both knees behind you, so that the heel on your injured leg is resting on the front of the ankle of your other leg. Starting with your legs bent to right angles, press your injured leg back, as though you were trying to bend your knee, while your other leg blocks the movement: hold to five, then relax. Repeat the exercise, gradually bending your knees further, to work your hamstrings in their inner, more difficult, range.

DYNAMIC STRENGTHENING EXERCISES

1. Lying on your stomach, keeping your knee straight, lift your leg backwards from the hip slightly, hold to three, then slowly lower. Build up to three sets of ten, then gradually add in weights over your ankle, or a weights boot strapped to your foot.

2. Lying on your stomach, bend your knee up behind you quickly, then slowly lower back. Three sets of ten, then gradually add in weights, strapped to your ankle or foot.

3. Lying on your stomach on a knee flexion weight-loading apparatus, bend your knee up behind you quickly, slowly lower back, making sure that you keep your hips down on the bench. Gradually increase the weights you are using, doing three sets of ten repetitions.

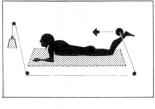

4. Fix three or four inner tubes from bicycle tyres, perhaps round a table leg, or attached to heavy furniture. Position yourself so that you are on your stomach, with your knee bent to a right angle, and the inner tubes are taut, against the back of your heels. Quickly bend your knees to kick your heels to your seat, then slowly return to the starting position. Build up to five sets of ten.

5. Standing up straight, with a light weight attached to your ankle, take your leg backwards slightly, keeping your hips forward and your knee straight, so that your back arches backwards, hold to three, then return to the starting position. Build up to three sets of ten, then increase the weight-loading.

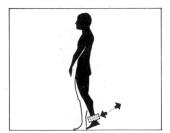

147

6. Standing with a weight attached to your ankle, bend your knee up behind you, trying to take your heel to your seat, then slowly lower back. Build up to three sets of ten, then increase the weights.

7. Lying on your stomach, with a light weight on your foot or ankle, bend your knee up to a right angle, then lift your leg backwards from the hip, keeping your knee at a right angle. Hold to three, then slowly lower, but keep the knee bent for the next repetition. Build up to three sets of ten, then increase the weights.

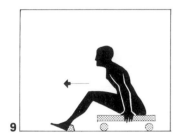

8. Standing, with a weight attached to your ankle, bend your knee to a right angle, and, keeping it bent, take your leg backwards from the hip, hold to three, then bring your leg forwards again to the starting position. Keeping the knee bent for the next repetition, build up to three sets of ten, then increase the weight-loading.

9. Sitting on a shiny-surfaced cushion, a soft towel, or, preferably, a seat on castors, with your heels fixed against an immovable wedge on the floor, pull yourself forwards by bending your knee, then push yourself back again, ten times in quick succession, building up to five sets of ten.

FUNCTIONAL EXERCISES

1. On a static bicycle, gradually lower the saddle height, and increase the resistance you pedal against. (Remember to straighten out your knees hard after this, to avoid knee-cap pain.)

2. Jog, forwards and backwards, then sideways, crossing your legs in front of each other in each direction.

3. Stride, at medium pace, so that you are stretching your legs forward as far as you can on each step.

4. Kick-backs. Run about sixty metres, kicking your heels to your seat at each step, then jog sixty metres before repeating the kick-backs for another sixty metres. Build up to ten sets of kick-backs in a session.

5. Sprint flat out for sixty metres, jog, then repeat the sprint. Build up to ten sets of sprints, gradually.

6. Jump backwards along a straight line for twenty paces, hop forwards to the starting position, then hop backwards again for twenty paces. Repeat the sequence three times at first, building up gradually to three sets of ten.

148

7. Sprint up a set of stairs (up to twenty steps), building up to twenty sprints.

8. Sprint up a set of stairs two at a time, building up to twenty sprints.

9. Hop backwards, up and down onto a low step or block. Start with ten hops, building up to twenty, then raise the height of the block or step.

10. Place three skittles or markers in a line, two roughly three metres from each other, and the third one metre away. Starting at the one-metre skittle, run backwards, weaving round the skittles, so that you run in a figure-of-eight pattern. Start with three circuits round the skittles, and build up to twenty.

Complications

If your hamstring injury does not improve, despite careful rehabilitation, it may be that there is an underlying problem. Hamstring pain and spasm can be caused by a stress fracture in the thigh-bone, so if you are aware of having stepped up your activities immediately before you first felt the pain, and if you feel a lot of pain deep inside the thigh, you should refer back to your doctor for further investigations.

Complications that can arise as a result of a direct injury to the hamstrings are avulsion fractures, or chips of bone torn away when the hamstrings are damaged near their attachments to the bones, either in the seat, or behind the knee; or cysts may form, giving rise to very localized spots of inflammation and pain, where you normally have bursae, or friction-reducing sacs of fluid, lying under the hamstring tendons where they lie over bones or other tendons. This problem may occur in your seat, or behind the knee, like the avulsion fractures. In either case, the symptoms initially will seem no worse than those of a simple muscle or tendon strain, but if these complications are present, they will show up as continuing, very localized, areas of tenderness and pain, inhibiting full recovery in the hamstrings. If they give a lot of trouble, they will probably need specialist treatment, so you must refer back to your doctor in the first instance.

The Adductors
(The inside thigh muscles)

STRUCTURE

The most important of the inside thigh muscles are the adductors, which are three muscles, with the descriptive names of longus (long), brevis (short) and magnus (large). All three are attached to the lower edge of the pubic bone at their origin, and spread out to be fixed along the inner edge of the thigh-bone.

Adductor longus lies to the front of the other two muscles, and starts with a cord-like tendon attached just to the side of the pubis, spreading out sideways, to cover the central third of the inner thigh-bone. Adductor brevis is, logically, the shortest of the muscles, lying just under adductor longus, and fixing onto the thigh-bone at a higher point. Adductor magnus, lying under the other adductors, spreads out to cover the whole of the inside thigh area, and it is attached to almost the whole length of the thigh-bone. Being such a deep-lying and extensive muscle, adductor magnus is very close to the inner hamstrings, semimenbranosus and semitendinosus, in their lower part (see p. 136).

The adductors are not as fleshy or as prominent as the muscles on the front and back of the thigh, but some parts of them can be felt and seen when they are contracting. If you press your fingers over the lower end of the inside of the thigh-bone, just above the enlarged knuckle which forms the upper part of the knee-joint, you are touching the lower attachment of adductor magnus. Keeping your fingers over the muscle, stand with your feet apart, and then press your legs towards each other, as if you were trying to draw them together, but without moving your feet. You will feel adductor magnus contracting isometrically under your fingers. The other place where you can feel and see the adductors is in the groin. Just to the side of the pubis, the cord of the adductor longus tendon stands out whenever you move your thigh. If you press your legs together, you can feel the tendon contracting, and you can also feel the adductor brevis tendon behind it, if you feel along the edge of the pubic bone, with adductor magnus forming a fleshier bulk underneath the tendons.

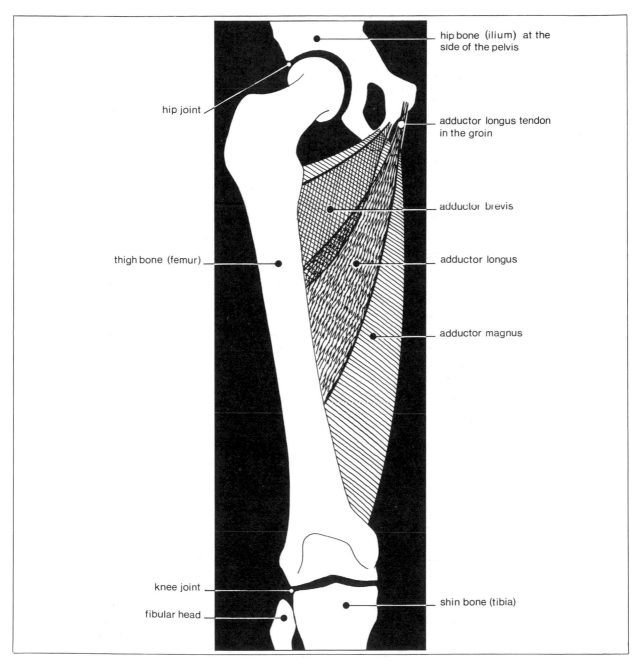

hip bone (ilium) at the side of the pelvis

hip joint

adductor longus tendon in the groin

adductor brevis

adductor longus

thigh bone (femur)

adductor magnus

knee joint

shin bone (tibia)

fibular head

Adductor muscles, front of right thigh.

151

The three adductors pull the thigh-bone inwards, towards and across your other leg, from the hip. They also turn the thigh-bone inwards, to turn your toes towards your other foot. They are especially active in a variety of movements of the leg. If you run sideways or side-step, your adductors contract to bring your trailing leg up to or past your other leg. If you run up stairs or up a hill, your adductors work to pull your thigh in as your leg moves forward, to give you greater economy of movement. Kicking a football with the inside of your boot, or kicking it across your body, is another movement which involves action from the adductors. When you ride a horse, your adductors pull your thighs inwards against the saddle to hold your knees fixed so that you can keep your balance.

PAIN IN THE ADDUCTOR REGION

Pain in the groin can be due to an inguinal hernia (see p. 163), or one of a variety of conditions affecting the pubic bones and joint, or referred symptoms from a back problem. A hip condition can cause pain felt in the groin area. A systemic infection can make the lymph glands in the groin swollen and painful, giving you localized groin pain. Pain felt down the length of the inside thigh can also be caused by hip or back conditions giving referred pain, without necessarily causing direct pain in the affected joints themselves. A stress fracture at any point along the inner side of the thigh-bone can cause pain and spasm in the adductor muscles over the crack.

    You must therefore try to establish the details of your pain, to help your doctor identify its cause. You should note down when and how the pain started, what you were doing at the time, and what has brought on the pain after you first felt it. Other relevant details to note would be any other aches or pains you noticed at the time, whether your thigh or groin hurts when you cough or sneeze, and whether it hurts only during exercise, or at rest and in bed at night.

Injuries to the adductor muscles

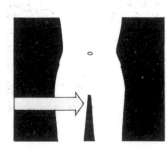

COMPLETE TEAR

A severe stressing force can cause a complete tear in one or more of the adductors. It usually happens when your leg is forced outwards at the hip, and perhaps twisted at the same time. Your leg may slide away from you as you run on muddy ground and an opponent comes to tackle you.

In this situation, the injury is even more severe if the opponent falls across your leg to force your hip into an awkward abnormal position. A fall in ski-ing or water ski-ing can twist your hip and force it out, tearing the inner thigh muscles.

What you feel is a sudden searing pain over the injured muscle, which makes it difficult for you to move your leg from the hip. You may see swelling or bruising, either immediately, or some time after the injury has happened. Because the pain is so severe, you will find it difficult to localize the main area of the injury, and the whole of your inner thigh or hip will feel sore. The torn muscle may bunch up when you move your leg inwards, forming a bulge or lump, on one or both sides of the gap which the ruptured muscle no longer covers. This is especially likely to happen if the muscle is torn close to or at its attachment, at the pubic bone or the lower end of the thigh-bone. However, this visible defect may not become obvious until after the acute stage of the injury, when you have reached the stage where the pain has subsided enough for you to be able to move your leg without excessive discomfort.

After immediate first-aid has been applied, you must attend a casualty department, to assess the extent of the damage, and to make sure that there has been no damage to any of the bones in the injured area. If the complete tear is diagnosed immediately, the orthopaedic surgeon may decide to stitch the two ends of the muscle together again, putting you under general anaesthetic. However, it may not be immediately apparent that complete rupture has occurred, as the swelling and pain will inhibit a full examination, so the decision may be taken to treat the injury as a partial tear. If, later on, it turns out that the muscle was completely torn, and therefore gives continuing trouble, surgery may be needed to clean out any adhesions formed in the torn muscle, and to repair the broken ends.

PARTIAL TEAR

Less severe stresses which force your leg outwards may cause partial tears, or strains, rather than tearing the muscle fibres completely. Partial tears may also happen if your inner thigh is kicked while the muscles are contracting, or if you over-stretch or overwork the muscles. Forcing the movement while you are trying to do the splits sideways is an example of over-stretching the inner thigh. Striding up a steep hill, or sprinting up a long flight of stairs can overwork the adductors.

What you feel is a sudden pain in the injured part of the muscles, and they then hurt when you stretch or contract them. You may see some swelling or bruising around the injury, but more often than not there is

153

no visible sign of damage. If you press the injured area with your fingers, it will feel sore. However, the pain is not bad enough to prevent you from walking, although you may limp a little, and you will probably feel the injured part of the muscles hurting at each step.

If you do have a lot of discomfort from the injury, you should attend a hospital casualty department for assessment and treatment. If the injury is not severe, you can wait before seeing your doctor about it. Specialist treatment may consist of anti-inflammatory drugs, and possibly injections. In most cases, however, your doctor will recommend recovery through rest and graded exercises.

OVERUSE STRAIN

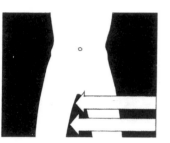

The gradually increasing pain of overuse injury to the adductors can be due to overworking the muscles so that they progressively become less efficient, rather than breaking down suddenly under the strain. A long-distance run on hilly ground can cause the strain. Horsemen often suffer the injury, especially in the adductor longus tendon: it can be caused by an unaccustomed long ride, or a change of horse, altering the normal mechanics of the adductors in their gripping action against the saddle.

At first, you feel only an ache over the injured muscle, which gradually gets worse if you continue to use it. The muscle or tendon feels tight, and may even tear completely, if you severely over-strain it while it is shortened. Initially, the injured muscle or tendon only hurts when you use it, hurting more when it is contracted than when you stretch it. If the strain develops to the more severe stage, you may find that it causes an ache in the inner thigh or groin after exercise, as well as during activity.

Rest from any pain-causing activity is essential to curing the problem. As there is rarely any swelling or bruising in an overuse strain, unless it has been allowed to develop to a very severe stage, there is no need for first-aid treatments. Once the diagnosis of the strain has been established, and your doctor has differentiated between all the other possible causes of inner thigh or groin pain, you have to start on the rehabilitation process.

Self-help measures for adductor injuries

• You should apply ice to the painful area immediately after you have suffered a traumatic injury to the adductors (p. 15). If the area is swollen, you should wrap a bandage round the whole thigh, using either a wide tubular bandage, or a wadding of cotton wool covered with a crepe bandage (p. 11).

154

- If the injury is too painful for you to walk on, you will probably need to be carried. It is difficult to ease adductor pain by using crutches, as the muscles have to contract as you hold your leg off the ground, and this inevitably causes pain over the injured part. It is best therefore to avoid walking, if at all possible, for the first few days after a bad injury.

- As soon as the initial pain has subsided after a traumatic injury, you should start stretching the injured muscles, within pain limits (p. 156). Do the stretching exercises only to the extent which does not cause more pain, and take care to hold the stretch positions absolutely still, to avoid causing further damage to the muscles. In overuse injuries, stretching must be started straight away. When you are stretching the injured muscles, try to localize the 'pulling' sensation to the damaged area. You will probably find that only some of the suggested stretching exercises affect your specific injury, so choose those to do intensively, and repeat the exercises frequently throughout the day.

- When the injured muscle or tendon begins to feel less tight when you stretch it, you should start doing the isometric exercises (p. 157). Try to do one or two of these every hour. Start with your leg straight, then gradually take your leg out sideways for the isometric contraction. Do not do isometric exercises with your leg in a position which causes increasing pain over the injured muscle or tendon. As the injury heals, you will find you can take your leg out further without feeling pain when you contract the adductors isometrically.

- When you can do isometric exercises without pain in an increased range of hip movement, you can start doing the strengthening exercises, gradually adding weight-resistance to the movements (p. 158). Do not forget to stretch your adductors before and after every strengthening session, doing at least three stretching exercises each time. If you can, do two strengthening sessions daily, starting with just one or two exercises, and progressively increasing the amount you do.

- Once your injured muscle or tendon feels stronger, but still flexible when you stretch it, you should progress to the functional exercises (p. 159). These exercises increase co-ordination between your injured muscle and the leg's other major muscle groups, and they stress the injury under increasingly difficult conditions. Once you can run up stairs, or kick a football without pain, you are fit to return to your sport. Remember to maintain a daily programme of adductor stretching exercises, using them as the first part of your warm-up before doing your sport. Loosen the muscles by stretching if they tighten up again, and rest from sport if you find that for any reason they remain tight despite stretching.

Inner Thigh

If the traumatic injury is treated correctly from the moment it happens, recovery should be complete within three to eight weeks, depending on the severity of the injury. However, if you have had a niggling overuse strain which has built up over a long period, full recovery can take between three and six months. You must regain flexibility in the first instance, and secondly power and co-ordination. Your guide to progress is the pain you feel while doing the therapeutic exercises. If the pain increases at any stage, or if the muscles tighten up, you have done too much, and you must cut back, reverting to stretching exercises only, if necessary, and gradually building up the other types of exercise again.

Exercises for the adductor muscles

STRETCHING EXERCISES

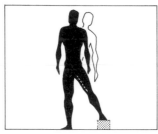

1. Standing with your legs apart, lean sideways over your injured leg, and then gently shift your weight towards your other hip, so that you feel a 'pulling' sensation over the injured inside thigh muscle. Hold the position absolutely still for a count of ten, then gently relax.

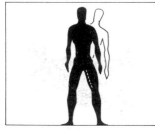

2. Rest your injured leg sideways on a support, keeping your knee straight. Gently lean sideways over your injured leg, without bending forward, until you feel the stretch on the inside thigh. Hold for ten, then relax.

3. Stretch your injured leg straight out sideways, then bend the other knee, until you feel the stretch on your straight leg. Hold to ten, then relax.

156

4. Sitting with your knees straight, and your legs stretched as far apart as possible, gently bend forward from the hips, keeping your back straight, until you feel the 'pull' on the inside of your thighs. Hold the position for a count of ten, then relax.

5. Sit with your knees bent, and the soles of your feet together. Let your knees fall out sideways as far as possible, and then pull your feet towards you gently, without letting your knees lift. Lean gently forwards towards your feet, keeping your back straight, until you feel a 'pull' on the inside of your thighs. Hold for a count of ten, then relax.

6. Lie on your back with your knees bent, and your feet together. Keeping your feet together, let your knees fall sideways, until you feel the 'pull' on your inside thighs. You may need to press your knees down gently with your hands to achieve the stretch. Hold for a count of ten, then relax.

ISOMETRIC STRENGTHENING EXERCISES

1. Lying on your back, with your legs straight and resting on the floor, press your feet inwards against each other, so that your legs are pressed together. Hold for a count of five, then relax completely.
2. Sitting in a chair, with your legs straight, and your feet resting on the floor. Press your legs together against each other, hold for a count of five, then relax.
3. Sitting in a chair, with your knees bent and feet resting on the floor, press your knees and thighs together against each other. Hold to five, then relax.
4. Standing with your legs apart, and a medicine ball or block between your feet, press both your feet inwards against the medicine ball, holding the isometric contraction for a count of five, then relaxing completely.

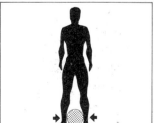

157

Inner Thigh

5. Sit in a chair, with your legs straight, feet on the floor, and the medicine ball or block between your feet. Press your feet inwards against the resistance, hold to five, then relax. (Do not lift the block up from the floor, as this can put a lot of strain on your back and hips.)

6. Stand with your legs apart, press your feet downwards into the floor, so that you feel the inner sides of your thighs tense up. Hold the contraction for a count of five, then relax.

7. Gradually spread your legs further apart, to do the isometric contractions in a wider range of hip movement.

8. Stand on one leg, and balance your injured leg sideways on a step or block, about thirty centimetres high, keeping your knee straight. Press your foot downwards against the block, hold for a count of five, then relax.

9. Increase the height of the step or block, so that your leg is resting on it at a wider angle from your hip. Take care to keep your trunk straight, so that you do not lean sideways as you press your leg down against the block.

STRENGTHENING EXERCISES

1. Lie on your back, with your legs straight, and a light weight attached to your ankle on your injured leg. Take the injured leg straight out sideways a little way, lifting it just enough to clear the floor or bed, take it back to the other leg, then slowly lower. Build up to three sets of ten, then gradually increase the weight.

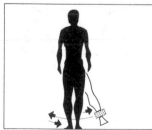

2. Standing, with a weight on your ankle, take your injured leg straight out sideways, then bring it back across your other leg, then back to neutral and lower. Build up to three sets of ten, then increase the weight.

3. Lying on your back with your knees bent and your feet close together, let your knees fall sideways, then pull them in together quickly. Build up to three sets of ten, then attach a weight over the inside of your knee.

4. Lying on your back, at the edge of your couch or bed, so that your injured leg can trail over the side, with your knee straight, take your injured leg up and across the other leg, hold to three, then lower back. Repeat in quick succession ten times, building up to three sets of ten, then adding in weights over your foot.

5. Using a weights pulley system, or three bicycle tyre inner tubes attached to a piece of heavy furniture, stand sideways to the resistance cord, with your injured leg attached to the resistance and closest to it. Take your injured leg straight across the other leg, against the resistance, hold for a count of two, then lower back. Try not to swing your hips across as you do this. You may need to hold onto a firm support to avoid 'cheating'. Start with five repetitions, build up to three sets of ten, then increase the resistance.

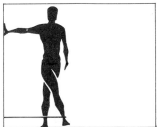

FUNCTIONAL EXERCISES

1. Start by jogging short distances forwards and backwards, then try lifting your knees up a little higher, and increasing your pace.

2. Side-slip, doing fast bouncing steps to each side, without crossing your legs over. Start with ten paces in each direction, building up to three sets of fifty.

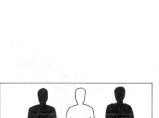

3. Jog up a hill or a set of stairs, starting with a short distance slowly, and gradually increasing speed and distance. Walk down at first, then jog down between each uphill run.

4. Side-slip, thirty paces in each direction, crossing your legs in front of each other. Build up to one hundred paces each way.

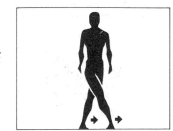

Inner Thigh

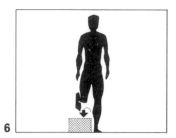

6

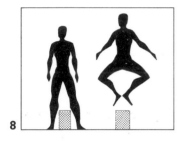

8

5. Hop sideways in each direction, starting by hopping on the injured leg, towards the injured side. (If your left leg is injured, hop towards your left first, then right.) Start with twenty hops along a straight line, building up gradually to a hundred hops in each direction.

6. Stand on your injured leg, with the inside of your foot alongside a low step or fixed block. Hop sideways, up onto the block, then hop down, starting with five hops, and building up to three sets of ten.

7. Kick a light ball with the inside of your foot, so that it goes diagonally away from you. For instance, if your left leg is injured, kick the ball against a wall so that it strikes the wall about one metre to your right. Start fairly close to the wall, kicking lightly, and gradually increase your distance away. You can progress to using a heavier ball when the movement feels easy.

8. Stand with your feet astride a low bench or block. Jump up, kick your feet together above the bench, and land with your feet on either side of the bench. Start with five, building up to three sets of ten.

9. Using a short slope, or if necessary a set of stairs, stand sideways on the bottom edge of the slope, with your injured leg lowest, and side-step up the slope, crossing your legs over, and moving as quickly as you can. Then hop sideways for ten paces, with your uninjured leg leading, jog back down the slope, then sprint forwards up it as quickly as you can, hopping sideways again as before, then jogging down, back to your initial position. Repeat the sequence three times at first, building up to twenty times.

Complications

If, despite care and gradual progress through the rehabilitation programme, you are left with continuing pain in the adductor region, you should refer back to your doctor, to check whether you have an underlying, more subtle problem, such as an inguinal hernia, a hip or back problem, or a stress fracture.

You may find that you have continuing pain in the groin or above the inner side of your knee, following injury to the adductor muscles. In this case, it is possible that a chip of bone has been pulled away where the adductors are attached to the bones, either in your groin or at the lower end of your thigh-bone. An X-ray would show whether this has happened, and treatment might consist of anti-inflammatory injections, or, if necessary, surgery, to remove the troublesome bone chip.

160

The Hip Flexors
(The muscles at the top of the thigh)

STRUCTURE

The main muscles which draw the thigh-bone forward at the hip are known collectively as the hip flexor muscles. The two most important of these are iliacus and psoas major, which, although separate muscles, are given the combined name of iliopsoas, because their functioning is so closely interlinked.

Psoas major is attached to the front of the lumbar vertebrae, the lowest blocks of bone in your spinal column. It extends down across the front of your hip joint to fix onto a small bump of bone on the inside of the top of the thigh-bone, called the lesser trochanter. Iliacus spreads right over the inside of your hip-bone (ilium), round to the inner edge of the front of your sacrum. It extends down over the front of your hip joint, joining

Hip flexors, over front of right hip.

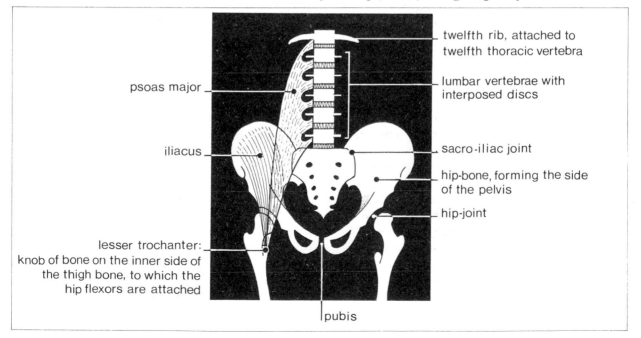

psoas major

iliacus

lesser trochanter:
knob of bone on the inner side of
the thigh bone, to which the
hip flexors are attached

twelfth rib, attached to
twelfth thoracic vertebra

lumbar vertebrae with
interposed discs

sacro-iliac joint

hip-bone, forming the side
of the pelvis

hip-joint

pubis

161

onto the outer side of the psoas major tendon, so that it is fixed with the psoas tendon on the inner edge of the thigh-bone.

It is difficult to feel the hip flexors. The adductors form a fleshy covering over them at the top of the inner edge of the thigh-bone, and in the pelvis they lie under organs and the thick layers of your stomach muscles. In the groin, iliopsoas lies between the strong cords of sartorius and rectus femoris, which stand out over the front of the hip when you lift your leg forward, and the adductor tendons at the inner edge of the groin crease. But the hip flexors are crossed by a main artery and nerve in the groin, so the discomfort you feel if you press your fingers over these structures prevents you from being able to feel the muscles moving when they contract to take your leg forward at the hip.

FUNCTIONS

The hip flexors bend the thigh up at the hip, so they are working when you walk forward, and they have to contract harder when you run, especially up stairs or hilly ground. All forward kicking movements involve the hip flexors. If you lie on your back, and lift one leg up from the hip, with your knee bent or straight, the hip flexors perform the movement. If you lift both legs straight up in the air, lying on your back, you will feel your lower back tighten up into an arch, because psoas major fixes its attachment point on the vertebrae, in order to exert greater power in lifting the long lever of your legs. You will feel a similar effect in your lower back if you sit up with your back straight from lying flat. It is because of this tension effect in the back that double-leg-raising exercises in the forward direction can create back problems. In leg-raising, the main work is done by the hip flexors, with the abdominal muscles stabilizing the trunk by contracting isometrically, so this type of exercise, which is often used to 'strengthen the stomach', is not even an effective way of doing that. Besides carrying the danger of damaging the back, it can cause a hernia in the abdomen or the groin.

The hip flexors also act to pull your lower back forward over your hips, for instance if you lie flat on your back and then sit up, keeping your back straight. When you sit upright on a chair or stool, your hip flexors work posturally to hold you, and counteract any tendency for your trunk to sway backwards. If your hip flexors are shortened or tight, whether as the result of injury or simply through your natural build, your lumbar spine will tend to curve more than the accepted normal, so that your back will be noticeably arched and hollow in its lowest part just above the pelvis. Problems with the hip flexors can relate directly to back problems, and can be either the cause or the result of spinal problems. This is especially

162

true if the hip flexors on one side are shortened relative to the other side, for any reason. The asymmetry between the hips can cause distortion in the pelvis and lower spine, so that there is a functional imbalance. This can lead to over-strain during movements and activities involving the lower back.

PAIN IN THE GROIN

Problems in the hip-joint, or at the upper end of the thigh-bone, can cause groin pain. Back problems can cause referred pain over the front of the hip. These problems may involve mechanical strains, inflammatory conditions, or disease processes. Your doctor has to distinguish between these various possible causes of your pain. Your accurate record of how the pain came on will help him to decide on which investigations would be appropriate, after he has examined you.

Inguinal hernia

A fairly common cause of pain over the front of the hip is an inguinal hernia. The inguinal ligament is a band which crosses the top of your leg, almost exactly where the skin crease shows when you bend your leg at the hip. The ligament forms part of the containing tissue which divides your abdomen from your leg, and it is formed in parts, so that it contains 'gaps' through which nerves and other structures like the male spermatic cord can pass.

Too much pressure in your abdomen can force other tissues down through these gaps, so that they get caught on the wrong side of the separating ligaments: this is the hernia. The pressure in your abdomen is increased by such movements as lifting a heavy weight, especially if you bend forward as you lift, or lifting both legs straight up while you are lying on your back, or simply coughing or sneezing, so a hernia can be caused in a variety of situations. It can cause pain all the time, or only when your abdominal muscles contract to increase the pressure over the hernia. If the pain is intermittent, it may be difficult to distinguish from the pain of a muscle strain in the abdomen or hip flexors, so you have to keep a careful check of the pattern of the pain, and how it started, to help your doctor make the correct diagnosis.

If a diagnosed hernia causes a lot of pain, it is usually necessary to have an operation to replace the protruding tissue in its correct compartment in the abdomen, and to tighten up the gap through which it pushed. Progress back to sport after the operation is guided by the surgeon. Usually you start by straightening up gradually, as the pain makes you bend forward. As you begin to stand straighter, you start doing a gradually increasing amount of walking. At the same time, you start to try gentle and controlled stretching exercises for the abdominal and hip flexor muscles (p. 166, p. 206). As pain allows, you start jogging, then running, until you feel fit enough to resume sport.

You have to avoid heavy lifting, and any activities which might bring on a recurrence of the hernia. You can protect yourself by learning how to look after your back and abdomen, for instance by bending your knees and keeping your back locked as straight as possible whenever you have to bend down to the floor, and especially if you have to lift even a light weight up. Whenever you cough or sneeze, you should take care to keep your back stiff and straight. You should never do exercises which place a strong strain on the stomach, for instance isometric exercises like lying on your back and lifting both legs up straight. However, you should stretch your stomach and hip flexor muscles, to maintain good flexibility, and you should actively strengthen these muscles with dynamic exercises which do not create an excessive increase in abdominal pressure (p. 199).

Injuries to the hip flexor muscles

Causes

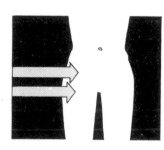

The hip flexors can be damaged by the same stresses which injure the adductors on the inner thigh. Your leg may be blocked as you take a kick in football or rugby. Your leg may be forced backwards at the hip by a tackle in football or hockey. If you catch your foot in a game like lacrosse, your trunk may be forced backwards over the hip.

Overuse strains happen to the hip flexors in long-distance running. The muscles perform most of the work of taking your leg forward at each step, so they can be strained simply by the fatigue of a distance run, or by the extra effort of increasing your speed, or running up a hill. Any exercise directly involving the hip flexors can cause an overuse strain if you do too much of it. A sudden enthusiasm for double-leg-raising exercises lying on your back can strain the hip flexors or cause a hernia. Extended sessions of interval running up and down hills can strain the muscles. The same problem may arise if you suddenly start doing drills, such as kicking a football forward over and over again with the same leg, or practising run-ups for the pole vault.

Extent of the damage

A sudden, very severe, shearing force can tear the hip flexors completely, where they form the tendon that attaches to the thigh-bone. Sometimes, the tendon may hold, but the lesser trochanter, the bump of bone to which the tendon is stuck, may be sheared away from the main thigh-bone. If the damage is severe enough to cause a total tear of the tendon, or an avulsion fracture in the bone, there is usually damage to the adductor tendons as well, and sometimes to other structures around the hip and the top of the thigh.

A less severe strain may cause a partial tear or over-stretch in the hip flexors. An overuse injury causes gradually increasing pain over the muscles, relating directly to the causative activity. On occasion, the injury may affect one of the bursae (natural cysts) which lie under the tendons, rather than the tendons themselves.

What you feel

In a sudden severe strain, you feel a lot of pain over the hip flexors, which stops you from being able to draw your leg forward at the hip, and which creates discomfort when you take your leg back at the hip, stretching the hip flexors. Walking is difficult, but not impossible, and you may find that you lessen the discomfort if you turn your foot inwards or outwards as you walk. The degree of pain you feel is directly related to the amount of damage done, and the number of structures hurt, if other muscles and tissues besides the hip flexors are involved.

The gradually increasing pain of the overuse strain at first only comes on while you are doing the activity which has caused the injury. If you carry on with the activity, increasing the damage to the hip flexors, the pain increases, and you start to feel it whenever you work or stretch the muscles. You may feel pain walking forward, and especially up stairs, or if you press your leg forward against a resistance, for instance by pressing your foot against a wall. The injured hip flexors will feel sore, and tighter than the other side, if you swing your leg backwards, or do exercises which stretch the front of the hip.

Self-help measures for the hip flexors

- Apply ice over the painful area, if the injury is sudden and severe (p. 15).
- Rest it from any movements which cause pain. This probably means that you should avoid walking in the initial stages of the injury. It does not help you to use crutches, as you would have to hold your leg forward at the hip to do so, and you would therefore be working the injured hip muscles.

165

• As quickly as possible after a traumatic strain, and as soon as an overuse strain has been diagnosed, you should start stretching the hip flexors. In the initial stages, this may involve no more than straightening your leg at the hip, while you are standing up, to counteract the tendency of the hurt muscles to shorten. As the pain decreases, you should gradually take your leg behind you, keeping your hip well forward, and holding the position at the point where you feel a 'pulling' sensation over the injury for a count of ten. As you regain flexibility in the muscles, you should then be able to place your injured leg behind you, and bend the forward knee increasingly, until you can hold the full-stretch position. At no stage should you push through the pain to increase the stretch over the muscles. Any increasing pain during or after stretching exercises means that you have forced the movement and over-stretched.

If the adductor muscles have also been injured, you must do stretching exercises for them too (p. 156). Hip flexor stretching can also be combined with abdominal stretches, so the exercises on p. 206 are useful to add variety to your stretching programme.

• While you are unable to do your sport, you should use swimming as substitute exercise for fitness. Any stroke which does not cause pain is suitable, so you will probably find that, while you can swim crawl or breaststroke comfortably fairly soon after the injury happens, backstroke will be uncomfortable until the injury has almost healed.

• Once you have regained flexibility in the damaged muscles, you should start to use them, perhaps by jogging, then gradually increasing speed, and finally by running up stairs and hills. If you play football, you can practise kicking a ball straight, against a wall, at a gradually increasing distance. You must take care to maintain full flexibility in the muscles while you begin to work them, and stretching should remain the first part of your warm-up and the last part of your warm-down whenever you do sport after you have recovered from the injury.

How long?

A mild overuse strain may clear up within a couple of days, if you rest the injury from painful activities and start to stretch the muscles immediately. However, a severe strain may take between three and six weeks to be cured. During that period, you should feel progressively less discomfort, and more freedom of movement in the muscles, as you advance through the rehabilitation process. If your pain remains constant, or if you feel it at times when the muscles are completely at rest, you must suspect that there may be complications, so you should check back with your doctor for further investigations.

166

Complications

An injury to the hip flexor muscles may coincide with any of the medical or inflammatory conditions that cause pain over the hip, so the diagnosis must be re-assessed if your pain does not resolve despite correct care. An avulsion fracture to the lesser trochanter may need surgery, if it causes continuing problems, and prevents functional healing. A more subtle complication may arise if the original injury causes you to adopt a bent-over posture at the hip. This can set up stress on the lower back, causing symptoms arising from the back as a secondary effect, which would not have been present at the time of the injury.

The Hip Joint

Bones

The rounded head of the top of the thigh-bone fits into a shallow cup-like formation called the acetabulum which forms part of the outer side of the hip-bone (see illustration on p. 161).

You cannot see or feel your hip joint, because it is covered with thick muscles. You can feel the prominent edge of the thigh-bone, called the greater trochanter, at the side of your hip. The trochanter forms the junction between the thigh-bone and its neck, which is directed inwards, and your hip joint is about six centimetres in towards your groin from the trochanter.

Soft tissues

Your hip is totally enclosed by a fibrous capsule, which is thickened over the front of the joint to form one of the strongest ligaments in the body, the iliofemoral ligament. Other ligaments protect the joint from behind and underneath. A central ligament binds the middle of the thigh-bone head to the acetabulum, but it is relatively weak, and in some people it does not exist.

Functions

Your hip is a ball-and-socket joint. Your hip flexors bend your hip forwards; your glutei and hamstrings take your leg backwards; the hip abductors take it sideways; your adductor muscles take your thigh in towards and across your other leg; small muscles at the front of the joint turn your thigh-bone in towards your other leg, while similar muscles over the back of the hip twist your leg outwards.

Structurally, your hip is a very stable joint. Its tight enclosing capsule creates a negative pressure in the joint, which is further strengthened by the ligaments and bone formation. Your hip helps to absorb shock taken through your legs or trunk, when you jump or fall down.

Functionally, your hips combine stability and motion. When you kick a ball, or balance in the ballerina's arabesque position, you pivot your whole weight over one hip, while the other hip creates free movement. Your hips co-ordinate with your pelvis and lower back, compensating for

168

the movement limitation due to the stability of the hips. If you do the splits, in either direction, your pelvis rotates, to achieve the movement, as your hips do not have enough freedom of movement to achieve such an extreme range.

Although your hips function as a pair, they are rarely symmetrical. You may be born with structural differences, or your postural habits may create these differences. If you lie on your back with your legs straight and completely relaxed, you may notice that one foot splays out sideways more than the other, indicating that rotation in one hip is greater than the other. You may notice that you can cross your legs more easily in one direction than the other when sitting. Or you may habitually stand with your weight resting over one hip when you are standing. When you do stretching exercises, you may find that some muscle groups feel tight round one hip. If you notice this type of asymmetry, you must try to correct it by adopting good posture at all times, and stretching any tight muscles every day.

HIP PAIN

Pain in the hip may be due to an inflammatory joint condition, which may affect only the one hip-joint, or it may be part of a syndrome affecting a number of joints with intermittent, unexplained pain. Osteo-arthritis often affects the joint when you are older, because the hip is such an important weight-bearing joint, and therefore subject to hard wear-and-tear. Disease, such as tuberculosis, can affect the joint. Pain felt in the hip may be referred from other areas, such as the back, the groin, or the knee. A stress fracture at the upper end of the thigh-bone may also give a feeling of pain around the hip.

It is therefore very important to be able to describe to your doctor how your hip pain came on, when it occurs, and whether any particular movements make it worse or better. It may also be relevant to remember any other aches and pains in your legs and back. For adults, childhood problems in the hips or knees may have a bearing on later pain.

Hip injuries

Because the hip-joint structure is so stable, it is rarely injured in itself through accidents in sport. You are much more likely to fracture your thigh or pelvis in a severe injury than to disrupt the hip-joint. In children, however, structural defects in the hip-joint may become noticeable problems as the result of doing sport, although the problems are unlikely to

169

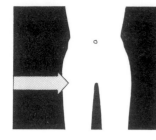

have been caused by sport. In children and adults, the structures around the hip-joint may be injured during sports. In adults, the pain of osteo-arthritis may be felt most during sport, although it may also be evident at other times.

PERTHES' DISEASE

This is a childhood problem affecting the hip-joints, and it usually happens to boys under the age of twelve. What happens is that the child's femoral head, in one or both hips, becomes flattened, and so no longer fits properly into the acetabulum on the hip-bone. This badly disrupts the working of the hip-joint, so the child starts to limp. What he feels, however, may be no more than a slight ache, which may happen either in the hip or in the knee. If the child is examined by a doctor, his hip will be visibly very limited in its movements, so the doctor will probably have X-rays taken which will reveal the extent and nature of the problem. The cure is usually a period of total rest, until the bones in the hip-joint have recovered their normal shape. The sooner the diagnosis is made, the better and quicker the cure. If the problem is allowed to drag on for some time without being diagnosed, the long-term result is likely to be very early osteoarthritis in the joint, which may come on even as early as twenty to thirty years.

SLIPPED EPIPHYSIS

This condition affects teenagers, between twelve and seventeen years old. Like all the body's other bones, the thigh-bone is formed in parts. Sometimes without any apparent cause, the growth of the head of the thigh-bone becomes softened, and so, under the pressure of bearing the body's weight, the bone slips downwards. This may result in only slight pain, felt either in the hip or the knee, but it will grossly limit hip function. It may occur in both hips at once, or just one. Sometimes, a fall or a blocked tackle may trigger an acute slip in the epiphysis, causing sudden pain and the symptoms of limitation. It is vital that the teenager should be checked immediately by his doctor, as the correct treatment for the problem can greatly reduce the danger of long-term problems arising from it. If this type of hip pain is suspected, the doctor will usually refer the teenager for X-rays and a specialist orthopaedic opinion.

BURSITIS

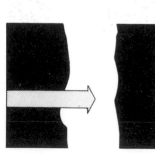

There are many bursae, or fluid-filled sacs for friction-free movement,

170

around the hip-joint. They separate the tendons and other moving structures from the joint covering, so you find them at the front of the hip, under the hip flexor tendons, at the side, between the greater trochanter and the iliotibial tract, and at the back, between the gluteal muscles and the joint. Where the bursa is close to the skin surface, as over the greater trochanter, it can be damaged by a direct blow, if you fall over and hit the side of your hip, or if you are hit with a stick or bat. Otherwise, the most common cause of damage to the bursae is friction, usually from unaccustomed repetitive movements, and sometimes due to muscle or tendon tightness, causing a loss of the free play in the tendon. Once the bursa is damaged, it becomes inflamed, and then sets up a very localized area of pain, which you feel when you press over the area, and when you move your leg in certain directions. It feels equally sore when the tendons over it are contracted or stretched, and this helps to distinguish bursitis from a simple tendon strain. It also feels sore on direct pressure, so if you have bursitis under the gluteal muscles at the back of the joint, it hurts when you sit down on a hard chair.

To ease the discomfort, you can apply ice (p. 15) over the area, and gently stretch the tendons over the bursa. You must rest from any activities which cause or increase the pain. Your doctor may decide to treat the bursitis, possibly with an anti-inflammatory injection. Once the soreness has gone, you can safely resume your sport, provided you do so gradually, and you try to avoid repeating the activity which caused the problem.

'SNAPPING HIP'

This is a condition caused by long-standing bursitis over the greater trochanter. It tends to happen in young girls, but can happen to older people of either sex. If the bursitis has happened, and not been allowed to heal, the bursa becomes very thick, and obstructs the tendon which should ride over it. This causes a snapping sound each time the tendon goes over the thickest part of the bursa. If it is painful, surgery may be needed to cure the problem. Quite often, the condition causes only the noise, but no pain, and in this case it is better not to worry about it.

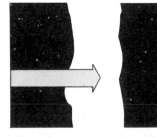

OSTEOARTHRITIS

Like all the joints we subject to loading, the hip is vulnerable to wear-and-tear degeneration. Injuries to the hip in childhood make the joint more vulnerable to arthritis later on. A major injury like a slipped epiphysis which is not recognized and treated immediately can lead to arthritis before the age of thirty. More often, wear-and-tear arthritis comes on after the age of forty. In arthritis, the joint's cartilage surfaces are damaged, especially over the head of the femur. When the cartilage tries to heal itself, it forms a new rich blood supply, which in fact weakens the cartilage and the bone underneath it. This can lead to cysts forming in the bone, flattening of the head of the femur, and sometimes knobs of bone forming over the damaged area, which may break off into the joint, or which may stay stuck to the edges of the head of the femur.

When the degenerative process has developed to a severe stage, it causes a gross limitation of movement, and usually a lot of pain. Your hip tends to be pulled inwards, and twisted, so that you can no longer take the joint through its full arc of movement. Pain in osteoarthritis can seem arbitrary. A lot of degeneration in the joint, which may show up as gross changes on an X-ray, may cause no pain at all, while conversely minor degeneration may be very painful. If there is pain, heat will tend to make it worse, by increasing the blood flow into an already congested joint, so you will probably feel pain at night, if you sleep under very warm blankets. Most arthritis sufferers feel more pain in damp weather, because this causes changes in the pressure within the joint.

Exercise is very important in preventing degeneration in the hip-joint, as movement can help to keep the joint surfaces healthy. However, too much weight-bearing movement can speed up the degeneration, especially if the joint has been distorted by childhood injuries. Free exercises to maintain a good range of movement and good muscle strength around the joint are the best antidote to arthritis. Swimming is the best form of 'unloaded' exercise, promoting full movement in the hips. Other sports can be continued, provided that they do not cause pain. You may find that you can play tennis or squash without any problems. You may be able to go jogging, and run moderate distances, although long-distance running and marathons may prove to be too much.

If you have pain in your hips which is diagnosed as being osteoarthritis, you should try to do a daily routine of mobilizing and strengthening exercises. It is essential to obtain an accurate diagnosis from your doctor, and to follow his instructions. Firstly, your doctor has to distinguish between this type of osteoarthritis and the inflammatory joint conditions or diseases which could give you similar hip pain. Secondly, he will advise you on the amount and type of exercise you should be doing. And thirdly, if there is severe distortion in the joint, or if it is too painful to allow you to carry on your normal activities, he may refer you to an orthopaedic specialist, with a view to having one of the corrective operations.

Hip exercises

The muscles surrounding your hip joints should be kept flexible by passive stretching, and they should be strengthened. Therefore, you should compose a selection of exercises for each of the muscle groups as a general daily routine, choosing from the sections of exercises for the hip flexors (p. 166), the thigh muscles (p. 133), the hamstrings (p. 144), and the back extensors (p. 206). If you go swimming regularly, you should try doing some of the exercises in the water, in the shallow end. Mobilizing exercises can be especially effective when done in water, if you use the water flow to help your hip to move in as wide a range as is practical. Striding through the water is a good strengthening exercise, if you start in water up to your waist, and then make the exercise harder by walking through water up to your chest.

MOBILIZING EXERCISES

1. Stand on one leg, holding onto a support with your hand; swing your free leg forward and backwards as far as you can, keeping your hip forward, back well arched. Start with ten swinging movements, and build up to thirty, on each leg in turn.
2. Stand on one leg, holding a support; swing your free leg out sideways, and then across the other leg, keeping your knee straight but relaxed. Start with ten, building to thirty on each leg in turn.
3. Stand on one leg, holding a support; swing your free leg round in as wide a circle as you can. Start with ten, building to thirty, on each leg in turn.
4. Lie on your back with your legs straight and resting on a smooth even surface covered with talcum powder; swing both legs sideways as far as you can, sliding them along the powdered surface, then swing them together again. Start with ten movements, and build up to thirty.

You can do this exercise in the swimming pool, lying on your back, floating, supporting yourself with your hands on the rail, or a float behind your back or head. You can also do the same movement lying on your stomach.
5. Lie on your back, on a firm surface; bend up one knee and clasp it in your hands. Pull the knee as close as you can to your chest, and then gently swing it from side to side, keeping your hip well bent. Start with five on each leg, building up to twenty.

173

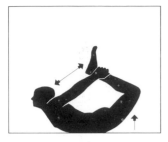

6. Lie on your stomach, on a firm surface. Bend one knee up behind you, and clasp your ankle in your hands. Gently pull your ankle, to rock your leg back at the hip, starting with ten movements on each leg, building up to thirty.

7. Sit on a firm surface with your legs as wide apart as possible, knees straight. Keeping your back straight, gently rock forward over your hips, reaching forward with your hands onto the floor in front of you. Start with ten movements, build up to thirty.

8. Lie on your stomach on a firm surface, with your knees slightly apart. Bend your knees so that your legs are at right angles to your thighs; swing your feet towards each other, then away sideways, starting with ten movements of hip-twisting and building up to thirty.

9. Lie on your back on the edge of a bed or couch, so that one leg can swing over the side; letting your knee bend slightly, swing your leg downwards to tap the floor with your heel rhythmically, so that your hip extends. Start with ten movements, and build up to thirty, on each leg in turn.

10. In the pool, stand facing the rail, with water up to your chest level. Holding on to the rail, bend both knees to swing your legs up towards your chest, then straighten them and swing your legs behind you to extend your hips. Start with ten continuous movements, building up to thirty.

174

1. Stand on one leg, with a weight attached round the ankle of your free leg. Holding a support with your hand, take your leg as far back as you can without bending forward at the hips, hold for a count of three, then take your leg forward as high as you can without curving your back, and hold for three. Start with ten movements on each leg, building up to three sets of ten.

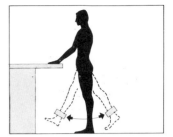

2. Stand on one leg, with a weight attached to the ankle of your free leg. Holding a support with your hand, take your leg sideways as far as you can without bending your trunk at all, hold for a count of three, then relax. Start with ten on each leg, building to three sets of ten.

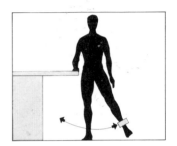

3. Standing on one leg with the weight on your free leg, and your hand holding a support, take your leg sideways, fairly slowly, then swing it in controlled fashion across the front of your other leg, then sideways again, then swing behind your other leg, out sideways again, then rest. Start with three movements on each leg, building up to ten.

4. Standing on one leg, with the weight on your free leg, hand holding a support, swing your leg round and out sideways in as large an arc as you can comfortably do, without bending your trunk at all. Start with five on each leg, and build up to twenty.

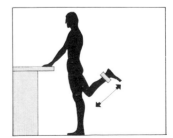

5. Standing on one leg, with a weight on your free leg, and your hand holding a support, bend your knee to a right angle, and take your leg backwards in a bouncing, rhythmical movement. Start with ten on each leg, building up to three sets of ten.

175

The Pelvis

The pelvic bones form a kind of basin. The flat bones at the sides are your hip-bones (ilia), which form fine ridges of bone where they meet at the front. The back of the basin is your sacrum, a wedge-shaped bone tapering to the tiny bones of your coccyx, or 'tail'.

The symphysis pubis is a strongly bonded joint at the front of the pelvis. The two sacro-iliac joints are also firmly bound by strong ligaments, but, unlike the pubis, they do have fluid between the bones.

You can feel your pubic joint clearly, and the sacro-iliac joints where they form dimples in your lower back. Your coccyx is easy to feel in the cleft of your buttocks, while under your buttocks you can feel the hard bones of your ischial tuberosities, or seat-bones.

FUNCTIONS

You cannot move the pubic or sacro-iliac joints voluntarily. The pelvic basin serves mainly as a protective structure holding your abdominal organs. The female pelvis is wider and shallower than the male, giving space for the womb. In childbirth the pelvic joints loosen. During the phases of the female menstrual cycle the sacro-iliac joints may slacken slightly.

Some sacro-iliac movement occurs in both men and women, when you move your hips or trunk relative to your pelvis. When you lift one leg forwards at the hip, your hip-bone twists backwards slightly over the sacrum, and conversely twists forwards when you extend your leg behind you. The sacro-iliac joints function as a pair, so when you stand on one leg, any movement on one side is balanced by the opposite motion on the other. This happens when you kick a football, reach for a low shot in tennis, or throw the javelin.

When you move both legs in the same direction, or bend and straighten your back without twisting, your pelvis moves as a whole. If you lie on your back and bend your knees up to your chest, the top of your pelvis rolls backwards to complete the curve in your back. You can feel this movement of pelvic tilting if you sit in a chair with your hands over the bone ridges below your waist, and then arch and relax your back,

176

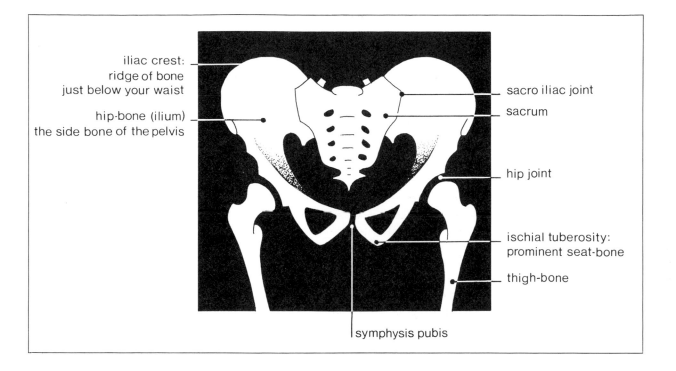

iliac crest:
ridge of bone
just below your waist

hip-bone (ilium)
the side bone of the pelvis

sacro iliac joint

sacrum

hip joint

ischial tuberosity:
prominent seat-bone

thigh-bone

symphysis pubis

accentuating its lower curve, then flattening it. This is a useful postural exercise which you can do when you are sitting or standing for any time.

Posturally, the pelvis is affected by your leg and trunk positions. If you habitually stand with your weight over one leg, or sit with your legs crossed, you cause a twist in your sacro-iliac joints. Holding your head to one side, dropping one shoulder relative to the other, or habitually carrying loads in one hand or on one shoulder, are all postures which cause stress on one side of the pelvis. Slouching in an easy chair makes the top of the pelvis tilt backwards, so that your lower back is slumped instead of arched. Women who wear high-heeled shoes tilt their pelvis forwards, as the back must arch to maintain stability. If young girls wear very high shoes during their growth years, their lower back may develop with an abnormally pronounced curve, or lordosis, which may cause problems later. Excessive weight over your stomach also tilts the pelvis forwards: this inevitably happens to some degree during pregnancy, but is an avoidable problem in men who have a beer gut.

Good posture depends on good trunk muscles, and an awareness of the importance of symmetrical alignment. Your back has natural curves, which you should maintain, possibly by doing the pelvic tilting exercise

The pelvis, from in front.

177

(p. 203), arching and relaxing your lower (lumbar) curve at intervals during each day, and by supporting the curve with a small cushion or rolled towel whenever you have to sit in an easy chair or car seat. Rigid, military posture is no better than a lazy slump, in terms of spinal alignment, but you should try at all times to sit or stand with your hips and shoulders level, to avoid twisting stresses. Symmetrical posture is especially important for children during their growth phases, as poor posture leads to muscle imbalance, and can cause a fixed twisting deformity (scoliosis) in the spine. A daily routine of trunk exercises will help to ensure that your muscles are strong enough to maintain good posture.

Lifting weights places stress on your pelvis and spine. To lift safely, you must co-ordinate the effort through your legs, back and arms, using your legs by bending your knees, holding the weight close to you in your arms, and keeping your back as rigidly straight as possible. If you have to turn with the weight, do not twist, but walk round. If you have to carry the weight in one hand, change hands frequently to balance the loading on each side of your back. These guidelines apply to any light weight you have to lift up from the floor, but you have to be especially careful when you handle heavier weights while weight-training. If you handle even a weight as light as ten kilogrammes with your back bent, legs straight, the combination of compressive loading coupled with muscle stress at a particular point in your back can cause harm.

Pelvic problems

PAIN IN THE GROIN

Groin pain may be caused by internal problems, for instance bladder or prostate problems. It may be referred from your back or hips, without necessarily causing symptoms in the joint which is the source of the pain (p. 207). An inguinal hernia (p. 163), injury to an adductor tendon (p. 152), or a stress fracture in one of the pubic bones, can all cause pain in the groin region.

As soon as you have noticeable pain in your groin, you should refer to your doctor with details of how it came on, what makes the pain worse, whether it eases at all, and whether it is aggravated by such movements as coughing, sneezing, or passing water. To make an accurate diagnosis of your problem, your doctor will probably want to do investigations such as X-rays, bone scans, blood tests and internal checks, as appropriate to your symptoms.

The pubic symphysis is such a strongly bonded joint that it is rarely injured on its own. In a severe injury involving shearing stresses, for instance a fall in which a motorcycle or a horse rolls across your pelvis, you are as likely to fracture the pelvic bones as to disrupt the symphysis pubis.

However, the pubic joint can be damaged by repetitive stress. If a particular movement or activity causes a continual slight separation or shearing in the symphysis, the joint surfaces can be eroded, causing a kind of roughening in the cartilage and bones forming the joint. This condition is called osteitis pubis, meaning inflammation of the pubic bone.

Footballers can suffer this injury, simply from the cumulative effect of the shearing movement involved in kicking the football. The condition can be triggered by a sudden injury, like a fall with the legs stretched wide apart, especially if there is external pressure, like a push or a violent tackle at the same time. Race walkers sometimes suffer from repetitive stress over the pubic joint, simply because of the exaggerated pelvic motion inherent in the sport. Runners may suffer similar stresses through over-striding, especially on hills. Previous hip problems, or limitation in your hip movements for any reason, can contribute to the pubic problem.

What you feel is pain directly over the symphysis pubis, which comes on when you do sport, and gradually gets worse if you continue with your sport. Usually the pain starts as no more than a mild ache during sport. However, if it is triggered by a sudden violent injury, the initial pain may be severe. Generally, the pain eases if you rest for a few days. The pubic joint feels sore if you press it, and you may be able to feel fluid swelling over the front of the joint. When the joint is painful, you may feel the pain radiating out over the genital area, or into your hips. The pain may be aggravated if you do violent movements with your hips, or if you contract your abdominal muscles hard, for instance by doing sit-ups on an inclined bench. If you continue with your sport, the pain gradually gets worse each time until you have to stop altogether.

When you have this type of groin pain, the earlier you refer to your doctor for help, the better. Your doctor has to differentiate between the various diseases and internal problems which could account for your pain.

Rest is an essential part of the cure for this problem. You have to avoid any pain-causing activities for anything up to six months. Your doctor may decide to give you drugs against the inflammation in the pubic bones. If the problem is severe enough, your doctor may refer you to an orthopaedic surgeon, with a view to your having an operation to fuse the two bones in the symphysis together. Apart from maintaining as much power and flexibility in the pelvis as is possible without causing further harm, and doing such sports as do not cause pain, there is no self-help measure to speed up healing in this condition.

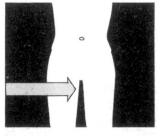

GROIN FRICTION

An uncomfortable condition which can happen to cyclists is friction directly under the groin from the saddle. The friction may cause pain, numbness or tingling. A very uncomfortable secondary effect in men can be a constant, painful erection, due to pressure on the nerves in the groin.

Specialist treatment may be needed, but analysing the cause of the problem is essential to avoid recurrences. The saddle may be too wide, so it should be changed for a narrower one, preferably with furrowed edges. Some soft padding along the edges of the saddle may help. The cyclist should avoid pressing inwards against the saddle with his or her thighs. Standing up in the pedals whenever possible can help to relieve the constant pressure on the seat and groin.

PAIN IN THE SACRO-ILIAC REGION

Pain in the pelvic region of the lower back may be due to internal problems, perhaps in the urinary system, or the gynaecological system in females. Pain can be referred to the back of the pelvis from the groin or hips.

ANKYLOSING SPONDYLITIS

Of the inflammatory joint conditions which can cause intermittent, unexplained pain, one in particular tends to affect the sacro-iliac region specifically. Ankylosing spondylitis is a progressive disease, causing stiffness and gradual loss of function. It usually starts in the back, and spreads up the spine, but it may affect other joints like your shoulders, elbows and hips, and it can cause the pain and tightness of plantar fasciitis under the soles of your feet. Quite often, the first sign of ankylosing spondylitis is stiffness in the sacro-iliac region. The disease tends to affect teenage boys, so the pain may be mistakenly related to over-exercising on the previous day. Diagnosis of the problem is usually made on the basis of the history of the pain, X-rays and blood tests. Once ankylosing spondylitis has been diagnosed, your doctor may treat the condition with appropriate drugs to ease immediate pain. The most important factor in controlling the disease is to maintain good power and flexibility in the trunk, while avoiding activities which tend to increase or bring on the pain. Anyone suffering from the disease is normally recommended to do a daily routine of back exercises aiming to keep the back fully mobile. The pain of the disease is intermittent and arbitrary, so while you should not try to do sport during an episode of pain, you can usually continue with any sports you like in between. The more sporting activities you can maintain, without aggravating any pain, the better off you are in the long-term. Swimming is a very useful activity for maintaining power and movement in your spine and limbs, without overloading the joints.

SACRO-ILIAC INJURIES

Because of the particular way in which the sacro-iliac joints move during most activities, they can be damaged in a variety of different situations. Over-balancing or over-hitting during ground strokes in racket sports can cause sacro-iliac strains. The injury can happen if you catch your foot during the run-up for a javelin throw. When you are at full stretch for a kick in football, the injury can happen if your foot slides on the ground, or if an opponent tackles you and twists your trunk over your hips. Over-striding in running can damage the sacro-iliac joints.

You will be more prone to sacro-iliac strains through minor stresses in sport if you have any kind of muscular imbalance round your hips or lower trunk. For instance, you may have tighter hip flexor muscles or hamstrings on one side than the other, or stronger abdominal muscles to one side of your trunk's mid-line. Childhood hip problems or injuries make it easier for you to strain your sacro-iliac joints in adult life. In women, the sacro-iliac ligaments loosen according to hormonal changes during the menstrual cycle, so sacro-iliac strains often occur through apparently minimal stresses at these times, usually just before a period, or in the early stages of the period. Because the pelvis alters position greatly during pregnancy, women frequently suffer from backache before child-birth, and then find that lifting the baby causes repetitive sacro-iliac strains because the joints have been 'weakened'.

What you feel when one or both sacro-iliac joints are strained is pain over the lower back. You may be able to localize the pain over the dimples of the sacro-iliac joint. The pain is usually worse when you stand up and bend backwards, and when you bend to either side. Bending forwards may hurt, or you may find that it only hurts when you reach a certain angle. If you have to spend time leaning forward, for instance over a drawing board, or leaning over a desk to answer telephones, you often find that your back becomes increasingly stiff and painful throughout the day, especially if you have to turn to one side constantly. Sitting in easy

181

chairs may feel comfortable at the time, but the back pain is worse when you get up. Or your back may feel painful even when you are sitting down. Besides back pain, you may feel a referred pain, or 'pulling' sensation down the back of your thigh, making you think that you have strained a hamstring.

The pain may not follow any easily identifiable pattern. It is often difficult to localize back pain, so you have to try to assess carefully exactly what you are doing, and have just been doing, at each phase when your back hurts or eases. This will help your doctor to make a reasoned diagnosis of the problem.

Self-help measures for sacro-iliac injuries

• If the initial pain in your back is severe, you should try to lie down as much as possible, and avoid sitting for any length of time. Ice applications may ease the discomfort (p. 15). You should not try to do any exercises, unless your doctor recommends you to. If you try to do back exercises and they cause pain, you are likely to do yourself more harm. In the first instance of any back problem, you must aim to reduce pain and muscle spasm by resting and avoiding painful movements and activities, and to obtain specialist help through your doctor.

• You must remember that easing pain through 'bad' posture is likely to increase your pain when you straighten up again. Avoid sitting slumped in an easy chair, but support your lower back in its natural forward curve with a small cushion or rolled towel. Do not cross your legs while sitting, or stand with your weight balanced on one leg, even if you feel these positions ease your pain.

• When you are not lying down, try to keep moving around, rather than sitting or standing still for long periods. If you have to sit down, you will probably find that arching and relaxing your lower back and pelvis, pushing your seat and stomach out, and then pulling both in, in a repetitive, gentle movement, helps to ease any stiffness and aching. Lying completely flat may make your back ache. In this case, you will probably find it more comfortable to put an extra pillow under your hips if you lie on your stomach, or a couple of pillows under your knees, if you lie on your back.

• When you are recovering from the initial phase of the problem, as soon as your specialist allows, you should start to do exercises to strengthen your trunk. In pelvic strains, you often find that your stomach weakens very rapidly. One test for this is to lie on your back with your knees bent, feet on the floor, hands behind your head, and try to sit up to touch your elbows to your knees. If you cannot do this, your lower stomach muscles are too weak to stabilize your pelvis for the movement, and you should

182

work especially hard on the abdominal strengthening exercises (p. 199). To make up a reasoned programme of specific exercises, you should start with strengthening the back muscles and the abdominals (p. 196), and then progress to the mobilizing exercises. Any exercises which hurt should be modified or left out.

• Once the worst of the pain is gone, you should try to analyse what caused the problem, so that you avoid repeating it. During your recovery, you can swim for fitness, but avoid running until you are sure it does not cause pain. Try running on the spot before you run outside. Similarly, you should try out any movements relating to your sport as 'shadow' swings or patterns, before you try the full activity. A good warm-up is essential before any exercise session, as you will certainly increase a back problem if you try to do sport while it is stiff.

• It is impossible to predict how long it takes to recover from an episode of back strain. Each case is different, with different factors involved. Much also depends on whether your particular sport places special strains in the normal way on the lower back, as this means that you have to be extra cautious in your return to sport. Specialist treatment for any kind of back strain may vary from rest and immobilization to active manipulation and early exercising. To help immobilize the sacro-iliac joints, as far as possible, your specialist may recommend a hard or soft corset, or a strap which attaches round your hip-bones and stretches the sacro-iliac joints slightly. Your specialist may find that you have differing leg lengths, and recommend a shoe raise to correct this, and even out the level of your pelvis. Equally, a specialist may decide that unequal leg lengths are incidental to your problem, and therefore correction is not necessary. As there are so many different ways of treating back problems, your only guide to effectiveness is the progress you make. If your condition is not improving, or if it is getting worse, you must seek a second opinion through your doctor. The first essential is to obtain an accurate diagnosis of the problem: this is the hardest part, and may require a lot of medical investigations. Once the diagnosis is established, amd any medical complications ruled out, it is much easier for your specialist to institute a reasoned line of treatment.

Complication

SHORT-LEG SYNDROME

Most people have different length legs, to some degree, and this can normally be ignored. However, length differences can contribute to pelvic joint strains.

Pelvis

Measuring the legs is best done by a specialist, who will take into account two measurements. Firstly, the length of the leg bones themselves, from the top of the thigh-bone (greater trochanter) to the medial malleolus at the end of the shin-bone. Secondly, the length from the rim of your pelvis, measured from the top edge of your hip-bone, to the end of your shin-bone. These measurements tell you whether the bones themselves differ in overall length (real shortening of one leg) or whether a visible difference is due to sideways tilting in the pelvis and lower back (apparent shortening), giving the impression that one leg is shorter than the other.

If the specialist finds the difference significant, and feels that it has contributed to your pelvic or hip problem, he will probably try to correct it with a support under the heel of your short leg.

In many cases, sideways tilting over your hip is related to the particular position you adopt during your sport. Track runners lean into the bends, and distance runners may train consistently on the same camber in the roads. In this case, part of your recovery may be helped if you try to even out the stresses by running round the track in the other direction, or finding camber sloping in the opposite direction to run on.

The Hip Abductors

The hip abductors are the muscles behind your hip which pull your thigh outwards. They consist of two main muscles, gluteus medius and the smaller gluteus minimus, both of which lie under the main bulk of gluteus maximus, which forms the fleshy part of your buttock. The abductors are attached over the outer side of your hip-bone, spreading out in a fan shape over the bone. They narrow down into two tendons which are fixed onto the top of the greater trochanter, the jutting bone at the outer side of your hip.

FUNCTIONS

If you lie on one side with your legs straight, and lift your upper leg straight up sideways, your hip abductors create the movement in your hip. Similarly, if you stand on one leg and lift the other sideways from the hip, the action is performed by the abductors. Abduction is a term meaning movement sideways in the limbs, away from the mid-line of your body.

However, the abductors also have a more complex stabilizing function. When you stand on one leg, your abductors on the moving leg may be working to help create hip movement. But the abductors on your standing leg are also working, to help hold your pelvis level by pulling it in a downwards direction on the fixed side. This effort keeps your pelvis horizontal even though it is not supported by your leg on one side. If your hip abductors are paralysed on one side through disease, if you stand on that leg, your pelvis will sag down on the other side, because the abductors have lost their stabilizing influence. This deformity is known as the Trendelenberg sign, and causes a bad limp when you walk, because you cannot keep your hip up high enough to allow your free leg to swing through.

In sport, your hip abductors work whenever you use your legs to run and jump. The abductors create the outward part of your leg kick in breaststroke swimming. When you kick the ball across your body in football, your hip abductors work to balance your pelvis from your standing leg, while on the other side they create the movement of taking your leg out sideways and backwards for the kick.

185

Injury to the hip abductors

The hip abductors can be strained through overstretching or overwork. Repetitive strain, for instance while long-distance running, can cause a gradual pain in the abductors through overuse. Or a sudden violent movement can strain the muscles, for instance when you are performing a karate kick and an opponent blocks it unexpectedly, or if you are taking your leg back for a football kick and someone knocks your leg from behind. You are more likely to suffer this type of injury if your abductors are tight, whether through overuse in your sport, or previous hip or sacro-iliac problems.

What you feel

You feel pain over the injured muscles, to the side of the dimple in your lower back, or spreading outwards from there. The muscles hurt when you use them, so lying on your side and trying to lift your leg up is painful, especially if you are lifting a weight or someone applies resistance against your leg during the movement. You may feel the pain when you balance on one leg on your injured side, or the pain may only become noticeable when you stand on the leg and lean over to that side. The muscles also hurt when you stretch them, so any movement which takes your hip through a circular range is likely to cause pain both when you take your leg out sideways, and as you bring it forward across your other leg. If you press hard over the painful area, you feel a tender area where the muscles are strained.

What you should do

When you feel the pain firstly, avoid movements which make it worse, especially in sport. You can apply ice over the painful area (p. 15), to ease it, although the muscles are so deeply sited under the bulk of your gluteus maximus that the ice is unlikely to have a direct effect on the abductors. When your doctor has established that you have simply strained the muscles, you should start stretching the area with passive stretching exercises, but not pushing through pain. Little by little you will feel less discomfort when you stretch. You can then start to do the strengthening exercises, stretching passively before and after each session. You progress to the dynamic exercises as the pain recedes, and once you can manage these without discomfort, you are fit to return to sport.

Hip abductor exercises

Repeat these as often as possible, every day.
1. Lie on your back, and bend the knee of your injured leg. Pull your knee towards your chest with your hand, and then draw the leg across towards the opposite shoulder, so that you feel a 'pull' over the injured abductor muscles. Hold for a count of ten, then gently relax.

2. Standing on your uninjured leg, pull your other knee up towards the opposite shoulder with your hands, to feel the stretch over the abductors. Hold to ten.

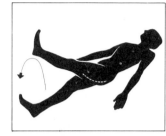

3. Lie on your back, and swing your injured leg over your other leg, keeping your knee as straight as possible. Take your foot up towards the opposite shoulder until you feel the pull over the injured abductors. Hold to ten.

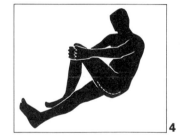

4. Sit on the floor with your legs straight in front of you. Bend your knee on your injured leg, and put your foot on the floor to the side of your other knee. With your hands, pull your knee over across your other leg, keeping your foot on the floor until you feel the pull over the abductors. Hold to ten.

STRENGTHENING EXERCISES

Start with five of each exercise, and build up to three sets of ten. Then use weights, attached to your foot or strapped over your ankle.
1. Lie on your side, with your injured leg uppermost. Lift your leg up sideways, keeping your knee straight, hold for three, then slowly lower.
2. Lie on your stomach; lift your injured leg backwards a little way, then take it out sideways, back to centre, and slowly lower.
3. Lie on your back; lift your injured leg up a little way, keeping your knee straight, then take it out sideways as far as you can, then back to centre and slowly lower.
4. Stand on your uninjured leg; keeping your back straight and your hip forward, take your injured leg out sideways and slightly backwards from your hip, keeping your knee straight, then slowly lower.

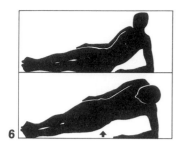

5. Stand on your injured leg, and lift your other leg straight out sideways; then bend sideways over your injured leg, hold the position for a count of three, then slowly straighten up.

6. Lie on your side with your injured hip underneath you. Resting your weight on your elbow and your foot, push your hips up sideways to arch away from the floor, hold for a count of three, then slowly lower.

To progress this exercise, when it becomes easy, balance your weight on your hand, keeping your elbow straight, and your foot.

DYNAMIC EXERCISES

1. Run sideways, starting by moving away from your injured hip, and then towards it. Build up to one hundred metres from thirty metres, starting with two runs in each direction, and building up to ten.

2. Hop sideways on your injured leg, in the direction of the injured side, along a line set to thirty hops. Start with two sets of hops in the same direction, and build up to ten sets of thirty hops in that direction.

3. Hop sideways up onto a stair in the direction of your injured leg. Start with ten hops, building up to three sets of ten.

4. Do sets of jumps, spreading your legs out sideways as far as you can. Start with ten jumps, and build up to fifty.

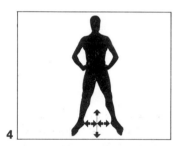

5. Sprint up stairs or a hill, starting with thirty paces on each leg, and building up to one hundred. Start with three sets of sprints, and build up to ten, jogging back to the start.

Complications

If the injury shows no sign of change within one week, despite care, it is likely that you have more than a simple muscle strain, so you should refer back to your doctor for further checks. Common complications are back problems underlying the muscle strain. The sacro-iliac joint is very close to the attachment of the abductor muscles on the hip-bone, so an injury to the muscles can cause damage in the joint and vice versa. Problems in the lower back can give referred pain into the buttock, making you think that you have localized muscle damage. Damage to the hip-bone can give rise to localized pain in the abductor muscles, but the problem is longer to heal than an uncomplicated muscle strain. All the structures in the pelvis are closely linked functionally, so you must suspect damage in more than one of the structures, if an apparent hip muscle strain does not gradually get better with due care.

188

The Lumbar Spine
(Lower spine)

STRUCTURE

The lumbar spine is the lowest part of your back, which curves forward to form a hollow above your pelvis. It consists of five bony vertebrae, linked together by ligaments, muscles, and soft-tissue discs between the bones.

Each of the five bones is in the form of a cylindrical block, backed by a triangular structure of finer bones. Each triangle of bone has short struts of bone protruding upwards, downwards, backwards, and to each side. The vertical struts interlink with the upward and downward struts on the vertebrae above or below, to form closely knitted joints. The backward and sideways struts also form joints with the equivalent fine bones on the vertebrae above and below, linked by ligaments, but the bones in each joint are not so close together.

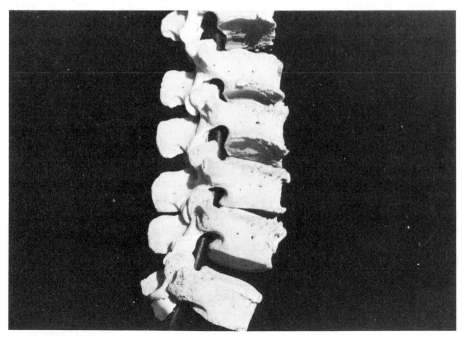

The five bones of the lumbar spine. The vertebral bodies are facing right, the spines jutting left. The spinal cord would run between the vertebral bodies and spines, like the rubber cord in the picture. The vertebral bodies would be separated in life by the soft-tissue discs.

You can feel the struts which project backwards from the vertebrae, as they form the spines which you can see and feel through your skin, down the centre of the whole length of your back. It is harder to feel the sideways struts, as they are covered by the thick masses of your spinal muscles, while the vertical struts are sited deeply, and so are equally difficult to feel.

The lowest of the lumbar vertebrae, called L5 for short, lies on top of the sacrum, which is flat and cylindrical in shape, to correspond to the block of bone forming the main body of the L5 vertebra. The body of L5 is slightly taller at the front than at the back of the block, to help form the curve forward of the lumbar vertebrae above the pelvis. Everyone has different degrees of curvature in the lumbar spine, so the degree to which L5 and the other vertebrae are wedge-shaped varies. If each vertebral body is uniform in height, the lumbar curve hardly exists, and the spine looks flat and straight where it spreads up from the pelvis.

As the spine is arranged in a series of blocks placed vertically one on top of the other, the ligaments joining the blocks together are also more or less vertical. A very strong ligament runs the length of the spine, attached to the front of each vertebral block. This is called the anterior longitudinal ligament, and it forms a long strap binding all the vertebrae together, from your skull down to the top of the front of your sacrum. A similar ligament runs the length of the vertebrae across the back of the vertebral blocks, from the top of the sacrum, up as far as the second vertebra in the neck. There are no ligaments at the sides of the vertebral bodies. Short strong ligaments bind together the struts of bone on the fine arches at the back of the vertebrae. Where the vertical struts lie close together to form their joints, they are bound by fluid-filled capsules, which enclose the joints. The ligaments binding the sideways and backwards struts are attached vertically between the corresponding bones on each vertebra. One long ligament covers the tips of the backwards spines spreading vertically from the lowest of the neck vertebrae to the top of the sacrum. In a bony person, you can see this long ligament spreading like a cord between the protruding spines when the back is bent forward.

The discs in the spine are connecting structures which lie between the bodies of the vertebrae. They fit neatly into the flat surfaces forming the top and bottom of each vertebral body. You have a disc between each vertebra, starting between the top of the sacrum and L5, up to the joint between the third and second vertebrae in the neck. Your discs make up about one fifth of the length of your whole spine, but they vary in thickness in each region, and are relatively thick in the lumbar region, compared to the thoracic region above it.

Each disc is 'stuck' to the bones between which it lies, and is constructed with two main features, which make it look rather like a raw egg. In the centre of the disc, like a yolk, is the nucleus pulposus, which is a water-filled transparent jelly. The nucleus is very elastic in children, but it gradually becomes harder, losing its water-holding capacity as you grow up. Surrounding the nucleus is the annulus fibrosus, which surrounds the nucleus as the egg-white surrounds the yolk. Around the nucleus, the annulus consists of fibrocartilage, while its outer edges are collagen, which makes it a stronger structure than normal ligaments. The nucleus does not lie quite in the centre of the protective ring formed by the annulus, but slightly back from the centre, so that it is closer to the back edge of the vertebrae than the front.

FUNCTIONS

Only slight movements happen between individual vertebrae, because the bone structure interlocks. However, the combined movements in the whole spine allow a good range. Your stomach muscles bend your spine forwards; long extensor muscles down your back pull your spine backwards; you bend sideways through the contraction of your trunk muscles on that side; and you can twist because of small rotator muscles in your back combining with the diagonal stomach muscles. In the lumbar spine, bending backwards and sideways are the freest movements, while forward bending is more limited, and twisting is very restricted.

Mechanically, your spine acts as a mobile series of levers when you bend and twist, or as a rigid single lever when you brace your back to lift a weight up. In throwing events, racket sports and rowing, your spine provides mobility and power. Twisting dives use the extremes of your spinal mobility, but you make your spine rigid for the moment of entry into the water. Your spine has to absorb shock and cope with compression forces. Your discs give at each level when you jump down from a height or land on your head in a fall, but if the jarring force is too great you may smash one or more of your discs, or crush some of your vertebrae. Normal discs have great resilience, but this is undermined as you grow older, or if you have had previous injuries to the back.

Posturally, your lumbar spine is influenced by various factors, including the effect of gravity; positions you adopt; your habitual patterns of movement; and extra loading when you lift, hold or carry weights. 'Good' posture holds your trunk and limbs in correct alignment, with minimal strain on your joints and soft tissues. Your lumbar spine is supposed to curve forwards, without strain, slouching or twisting. You may have to train yourself into good, symmetrical posture, remembering that your pelvis and shoulders also influence your lower back.

191

Your vertebrae have a protective role, as your spinal cord is enclosed within the bony arches at the back of the spine. The cord extends from your brain to about the level of the second lumbar vertebra, and is part of your central nervous system, which never heals once it is damaged. At each vertebra, tiny nerves lead off from the cord, forming part of your peripheral nervous system, which provides sensation and motor power around your body. The peripheral nerves from your lumbar spine supply your legs. A major injury to the spine can break the spinal cord, causing permanent paralysis. Sports like rugby, parachuting and gymnastics carry the risk of this type of accident, through direct pressure on the spine, or through falls from a height. If the peripheral nerves are damaged, giving referred pain, the problem is usually reversible with correct treatment.

BACK PAIN

A variety of medical conditions can make your back hurt by affecting your spinal joints, ranging from ankylosing spondylitis (p. 180) and the various forms of arthritis to tuberculosis. Apart from joint problems in the spine, problems in the various internal organs in the abdomen can give rise to lower back pain.

Therefore, your record of your back problem should include any details of illnesses just before the pain started: problems passing water, digestive problems, or gynaecological problems in women. You must also note down any apparently unrelated pains that you may have felt, before, during or after any episode of back pain. This will help your doctor to perform the relevant investigations and make the right diagnosis. The sooner you refer to your doctor for help once you start noticing back pain, the better off you will be in the long run.

Back injuries

Causes

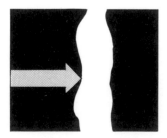

Any movement, or series of movements, which places abnormal stress or abnormal loading on the spine can injure it. This may be a sudden overload, if, for instance, you overbalance while lifting a very heavy weight. Or it may be a cumulative overload, if you repeatedly pull or lift a weight at an awkward angle. This kind of cumulative strain can happen to oarsmen who have to lean and turn to replace heavy boats onto low racks, or it can happen to racket games players through the repetitive twisting stress of ground strokes.

192

In principle, your back is a very strong structure. It can withstand a great deal of pressure. Equally, in certain situations, it can become vulnerable to strains. Often, the strain is caused by pressure or loading that seems trivial, and below the normal strength of your back. It is not surprising that a competitive weight-lifter, attempting a maximum lift beyond his previous known capacity for power, may exceed his muscles' ability to cope with the load, and so may suffer damage in his spinal joints. In this situation, as the trunk muscles fail to hold the load, the damage is usually caused by movement in the spinal joints, which are no longer held fixed, and this can cause tearing or fractures in any of the structures in the joints, including the bones. But the type of back injury which comes on when you feel you are doing no more than your accustomed activities is more surprising. This type of pain is usually associated with twisting movements in the spine, so it particularly affects people who play golf, tennis or squash. Sports which combine twisting movements in the spine with heavier compressive loading, like rowing, judo and rugby, carry the double risk of sudden, traumatic, back injuries, or the more gradual kind.

It is usually possible to identify a triggering factor for your back pain, even when the injury appears to have no particular cause at first sight. You may have changed your equipment, or your style of play; you may have been doing more of your sport than you were used to; you may have been feeling back stiffness due to fatigue; you may have over-twisted or over-loaded your back without a preparatory warm-up; you may have developed a faulty technique through carelessness in handling, lifting or carrying heavy weights; or a leg injury may have affected your back posture.

What you feel

Back pain, whether sudden or gradual, may be felt in one localized area of your back, or it may feel widespread over the whole lower back. If the injury is sudden, it is likely to cause a severe stab of pain, which may subside quickly or may persist. A more gradual pain usually starts mildly, but builds up to the stage of causing real discomfort. You may find that certain movements or positions aggravate your pain, while others relieve it. You may feel that your back hurts, whatever you do, but careful analysis may show that in certain positions you can relieve your pain. You have to be aware of cause and effect: poor posture may ease your pain temporarily, but make it worse as soon as you straighten up. Easing pain through twisting your back is likely to make your pain progressively worse over a space of time. Your back may hurt when you are at rest; when you cough; when you turn over in bed at night. But it may stop

193

hurting when you lie flat; when you are walking around; when you bend forwards, backwards or sideways; or if you hang from a bar by your hands, and take the weight off your feet.

You may also feel pain in one or both legs, associated with your back pain, and which gets worse when your back is moved in certain ways, for instance when you are sitting in an easy chair, or when you bend forwards. The leg pain may be directly traceable to your back, so that you feel a line of pain spreading down from your lower back into your groin, or down the back of your leg. The pain may spread only to your knee, or it may go right down to your foot. This kind of leg pain may come on without an obvious link to your back, making you think that you have a localized muscle strain in your leg. Although referred pain in the leg relates directly to a back strain, or sometimes to a hip problem, it can come on when you do not have noticeable pain in your back (p. 207).

What has happened

Because of the complex structure of your spinal joints, there are many different tissues which can be damaged in a back injury. A severe compression injury, like a fall from a height, can crush the body of a vertebra. A severe twisting injury can fracture the bony arch at the back of one of the vertebrae. Any of the ligaments guarding the spinal joints can be strained by abnormal movements. The small or larger muscles in your back may be strained by over-stretching or over-contraction. If a spinal joint is damaged, the muscles over it usually go into spasm, to fix the joint in a kind of natural splint. This stiffens that part of your back, creating even more pain if you then try to move it against the limiting factor of the tightened muscles. If you try to force movement, you may tear the muscles, adding to the original damage done in the injury.

The discs between your vertebral bones can be damaged in a variety of different ways. The danger of disc damage increases as you get older, because the strong outer part, the annulus fibrosus, begins to degenerate at any time after twenty-five years, while the nucleus pulposus begins to lose its pliability and water-holding capacity as early as in middle age. Minor damage to the outer part of the disc can be no worse in its effect than a strain to the ligaments covering the joints. But major disc damage is a much more serious problem. A rise in pressure over a degenerated disc can push the disc out from between the vertebrae, or it can create enough pressure to push the nucleus through the annulus, cracking its outer ring. Usually the broken disc protrudes backwards, so that it encroaches into the spinal canal, and lodges against the nerves there. This can cause severe and unremitting pain in your leg, in the pathway of the pressurized nerves, although the pain may be milder and intermittent. The cause of

194

this major injury can be minor: a degenerated disc may be disrupted by simple activities like coughing when you are bending forward, or lifting even a light weight with your back bent.

It is totally impossible for you to identify which of the various spinal structures has been damaged in any particular injury. This is a matter for specialist diagnosis. In most cases, damage is not isolated to a single structure, because the spine is a functionally linked series of joints. In many cases of back injury, accurate diagnosis is not possible, but functional recovery can be achieved just the same.

Self-help measures for back injuries

- If there is any danger at all that your back might have been broken in a very severe, traumatic injury, you should not be moved at all until specialist help arrives and you can be transported to hospital. Apart from back pain, the main signs that your back may have been broken are numbness, tingling or pain in your legs, and a feeling of total weakness in your trunk and legs.
- If the injury is less drastic, but very painful, ice can be applied to your back (p. 15). You should refer to your local casualty department or your doctor as quickly as possible, in case you need X-rays or other investigations.
- In the initial stages of a painful back injury, the more you lie down and keep the weight off your feet, the better. If possible, lie flat, and avoid propping your head up on pillows, or curling up on your side.
- If you have to sit down, especially at work, you must make sure that your back is well supported, preferably on soft cushions. Your doctor may provide you with a soft corset, to provide some support for your back, without limiting your movement too much. If your back is very sore all the time, your doctor may give you a firmer, boned corset, or even a plaster cast.
- You must avoid any activities which cause pain in your back, but you must also be aware of the importance of your everyday posture. Poor posture, which allows the back to sag, and stretches the ligaments, may feel comfortable at the time, but it can contribute to your pain afterwards.
- As soon as your back is less sore, and your doctor allows, you should start doing the simpler exercises to strengthen your back and abdominal muscles (p. 196). You should avoid any exercises which bring on pain.
- Once you can do the more advanced of the trunk strengthening exercises, involving spinal movement, without pain, you can progress to the mobilizing exercises (p. 202). The exact sequence in which you build up

195

your rehabilitation programme will depend on your particular injury and pain, and on the opinion of your specialist. In general, you will probably start exercising simply using small-range strengthening exercises. You should be able to progress fairly quickly to the freer exercises involving gentle mobilizing (p. 202). You may be able to start the hanging exercises (p. 204) fairly early, as they help to ease out a stiff back. But with all the exercises, the main guide-line is that any painful movement should be avoided.

• The stretching exercises (p. 206) should not be done until you have achieved a good programme of strengthening and mobilizing. You must be careful not to over-stretch your trunk, as you will find that this will cause a painful reaction afterwards, especially if you have suffered from leg pain in the course of your back problem.

• General exercising is best started with swimming and/or pool exercises, as you can achieve a good range of movement in the water, without loading your back.

• Your return to your sport should start with gentle jogging, building up to sprinting, and then sprinting and turning, and shuttle running (p. 47). If your sport involves twisting movements, you must practise those movements, without loading, preferably in front of a mirror. For a racket sport, for instance, you should start by simulating your strokes without a racket; then with a racket; and finally with racket and ball, shuttlecock, or other projectile. For any sport, you should try to rehearse the techniques of the sport without pressure before going into practice situations. You should not think in terms of competition before you are absolutely confident of your recovery. You must always remember to warm-up thoroughly before any exercise session; warm-down afterwards, and shower quickly, rather than sitting around getting chilled.

Trunk exercises

STRENGTHENING EXERCISES

Back extension exercises

All these exercises are carried out lying on your stomach. Except where otherwise stated, do three sets of ten for each exercise.

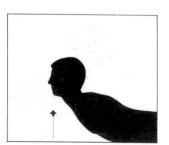

1. With your hands resting at your sides; lift your head and shoulders backwards, just a little; hold for a count of three, then gently lower.

196

2. With your hands clasped behind your back, elbows straight; lift your head and shoulders backwards just a little, hold for a count of three, then slowly lower.

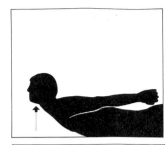

3. With your hands behind your head, fingers touching or interlocked, elbows bent; lift your head and shoulders just a little, raising your eyes so that you can see forward in front of you. Hold to three, slowly lower.

4. With your arms stretched out straight forwards, above your head; lift your arms, head and shoulders, hold for a count of three, then slowly lower.

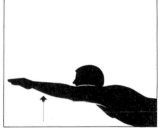

5. Lie over the end of your bed, so that your trunk bends forwards. (Fix your feet if necessary.) With your hands by your side, lift your head and shoulders backwards until you are arching back slightly; hold for three, then slowly lower down again.

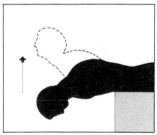

6. Lie as in (5), but with your hands behind your head. Lift your head and shoulders back, hold for a count of three, then gently lower back.

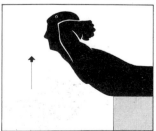

Lower Back

7. Lying flat, with your hands by your sides; lift one leg a little way backwards, hold for a count of three, then slowly lower. Repeat with the other leg. Do three sets of five, each leg in turn.

8. Lying flat, with your hands by your sides; lift both legs together a little way backwards, slightly arching your back. Hold to three, then slowly lower.

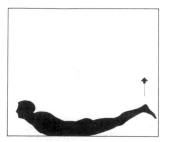

9. Lying flat, hands by your sides; lift both legs back a little way, separate your legs, bring them together again, then slowly lower.

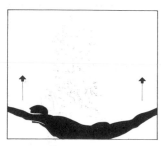

10. With your arms stretched out straight forwards, above your head; lift your arms, shoulders, head, together with both legs, just a little way backwards, so that your whole trunk arches slightly. Hold to three, then slowly lower.

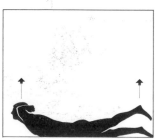

11. With your hands behind your head, fingers touching or interlocked, elbows bent; lift your elbows, head and shoulders, together with your right leg, then lower, and lift again, this time raising your left leg backwards a little way. Repeat in quick succession.

12. Lying over a bolster, or a bench covered with padding material, with your middle supported; with your hands held forward, above your head, raise your arms, head, shoulders and both legs, so that your back is arched slightly, and you are balanced on the support. Hold to three, then slowly lower.

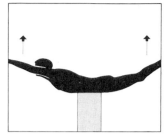

Abdominal exercises to strengthen the stomach

All these exercises are carried out lying on your back. Except where otherwise stated, do three sets of ten for each exercise.

1. Lying flat, with your hands resting on your thighs; lift your head and shoulders forwards a little way, sliding your hands down your thighs towards your knees. Do *not* sit right up, but just enough to see your feet. Hold to three, then gently lower back.

2. Lying on your back with your knees bent, feet flat on the floor; with your hands clasped behind your head, elbows bent, lift your head and shoulders to touch your elbows to your knees, then slowly lower back. (You may need to fix your feet.)

3. Lying on your back, with your knees bent, feet flat on the floor; with your hands behind your head, elbows bent, lift your head and shoulders to touch your left elbow to your right knee, then lower back, and lift forward again to touch your right elbow to your left knee.

4. Lying on your back with your knees bent, feet flat on the floor; lift your knees gently up towards your chest, then slowly lower, keeping your knees bent.

5. Lying flat, with your hands behind your head, lift your left knee towards your chest, as you raise your head and shoulders, to touch your knee with your right elbow. Lower back, and repeat touching your left elbow to your right knee.

6. Lying flat, with your hands behind your head; lift both legs back, bending your knees, and bring your head and shoulders forwards to touch your elbows to your knees. (Slowly lower back.)

7. Lying on your back with your knees bent, feet flat on the floor; with your arms straight out on the floor above your head, lift your hands, head and shoulders to touch your hands to your knees, then slowly lower back.

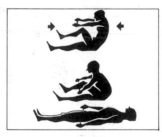

8. Lying flat, with your arms stretched straight above your head, and a band about forty-five centimetres long held between your hands. Lift your hands, head and shoulders up and forwards, and bend your left knee, so that you can slide the band under your knee as you straighten it out. Reverse the movement, then repeat, sliding the band under your right knee. Do two sets of ten.

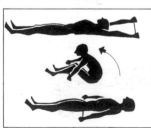

9. Lying flat, with the band held above your head, as in (8). Bring your hands and trunk up and forwards, while bending both knees towards your chest; slide the band under your knees, straighten your knees and lower your trunk back; then bend up your knees, lift the band over your feet, and lower back. Do two sets of ten.

200

All these exercises are carried out lying on your stomach. Do three sets of ten for each exercise.

For simple weight-loading, use a double oven glove with a weight in each compartment. Start with a very light weight (no more than 900 grammes), and build up gradually, increasing the weights once or twice a week, by no more than 900 grammes at a time. You can use an adjustable weights boot, a dumb-bell, or free weight discs, as appropriate to the exercises, if you find these more convenient. Handle the weights with care: do not pick them up by bending your back, but always make sure that your back is straight and your knees are bent when you pick up weights from the floor. Do not use the weights if they make the exercises painful. Do not increase the load unless you are sure you can manage the previous weight-load easily.

1. With a weight held behind your head, in your hands, lift your head and shoulders backwards a little way, hold to three, slowly lower.

2. With your arms outstretched above your head, and a weight held between your hands, lift your arms, shoulders and head back a little way, hold, then slowly lower.

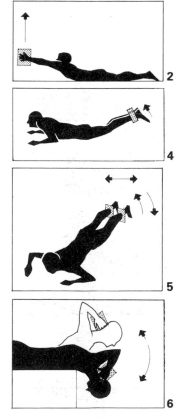

3. With a weight over each ankle, lift one leg back a little way, hold to three, then slowly lower. Repeat on the other leg.

4. With a weight over each ankle, lift both legs back together a little way, hold to three, then slowly lower.

5. With a weight over each ankle, lift both legs back a little way, separate your legs, bring them together again, then slowly lower.

6. Lie over the end of your bed, so that the top of your trunk bends forwards. With a weight in your hands behind your head, raise your head and shoulders until your back is slightly arched, hold to three, then slowly lower.

7. With your arms outstretched forward above your head, and a weight in your hands, more weights over your ankles, lift your arms, shoulders and head together with your legs, a little way backwards. Hold to three, slowly lower.

8. Lying over a bolster or padded bench, with a weight between your outstretched hands, and weights over your ankles, lift your arms, head and shoulders, together with your legs, a little way backwards, until your back is slightly arched. Hold to three, then slowly lower.

MOBILITY EXERCISES

Prone kneeling

These exercises are done kneeling on hands and knees.
1. Keeping your arms and legs still, arch your back to hump it upwards, while you bend your head downwards, then curve your back to hollow it out, while you raise your head up. Repeat the sequence in quick succession ten times.

2. Stretch one leg straight out sideways, turning your head to the same side to look at your foot; swing your foot round behind you, keeping your knee straight and your toes close to the ground, while you turn your head to the other side so that you can see your foot again. Swing your foot back to the starting position, turning your head too, repeating the sequence three times in quick succession on one leg, and then doing the sequence with the other leg.

3. Bend one knee forward as you bend your head down, so that you touch your forehead with your knee; then stretch your leg straight out behind you, as you raise your head so that your back arches slightly. Repeat in quick succession three times on each leg in turn, up to ten sets on each leg.

Lying on your back

These exercises are done with your knees bent and your feet resting on the floor.

1. Flatten your back into the floor, then arch it so that it lifts up from the floor, keeping your hips and shoulders in contact with the floor throughout the movement. Relax as you do this, so that the movement is free-flowing and unforced, and repeat the movement ten times in succession, three times over.

2. Keeping your feet and shoulders still, push your seat up into the air, then lower it, quickly ten times.

3. Keeping your feet close to the floor, let your knees fall to each side in turn, twenty times in quick succession, to create a 'rolling' movement at your waist and hips.

Standing up

1. With your arms held straight out at right angles to your body, turn your trunk to each side in turn in a free-flowing movement, keeping your arm straight on the side to which you are turning, but letting the other arm bend loosely across your chest in rhythm with the movement. Twenty times to each side, building up gradually to fifty.

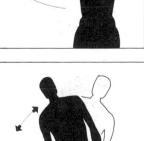

2. Keeping your arms by your sides, bend your trunk to each side in turn, without bending forwards, in a free movement. Twenty to fifty times.

3. With your hands together, stretched up above your head, arch your back and lean backwards with a gentle bouncing movement. Press back in sets of three, starting with three sets, and building up to ten.

4. Standing with your legs apart, hands on hips, circle your hips rhythmically, three times in each direction. Start with three sets each way, building up to ten.

5. Standing with your legs apart, bend forward at the hips; turn your trunk gently and rhythmically from side to side, letting your arms swing with the movement, so that one arm bends across your chest as you turn away from that side, while the other arm straightens and swings up sideways from your trunk.

Hanging

All these exercises are done hanging by the hands, from a beam, wall-bars or, if safe, a door-frame.

As soon as your hands feel tired, you should step down, as your back muscles will tense up when your arms tighten. This may happen within a few seconds when you start doing the exercises, but as you get used to hanging, you find you can do more. Like isometric exercises, hanging exercises are not suitable for people with blood pressure problems.

1. Simply hang, and let your body relax completely, so that you feel it gently stretching out.

2. Relaxing your arms and upper body as much as possible, swing both legs together from side to side.

3. Part your legs, hold them apart for a count of three, then close them again. Keep your body straight, and do not bend your hips at all.

4. Relaxing your body, but keeping it straight, pull each leg in turn upwards at the waist, without twisting forwards or sideways to any degree. (Hip hitching.)

5. Gently press your legs backwards, keeping them together, so that you arch your back slightly, rhythmically.

6. Bend your knees up to your chest, keeping them together, then straighten them downwards (not forwards), and gently press them back to arch your trunk, when they are straight. Repeat the sequence in a free-flowing movement.

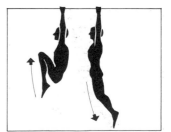

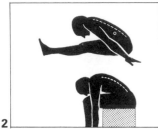

STRETCHING EXERCISES

1. Lying on your stomach, with your arms bent close to your sides so that your hands rest just under your shoulders, push your arms straight to arch your back, lifting up your head so that your whole spine curves back. Hold for a count of ten, then gently relax.

2. Sitting, either in a chair with your knees bent, or on the floor with your legs straight, lean forward from the hips, bending your neck forward, to try to take your head down to your knees. Hold at the limit of the movement for a count of ten, then gently relax.

3. Lying on your stomach, holding your ankles in your hands, stretch your shoulders and ankles upwards and backwards to arch your back. Hold to ten, then relax.

4. Lying on your back on a cushioned but firm surface, rest your weight on your shoulders. Gently take your legs over your head, keeping your knees bent at first, and gradually straightening your knees as you become more flexible with practice. (Do not do this exercise if it hurts your neck, or if you have blood pressure problems.)

5. From lying on your back, place your hands under your shoulders, and push yourself upwards to arch your back, so that you are balanced on your hands and feet. Hold to ten, then relax.

6. Sit with one leg straight in front of you, and the other knee bent and crossed so that your foot rests to the outside of your straight knee; turn your trunk towards your bent knee, so that you rest the opposite elbow against the outside of that knee. Hold the position to a count of ten, then reverse the position to twist in the other direction.

7. Standing with your legs slightly apart, bend sideways (without bending forwards) and take your uppermost arm over, above your head. Hold the position for a count of ten, then repeat, bending to the other side.

8. Lying on your back, with your legs straight, and your arms stretched out sideways at right angles to your body, lift one leg straight up in the air, then swing it down sideways, over the other leg, to touch the floor with your foot. Keep your shoulders as close to the ground as possible, so that your trunk twists as far as it can. Hold to ten, then repeat with the other leg, to twist your trunk the other way.

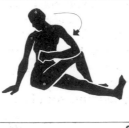

Complications

Problems in the spinal joints can cause referred pain, because the tiny nerves which emerge between the joints are interfered with. The actual interference may be very slight: an alteration in the normal blood supply to the nerves may impair their function. This may be the result of a trivial strain to one of the tiny ligaments binding the spinal joints together. Or there may be a major impedance to the functioning of the nerves, caused by a disc breaking and protruding backwards into the spinal canal, pressing against the nerves as they spread outwards from the spinal cord.

When the nerves are interfered with, you feel the effect throughout the pathway which would normally be under the influence of those nerves. The nerves from the lumbar spine supply sensation and nerve-muscle messages to your legs, so referred pain through low back problems affects your legs. If the damage is on one side of the spine, affecting the nerves emanating from that side, you will feel the effects in one leg. If the problem is more central, or widespread over both sides, both your legs will be affected. The effects vary from numbness, tingling, or an awareness of strange feelings in your leg, to pain down your leg. The symptoms may be intermittent, or constant. They may affect one part of your leg, for instance the back of your thigh from your seat to your knee, or they may seem to be more widespread, down your whole leg into your foot. The course of the pain or altered sensation depends on the exact level of the spine affected, as the nerves at each level have their own specific pathway. The amount of pain or alteration in sensation you feel depends on the nature of the damage to the spinal joint, and the amount of impingement or impairment over the nerves near the joint.

You may feel referred pain in your legs without necessarily being aware of having hurt your back. Usually this type of referred problem only affects the back of your leg, but it may travel down the whole leg. In your back, you may feel only a slight stiffness, or even no symptoms at all. Often, however, you know that you have had a back strain, just before the time you start noticing your leg pains. Because the leg pain seems localized, you may assume that you have strained a muscle somehow: to complicate matters, the referred symptoms do sometimes coincide with a localized muscle strain in the painful region of your leg. The signs that you have a referred, rather than localized, problem are, firstly, that your leg pain is intermittent, and seems to follow an arbitrary pattern, rather than relating to specific leg movements; it often feels worst when you are sitting down, especially if you slouch in an easy chair; bending your head forward may bring on the pain; if you feel gently over the painful region of your leg, and then compare the sensation with your other leg, you may find that your painful leg is not as sensitive to touch as the other; and you probably will not be able to find any localized tender spots over the area which you think is injured. A record of your symptoms will help your doctor to identify whether you have referred symptoms from a back problem, or a localized muscle injury, or a combination of both.

Meanwhile, to help yourself, you should try to work out if your pain gets worse according to your activities, and be especially aware of the importance of your back posture to avoid aggravating the pain. You should not try to do any sport which stresses your back while you have referred pain in your legs. It is also wise to avoid full stretching movements in your back, unless you are advised to do a particular movement by your specialist. You may find, for instance, that bending forward to touch your toes relieves the pain in your leg: but if the pain comes back immediately you straighten up, it is likely to get progressively worse if you persist in doing the exercise, so you must do specific exercises for your problem only under guidance from a specialist who can gauge the overall effects of each movement.

DISC PROLAPSE AND THE LAMINECTOMY OPERATION

Minor disc problems usually recover with appropriate treatment, rehabilitation exercises, and a cautious return to sport. However, a major disc injury may lead to continuing and agonizing pain in your back and/or your leg. There are various possible solutions to this problem, which your specialist may try, including total rest lying flat, or rest with your back held in traction, or traction or manipulation treatment on a regular basis. One more radical solution is for an orthopaedic surgeon to perform a laminectomy operation, in which he removes the damaged, degenerated disc, and fuses the two vertebrae between which it was lying together. Recovery following this operation may only take a few weeks, if your problem was not long-standing, and if there are no complications. Otherwise, complete recovery may take anything up to a year. However, it is usually possible to resume a reasonable level and amount of sport after the operation, provided your sport does not involve excessive loading on the spine. It is extremely important to regain good strength and mobility in your spine after the operation, as otherwise the joints above and below the fusion level will be at extra risk of injury.

In the long-term, you have to learn to assess the effects of your sport on your back. Heavy weight-training and contact sports are usually ruled out after a back problem serious enough to warrant surgery. But less obviously demanding sports may need a common-sense approach. If you run, you may find that long-distance training troubles your back or leg, whereas you can manage a reduced mileage without problems. In this case, you should consider avoiding marathon running, in favour of concentrating on half-marathons, or shorter distances, and you should assess whether doing most of your training on grass or soft surfaces helps you to maintain a reasonable training level. If you play tennis, you may find that a lighter racket places less strain on your joints. In golf, you may find that the only stressful part is carrying your golf-bag, so you should use a trolley or hire a caddie to reduce the loading.

STRESS FRACTURES

Like all the other bones in your body, your vertebrae are susceptible to cracks caused by excessive, repetitive muscle pull. The problem usually happens in one of the fine bones forming the arch at the back of the vertebrae. It occurs especially in sportsmen who have to twist and turn repetitively, against a certain amount of loading. Oarsmen are prone to this problem, as are tennis players, though to a lesser extent. The oarsman who has always rowed on the same side of the boat is, by definition, subjected to a continuing twisting and pulling pressure in his spine. The stress fracture may happen when you increase your training on the water, or when you resume rowing after a lay-off. A tennis player may suffer following a prolonged practice session of one particular shot, like the backhand, causing a more constant repetition of particular leaning and twisting movements than would normally happen in the varying pattern of the game.

The pain of the stress fracture may feel no worse than a slight backache, which comes on during or after sport, and which is directly related to an increase of the particular activity. Once the crack in the bone strut has occurred, the pain becomes progressively worse, if you continue with your sport. As it gets worse, you tend to feel the pain on other activities besides specifically during or after sport. You may be able to localize the pain to a spot a the side of your spine, although it is difficult for you to press the area for yourself, as you have to twist yourself to reach your back, and this distorts your spinal joints. If the problem is allowed to develop to a severe stage, the crack in the bone will show up on X-ray, although the X-ray may have to be taken at a certain angle to reveal it. Rest allows the problem to heal, and you should not try to resume sport until you are sure the bone has mended. Once your specialist lets you return to your sport, you must do so in gradual stages, to avoid a recurrence of the problem. As with any back problem, it is advisable to build up strength and mobility in your trunk before returning to full sport.

SPONDYLOLYSIS

The fine bones forming the arches at the back of your vertebrae may fail to bond together properly, leaving a gap in the arch. This is called spondylolysis, and, while it can happen without causing any problems or noticeable pain in your back, if it does cause pain, it can set up symptoms similar to those of a stress fracture. You feel pain just to one side of the spine, which is aggravated by sport. Usually, the problem shows up on an X-ray, especially if an angled view is taken. The fact that the bone has failed to fuse may not have anything to do with your back pain, so seeing the defect on X-ray does not necessarily give the diagnosis of why you have back pain. Often, the specialist will simply restrict your activities, until the immediate pain has subsided, and then allow a gradual return to sport. If you have continuing problems, your specialist may advise you to do less demanding sports, or perhaps to wear a corset support while you do sport. It is rare for a specialist to try to correct the spondylolysis surgically, as the problem is something you grow up with naturally, and it is not considered to be the kind of condition which inevitably causes pain. Generally, you will simply have strained your back through awkward movements or overloading, as anyone can, but the strain localizes itself round the weak part of the spine.

If you allow the strain to recover, and use the rehabilitation exercises and correct posture to help yourself regain good function, in most cases you will find that you can resume your normal level of sport, and you are not necessarily more prone to back problems than another sportsman who does not have spondylolysis.

SPONDYLOLISTHESIS

When the sides of the arch behind a vertebra are cracked, either through a stress fracture or because of failure to fuse as you grow, the vertebral body may slide forwards over the vertebra below, as part of its retaining structure is lost. Like spondylolysis, this may happen without causing any pain or other symptoms. But when it does cause pain, you feel quite a marked back-ache, usually at the very lowest part of your spine. The pain gets worse with exercise, and is often only relieved by complete rest from any active sports. The slipped vertebra shows up on an X-ray taken sideways on. If the defect is bad, and you are suffering from severe pain in your back, with pain radiating into your buttocks and legs, your

210

specialist may recommend resting in bed to allow your symptoms to settle. If your spine has also become unstable, and therefore prone to pain whenever you move it beyond a limited range, the specialist may consider performing a spinal fusion operation to stabilize the joints. Once the symptoms have subsided, there is usually no reason why you should not resume your sport, provided that it does not cause a return of the symptoms, and that it does not obviously overload the spine.

OSTEOARTHRITIS

Wear-and-tear arthritis can develop in your spinal joints as the result of simple overuse over a space of some years, or because you have suffered repeated episodes of back strain. It is more likely to happen if you have done a sport which involves heavy loading of the spine, like power lifting, but it can equally be due to repetitive rotational movements twisting the spine, as you would do in sports like golf and tennis. The pain of osteoarthritis comes on usually in late middle age, although it can happen sooner. Sometimes, it is triggered by an accident in which you know you have lifted a heavy weight awkwardly. If you have this type of accident, and you coincidentally have arthritis in your spinal joints, your pain will tend to persist longer than it otherwise would, despite treatment, rehabilitation and care. You may find that you have a certain amount of pain in your back when you are at rest in bed at night, and the pain increases on certain types of movement. Arthritic changes normally show up on X-ray: the most telling change is the formation of little offshoots of bone around the edges of your vertebral bodies. These may form at the front or the back of the bones, and if they grow large enough, they can severely limit your spinal movements. If the bony outgrowths, which are called osteophytes, form at the back of the vertebral bodies, they may impinge on the spinal nerves, and cause referred pain on certain movements of your spine.

If the wear-and-tear changes are severe, and causing you a lot of pain and hindrance to movement, your specialist may suggest an operation to relieve the pressure between the worst affected of the joints. If that stage has not been reached, common sense in trying to preserve as much function in your spine as you possibly can must prevail. This means that you must do daily exercises to maintain and increase the strength of your trunk muscles, and to keep your back as mobile as possible. Painful activities must be avoided, and you must take care to keep good posture generally, and to lift any weights with care. If you have to carry heavy bags, alternate the loading, so that you carry the weight first on one shoulder or in one hand, and then the other; or try to balance the loading,

211

so that you are carrying equal weights on each side. Exercise will help to maintain function in your spine, but only if you do it in moderation. Swimming, in which the trunk is supported during movement, rather than loaded, is one of the best forms of exercise for the back. Excessive amounts of sports which involve weight-loading, jarring, or rotational stresses, are likely to speed up the wear-and-tear processes in the spine. You must be guided by your specialist as to the amount and type of sport you should so. Once arthritis has been objectively diagnosed, the wear-and-tear process cannot be reversed. You can control your pain with correct care, but you must also be aware that you can make matters very much worse if you over-stress your spinal joints.

The Thoracic Spine
(Upper spine)

STRUCTURE

The upper part of your trunk is called the thorax. It extends from just above your waist to the level of your shoulders, and consists of twelve thoracic vertebrae and your rib cage. Your ribs are attached to either side of your vertebrae at your back, and to your breast bone in front, to form a rounded bony container covering your chest.

The thoracic vertebrae are similar in form to your lumbar vertebrae, in that they have a main block of bone, with fine struts forming a bony arch projecting from the back of it. However, the thoracic bones differ from the lumbar in detail: they are smaller than the lumbar vertebrae, and tend to be wedge-shaped, tapering forward so that the front edge of the block

The upper back muscles, made to stand out in detail by a top body-builder.

213

is shallower than the back. The joints at the sides of the arches are not interlocked at their sides in the same way as the lumbar vertebrae, but they overlap backwards.

Like the lumbar vertebrae, the thoracic bones are joined together by ligaments binding each vertebra in line. The bodies of the vertebrae are held by the same long bands which extend up the front and back of the bones. The struts of the arches are all bound to the struts on the vertebrae above and below with finer ligaments, while the bones which are close enough together on adjacent arches to form joints are bound in their retaining, fluid-filled capsules. Each vertebral body is separated and cushioned from the next by a disc, which is thinner than the discs in your lumbar region.

The main difference between your thoracic and lumbar vertebrae is that the thoracic bones form joints with your ribs. The ends of your ribs fit into a notch on each side of the vertebral bodies, and are held there by ligaments and a retaining capsule. Apart from your eleventh and twelfth ribs, which are short, your other ribs also form a joint with the sideways struts from your vertebral arches. Therefore the back edges of your ribs are held as if in two clamps to your thoracic vertebrae, and your ribs extend away from these attachments to enclose your chest cavity. Your thoracic spine forms a central pillar from which your ribs arch away symmetrically on either side.

In most people, the spines of your thoracic vertebrae stand out prominently, because this part of your vertebral column curves backwards. If you bend forward and look in a mirror behind your back, you can see the spines projecting out as individual points down your spine. If you are fairly thin, you may also be able to see how your ribs curve round towards the vertebrae. It is of course difficult to feel the rib joints with your fingers, because your spine twists and stiffens as soon as you lift your arm to reach back, but you can run your fingers over the vertebral spines quite easily, as they are so distinct. Over the back of your rib cage you can feel your shoulder blades, which extend from the level of your second thoracic vertebra to the seventh, roughly speaking, but which do not have any direct links with your vertebrae.

FUNCTIONS

Because the spines at the back of the thoracic vertebrae overlap closely in the backwards direction, there is little leeway for backward movement in this part of your spine. Forward movement is also limited by your ligaments and the shape of your thoracic bones. Twisting is the freest movement in the thoracic spine. As in the lumbar spine, movements are achieved through co-ordination between the complex muscles lining your spine, and the muscles projecting round your trunk.

All movement in the spinal column is interlinked so it is not possible to separate movement in one region from the other areas, nor can you achieve any active movement at all in an isolated reaction between two vertebrae. The functional co-ordination between all your vertebrae means that you have a good range of movements allowed by your spine, while it can also achieve its shock-absorbing and protective functions. In the thoracic region, the bones form part of the protective ring around your lungs and heart. The twisting movements allowed make the thoracic spine essential in any activities involving reaching round your body. When you hit a ground stroke in tennis, your legs and pelvis hold you stable, while your lumbar spine bends to some degree, allowing your thoracic spine to achieve enough rotation to swing your shoulders through the backswing, strike and follow-through pattern. All throwing movements involve twisting in the thoracic spine for greater impetus. If you throw the javelin, for instance, you twist first away from the direction of your throw, and then towards it, to achieve maximum projecting power.

Like the rest of your body, the thoracic spine is subject to the compressive pressure of gravity. Your theoretical line of gravity normally passes directly through the centre of one of the vertebral bodies in the middle of the thoracic region: in a 'normally' aligned person, the line of gravity is assumed to go through the body of the sixth thoracic vertebra. Wherever it passes, the line of gravity creates an effect of direct pressure. Under loading, however, the thoracic spine tends to take less direct pressure than the other parts of your spine.

Although your thoracic spine is protected by its central position in the vertebral column, if an applied force through the spine is great enough, it can crush one or more of the thoracic vertebrae, especially if abnormal movement in the region happens because of the stress.

Posturally, your thoracic spine acts, in a sense, as a linking section between your neck and your lower back. If you straighten your back, you tend to do so by extending your lower back, or lifting your head. Postural adjustments in the thoracic region consist mainly of bracing your shoulders back, and this is achieved by active movement in your shoulder girdle, without much direct influence over the thoracic vertebrae. It is a relatively immobile area, whose main function is to support the rib cage. Poor posture in the spine generally can make you look very hunched in the thoracic region, but this is correctible if you straighten your lower back and your neck. A true hunch is caused by a deformity accentuating the backward curvature of the thoracic spine, and you may

215

be born with this, or suffer it through disease. If you habitually carry your shoulders twisted, because your activities constantly make you drop or raise one shoulder backwards or forwards relative to the other, you can develop a twisting defect in your thoracic spine, which can cause an abnormal sideways curve, called a scoliosis. Correcting poor posture in the thoracic spine means strengthening the muscles of your whole trunk as it is not possible to isolate the central trunk muscles, and it would not be functionally efficient to try to do so. Remembering that your thoracic spine is influenced by the rest of the column, you have to try to maintain postural symmetry through your hips, lower back, neck and shoulders, in order to protect the thoracic region from abnormal stress.

PAIN IN THE THORACIC REGION

As the thoracic spine forms part of the protective structure for your heart and lungs, these internal organs may cause pain which you feel at the back of your chest. Pleurisy, or inflammation of the lining covering your lungs, can cause pain in your upper back which feels just like a muscular strain. Certain viruses, similar to 'flu, can also cause pain in your upper back. Problems in internal organs in other regions can give rise to referred pain which you feel at the back of your chest. A gastric ulcer or a liver problem can refer pain to the lower part of your thoracic region, on either side of your spine, as though you had strained the joints at the sides of the vertebrae.

Therefore, whenever you have pain in the back of your chest, you must try to remember any possible medical problems, including digestive difficulties or even common colds, to help your doctor decide on the nature of your pain. You also have to remember that you can have a mechanical strain and a medical problem at the same time, so even if you know you have suffered a specific injury, you must be aware of any other symptoms, like a chesty cough, which might be adding to your problem.

Injuries to the thoracic spine

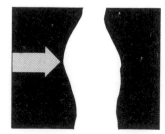

The joints of the thoracic spine can be injured by awkward movements involving twisting; by overloading, usually caused by twisting your shoulders with a heavy weight in your hands; by a sudden excessive muscle pull, for instance if you twist while you heave a dinghy off the water; or by repetitive twisting strains, causing a continual stress from the muscles pulling over the joints, which can happen if you do long sessions of practice on a particular stroke in tennis.

216

You feel pain in the back of your chest, which you can relate directly to your sport, or a particular movement you did. You may feel the pain in the centre of your spine, or on one or both sides of it. The pain may seem to radiate round away from your spine, as though it encircles your ribs at a particular level, because your nerves trace a circular course away from your thoracic spine, round to your chest, following the line of each rib.

The pain may be sharp, or it may start as a slight ache, and gradually get worse. You may feel it as you make an awkward movement, for instance if you hesitate or stumble just as you are about to throw a javelin, or it may come on immediately afterwards, or some time later. You then feel the pain every time you make the movement that caused the strain. You also feel pain if you do a similar movement during your everyday activities, because you inevitably have to make your spinal joints work during most of your activities. You may find that you feel a sharp pain if you cough or sneeze, and this may send radiating pain round your chest. Even slight movements may bring on your pain, once you have strained a thoracic joint, but if the problem is purely mechanical, the pain should be eased if you lie flat, comfortably. Deep breathing may cause pain, but you should not feel it when you breathe at a normal quiet level, unless the problem has become extremely severe.

What has happened

In any problem affecting your vertebral column, you may damage any or many of the structures of the spine. Minor injuries are virtually impossible to diagnose accurately, although specialists may assess that there is likely to be ligament, muscle, or disc injury approximating to a particular type of pain. The pain you feel may be entirely out of proportion to the exact amount of damage done. Muscle spasm around the injured joint may greatly increase the discomfort you feel, and it may occur as part of the cause, or the effect, of your injury. While it is possible to injure the muscles in your back in themselves, as you can injure any other muscles in your body, if the injured muscles are attached to your vertebrae, it is common for the spinal joints to be affected by the injury, setting up the symptoms of a joint strain. This makes the problem of diagnosis even more complex. Soft-tissue problems do not show up on X-ray, and even small fractures in the bones of the vertebrae may not be seen, unless the X-rays are angled very precisely.

Major spinal injuries are much easier to diagnose. Firstly, there is intense pain, and you feel unable to move. You may be unable to feel normal sensations, if the injury has damaged some of the sensation nerves leading away from the spine. Even lying still, you probably feel unable to

217

breathe without pain. This type of injury must be treated with extreme caution, and you should not be moved except by qualified and experienced first-aiders or ambulancemen. Anyone around you must avoid increasing the damage done, and allow you to be transported to hospital, where the casualty specialist can assess the injury and do appropriate checks, such as X-rays. This type of injury can only happen if your spine has been subjected to extreme stress, like a fall from a height, or a crushing blow from a heavy load, so your first guide to what has happened is the way in which it has happened.

Self-help measures for thoracic spine injuries

For minor injuries, you can safely apply self-help measures to ease your discomfort, but you must refer to your doctor as quickly as possible for an assessment of the extent of injury. If necessary, your doctor will refer you for appropriate treatment.
- Apply ice (p. 15) to relieve pain and muscle spasm over the injury. It is probably best if you lie on your stomach, on a soft surface, and have the ice placed over your back in a wet towel.
- Lie flat, either on your stomach or your back. If you lie on your back, have one or two soft pillows under your head, but do not prop your head forward, as this curves your thoracic spine. If you lie on your stomach, you may be more comfortable if you put a pillow under your chest, and perhaps another under your hips. Again, do not lift your head up too much, as this arches your back and can strain your thoracic spine into the extreme limits of its range of movement.
- Try to keep your general posture symmetrical (p. 177), and remember to keep your shoulders level but relaxed, without letting them slouch forwards. Keeping a good alignment between your pelvis and your head helps to protect your thoracic spine. Avoid leaning to one side or twisting your back, even if you feel this eases your pain at the time. Any movements which cause pain should also be avoided.
- As soon as your pain has subsided enough for your specialist to allow you to exercise, you should do the back strengthening exercises, and balance these with abdominal exercises (p. 199). As you improve, you should gradually start doing the mobilizing exercises (p. 202). If you do not receive guidance, your only way of knowing when to progress to the mobilizing exercises is whether you are free of pain in your back on normal activities. You should continue to do a daily session of strengthening exercises for your back and stomach until you are fully fit.
- You should not try to do sport again until you are fully recovered. You

218

may be able to swim, for fitness, if your specialist allows, although you should avoid any stroke which causes pain, and you should try to swim in as relaxed a style as possible. At the same time, you may be able to do stretching and general exercises in the pool, and even run in the shallow end. As you progress with your specific back exercises, if you have no setbacks, you begin your return to sport with jogging, and build up with stages which take you through running faster, to running and turning, and then running, touching the ground and turning. If you play a racket sport, you should practise the movements first without a racket, progressing to shadow play with a racket, and finally to practice with racket and ball or shuttlecock.

How long?

The whole rehabilitation process may be complete within ten days to two weeks following a minor strain which occurred suddenly. A more gradual, or more severe, injury may persist for several weeks. Your guide to progress is any pain you feel. If an exercise or activity gives you increasing pain, you must avoid it, and revert to simpler exercises which do not cause pain. If your pain appears arbitrary, without any direct relationship to your activities, you must check with your doctor, in case there are complications in the injury, or a medical cause underlying the pain.

Complications

As with other parts of the spine, thoracic injuries can be complicated, either through 'hidden' damage which is not obvious at the time of injury, but which becomes evident when it prolongs your pain; or through previously existing 'faults' in your spine, which you may not have been aware of, and which may not have contributed to the injury, but which start to cause pain as a result of the injury.

STRESS FRACTURES

In the thoracic spine, these can occur in the fine arches of the vertebrae, as the result of prolonged and unaccustomed activities involving twisting your spine. An over-enthusiastic practice session of discus throwing or tennis serving can cause the fracture, which typically starts as no more than an ache after the session, but gets progressively worse if you try to continue with your sport. Usually, you know that you have done too hard a session, and you can trace your pain directly to the session which

219

brought the pain on. Diagnosis is difficult, and it can only be made by a specialist. While the stress fracture can occur in the side bones of the thoracic vertebrae, it may equally easily happen to one of the ribs attached to the vertebrae. From your point of view, if you are aware of a gradually increasing pain, associated with a particular activity, and brought on because you suddenly increased the amount of that activity, you must rest from your sport until you are quite sure that you no longer have pain on the movements which originally caused your injury. This may take up to six weeks. After that, you must return to your sport only in very easy, graduated stages.

SCHEUERMANN'S DISEASE

This is a 'growing problem', in which the vertebrae fail to grow properly. It happens to young teenagers, between the ages of twelve and fifteen, usually, and it causes pain especially in the thoracic region. The pain may be triggered by a specific injury, but the condition is usually due to repeated injuries, or it may even come on without an obvious cause. The pain comes on when you bend forwards and backwards, and it is worst after sport, so your back may hurt most of the time, except at rest. What happens in the condition is that the front edges of the vertebrae become narrowed, losing their height, so the spine is curved abnormally. In the thoracic region, this means that you develop a pronounced hunch, which may extend into the lumbar region, making your lower back curve backwards instead of forwards, if the problem is severe and widespread.

If the specialist feels that the condition is bad enough, he will probably give you a brace to protect your vertebrae from further harm, and allow them to grow properly. This will mean resting from active sport for some time. On the other hand, if the problem is mild, you may be allowed to do sport, so long as it does not cause pain. In this case, you will probably also be given specific exercises to do, to strengthen and then mobilize your back.

The Abdominal Muscles
(Stomach muscles)

STRUCTURE

Over the front of your abdomen you have four large muscles, forming a solid wall. The muscles link the front and sides of your pelvis (p. 177) to the lower parts of your ribs, and are arranged at different angles, to form an enclosing sheet over your abdominal cavity. In the mid-line of your body, the muscles from either side of your abdomen meet in a tendon which forms a straight line down from your breast-bone to your pubis. Just below the central point of the line, which is called the linea alba, is your umbilicus, or navel.

Your abdominal muscles are arranged symmetrically on each side of the mid-line. Rectus abdominis forms two wide bands joining the front of your ribs to your pelvis in a vertical line. Under rectus abdominis you

The abdominal muscles and their intersections, clearly demonstrated by a top-class body builder.

221

have two diagonally arranged muscles. The obliquus externus (external oblique) extends from your ribs, covering the whole of the side of your abdomen, to be attached to the top of your hip-bone, over the iliac crest, just below your waist. The obliquus externus runs in the same direction as the sides of your ribs, so it curves downwards and inwards from its wide starting point on your ribs. The obliquus internus (internal oblique), underneath the externus, runs in the opposite direction, more or less, so its fibres are angled towards the mid-line at its upper end, just below your chest. The fourth abdominal muscle is the transversus, which lies under the other three muscles on either side of your abdomen, and whose fibres run in horizontal lines from your sides into the linea alba.

The linea alba forms a distinct line along the front of your abdomen. There are also horizontal lines crossing the rectus abdominis, dividing the muscle into square shapes in a muscular person. You normally have three of these lines, which are thickened fibres in the sheath which encloses your rectus abdominis. The lines may be straight across your abdomen, or they may seem to zig-zag. In women, they may not be very visible, because women naturally have more fat cover over their stomachs than men. But if you lie on your back with your hands spread over your abdomen, you can feel the horizontal lines cutting across the vertical bands of your rectus abdominis when you lift your head up and the muscles start to work. If you sit up in a chair, and place your hands over the top of your hip-bones, just below your waist, you can feel your oblique abdominal muscles contracting on both sides, if you turn your trunk from side to side, keeping your back straight.

FUNCTIONS

Your abdominal muscles have an important protective function, cushioning the abdominal organs. Their thick layers and the fat cover over the muscles form a thick padding, shielding the organs, which have no bony protective cover in front of them. Because they act over the abdomen, the abdominal muscles work to help your body do such activities as vomiting, or passing water or faeces.

The muscles also work when you breathe deeply. If you take a deep breath, you can help your chest cavity to open to its widest extent by pulling your abdominal muscles in. If you do this with your hands over your lower ribs, you feel your ribs pushing out and up, expanding your lungs. If you breathe deeply, allowing your stomach to push out, and keeping your abdominal muscles relaxed, you feel that the rib expansion movement is much less. When you breathe out hard, cough or sneeze, your abominal muscles contract automatically, to help increase the upward pressure under your chest, and so add to the expulsion force.

The abdominal muscles act to bend your trunk forwards, when you do this against gravity, for instance when you are lying down and you lift your head and shoulders forwards. When you bend sideways, the stomach muscles on that side contract in harmony with the muscles on that side of your back, to produce the movement. If you twist your trunk, your oblique abdominal muscles co-ordinate with the spine's rotator muscles to turn you. The internal oblique muscles work to turn you on the side to which you are twisting, while the external muscles pull on the far side, so that they are turning you away from the side on which they are working.

Posturally, the abdominal muscles are not very active when you are sitting or standing, but they play an important part in balancing the action of your spinal muscles. Weakness in the abdominal muscles, or an imbalance in strength between your abdominals and your back muscles, often accompanies back problems, sometimes as a cause and sometimes as effect.

PAIN IN THE ABDOMEN

A large variety of internal problems can cause stomach pain and cramp, including appendicitis, liver problems, stomach problems, and gynaecological problems in women. Some of these problems may be triggered by exercise, or they may co-exist with an injury to the stomach muscles. Any unexplained pains in your abdomen must be treated with care, and you must take note of any symptoms of digestive problems or other internal disorders, to help your doctor make the correct diagnosis.

The stitch

One problem that happens to sportsmen, but is not usually related to any particular injury or muscle strain is the stitch. This is a pain you feel in your side when you do hard exercise, but which eases quickly as soon as you stop. You feel it most often in the right side of your abdomen, although it can come on over the middle or the left side.

It is thought that a variety of factors can cause the stitch. One factor is spasm in your diaphragm, the main breathing muscle that spreads right across your body, dividing your trunk in half internally. The ligament linking your diaphragm to your digestive system can become tense during exercise which puts vibrating stress through your abdomen, like running, and this can give you a stitch. Other causes include gas in your large bowel, or liver congestion.

223

Unless you suffer from extreme problems due to repetitive stitch, there is usually no need to worry about the exact cause of the stitch, as you do not feel it apart from when exercising, and it has no lasting effects on your internal organs. When it comes on, you can usually ease it by breathing deeply, and perhaps bending forward if you are running. If it does not ease, you may have to stop and stretch gently, leaning away from the painful side. Once the stitch has passed, you can continue your exercise.

In general, the stitch is worst if you are trying to work yourself harder than your fitness allows, or if you are under special tension, for instance in an important race or competition. If you find you are suffering from the problem regularly, you should try to assess whether your training is wrong, and whether you should cut down on your activities, in order to build up again on a more gradual basis.

Injury to the abdominal muscles

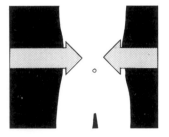

The abdominals can be injured suddenly or gradually. A direct blow to your stomach while the muscles are contracting, or over-contraction of the muscles, can cause a sudden tear. This kind of accident can happen in sports like lacrosse or boxing, or football and rugby, where a missed kick or a tackle while kicking can over-stress the abdominal muscles. More gradual strains can happen if you do excessive amounts of abdominal exercises, leading to fatigue and inefficiency in the muscles. Repeated twisting movements, for instance if you do long sessions of discus throwing or tennis serving, can over-strain the oblique abdominal muscles.

What you feel

A sudden or gradual pain comes on over your stomach muscles, which you can relate to a specific movement of your trunk. A sudden tear is felt while you are doing your sport; a gradual strain often comes on while you are doing a particular activity, but sometimes you only feel the discomfort afterwards. Once the muscles are strained, you feel pain whenever the muscles work or are stretched, so virtually all your trunk movements lead to some discomfort over the injury, which you also feel when you cough or sneeze. If you press over the area of pain, you find a tender spot, which may be small and very localized, or quite wide, depending on the extent of the strain. You may feel the tender spot when your abdominals are relaxed, for instance while you are sitting down, or you may have to put the muscles on the stretch, perhaps by lying flat on your back, in order to isolate the injured part.

The amount of pain you feel may range from a mild niggle to severe pain, depending on the extent of the damage to the muscle fibres. The initial severe pain of a sudden injury should subside within a few days, if there are no complications, but as the muscles tighten up to protect themselves from further harm, you may then feel a sudden stabbing pain, sharp enough to take your breath away, if you do any movements which over-stretch the taut fibres.

What has happened

This can range from a total tear through the stomach muscles to a minor strain of some of the muscle fibres. Total tears usually affect rectus abdominis rather than the other muscles. This severe injury may be complicated by a tear in one of your major abdominal blood vessels, causing internal bleeding.

Self-help measures for abdominal injuries

• In a sudden, severe injury, you should rest with your trunk bent forward, to take the strain off your abdominal muscles. If there is any danger that you may have burst a blood vessel in your stomach, you must be taken to hospital immediately. The signs of a ruptured blood vessel may not show up until some hours after the injury, when you notice swelling and bruising over your stomach: if you see these signs, you must refer to your doctor or casualty department straight away.
• For a more minor strain, you can apply ice (p. 15) directly over the injury.
• You should start stretching the abdominal muscles within a day of a minor strain, or as soon as the immediate pain of a more severe injury has abated, and your doctor decides you can start passive stretching.
1. Lying on your stomach, with your hands on the floor directly under your shoulders, straighten your elbows to lift your shoulders and chest off the floor, while keeping your hips on the floor. When you feel the stretch over the front of your stomach, hold the position for a count of ten. Repeat this exercise about three to ten times, three or four times daily.
2. Lying on your stomach, holding your ankles in your hands, lift your shoulders and knees backwards, to arch your back. Hold the stretch position, without forcing it into a painful limit, for a count of ten. Repeat about three times, twice a day.
• Once you have regained flexibility in the stomach muscles, and the pain and tenderness have gone, you should start strengthening exercises (p. 199). Do three or four abdominal stretching exercises before and after

225

each strengthening exercise. Select one or two easy exercises to start with, and gradually build up the amount you do, adding in new exercises as your stomach gets stronger. Do not do any exercises which cause pain.

• It is difficult to do alternative exercise while you are recovering from a stomach muscle strain, because any activity risks stressing the muscles. Any painful activity must be avoided, so you may have to rest from sport while you work through the rehabilitation exercises.

• When you can do full-range strengthening movements using the abdominals, without any pain, you can safely re-start your sport, taking care to build up in easy stages. Practise the appropriate trunk movements as shadow practice in the first instance, and then have a practice session using the techniques. If you throw the discus, practise the twisting techniques without the discus in front of a mirror first; then practise short, relaxed throwing with the discus, building up to full-blooded throws. The same principles apply if you play a racket sport, or any game in which you kick.

How long?

A sudden injury, properly treated, should recover within two to three weeks. A more minor strain should only last a week or two. If, however, you try to ignore the injury, your pain can last for anything up to several months, because you will continually be straining the injured muscles in your sport and your everyday activities. Your stomach muscles will tighten up each time you strain the muscles, making them progressively more vulnerable to over-stretching.

If, however, you have taken care to stretch your stomach muscles, and avoid painful activities, and you still have the same pain after a week or two, you must refer back to your doctor, as you may have an underlying medical problem, or you may have suffered a complication related to the injury.

Complications

TRACTION ON THE BONY ATTACHMENTS OF THE MUSCLES

A severe injury to the lower abdominal muscles can pull them away at their attachment over the front of your pelvis. This can affect the bones, either by irritating their surface, or by pulling away chips of bone. You then feel continuing sharp pain whenever you try to do sport, and the affected bone feels tender to touch, either over your pubis or over the crest of your hip-bone, below your waist.

226

Your doctor will firstly have X-rays taken, if he thinks these necessary, and then will probably refer you for specialist treatment. Meanwhile, you have to rest completely from any activities which cause pain.

ILIAC CREST EPIPHYSITIS

During the fusion phase of the growth of the hip-bone, the ridge along the top of the bone is very vulnerable to shearing strains caused by excessive muscle pull from the abdominals and the hip abductors. Fusion in this part of the bone normally happens at the age of sixteen in boys, but it may be delayed until twenty years, while the normal age for girls is fourteen, but the fusion may not happen before eighteen years.

Any sport which places undue stress on the hip-bone ridge can pull the growing crest away from the main bone. Long-distance running, hill running, hurdling, throwing events, racket sports and rowing are all sports which involve strong abdominal muscle work, and in which it is easy to exceed the load which growing bones are able to withstand. The problem may occur if the sport is new, or if you have re-started it after a long lay-off, or if you suddenly start to do intensive training for it.

Once this problem has happened, you feel pain over the affected area of the bone whenever you do the sport which caused the epiphysitis. The bone feels tender to touch, and X-rays show up the separation of the crest from the rest of your hip-bone. The only cure is to rest from any painful activity. Unfortunately, as with any other growing bone, this disrupted fusion can take a long time to heal, sometimes years, so it is a fairly disabling condition. While you are resting, you should try out alternative sports, gently, to see if there are any activities which do not cause painful stress over the damaged bone.

HERNIA

A hernia is a protrusion of an organ or other internal tissue through tissues which are supposed to bind and enclose it. Your abdominal wall is elastic, but held together by binding tissues. Any part of it may herniate, because of a sudden, excessive increase in abdominal pressure, for any reason, and then you can suffer from the protrusion of some internal tissue through the break. You may actually feel the protrusion coming forward through your stomach wall when certain movements of your trunk tense your muscles and push the protrusion out.

The hernia may not be directly related to sport, but the increased abdominal pressure caused by muscle contraction during exercise can aggravate the condition, or even make you notice it when you might not

227

Abdominals

have if you did not exercise strenuously. Certain exercises can cause a hernia, if they raise the pressure in your abdomen to an excessive degree. Raising both legs up straight when you are lying flat or hanging from a bar is one of these exercises. Struggling to lift heavy weights is another possible cause of abdominal hernia.

The pain of the hernia seems very similar to that of an abdominal muscle strain, except that it can feel at its worst when you cough or sneeze. The pain continues when you would normally have expected the muscle strain to heal. In this situation, your doctor will be able to identify the hernia: if it is bad enough, he may refer you for surgery to reduce the gap through which the tissues are protruding, as leaving it to settle spontaneously carries the risk that the gap will widen under pressure.

The Chest Muscles

The main muscles covering the front of your chest are your pectorals. You have two pectoral muscles, pectoralis major and minor, indicating their relative sizes. Pectoralis minor lies under the larger major muscles, and functions slightly differently from it. Pectoralis major is the largest muscle over your chest, extending from your collar-bone, down the whole side of your breast-bone, and across the inner edges of your upper six or seven ribs; it spreads sideways in a tapering fan shape on either side of your chest, to form a tendon which joins the top of your arm-bone, or humerus, just below your shoulder.

The pectoralis major tendon forms the fold at the front of your armpit. If you put one hand over the front of your chest and armpit on the opposite side, and stretch your arm forward on that side, you can feel your pectoralis major contract, if you push your outstretched hand inwards against an immovable object. In a well-developed male, the pectoral muscles form the bulge of the chest. In the female, the pectorals are only really visible over the upper part of the chest and the armpit, because they are covered by the breasts in their lower part.

FUNCTIONS

Pectoralis major works to pull your arm forwards and inwards. Therefore it helps perform throwing movements, punches in boxing, and forehand strokes in racket sports. If you hang by your hands, and then pull your body upwards, as in doing chins on a bar, or rock climbing, pectoralis major works to achieve the movement, in conjunction with the strong sheet muscles down your back.

PAIN IN YOUR CHEST

Medical conditions affecting your heart and lungs can cause pain in your chest. Over the front of your shoulder you can also feel referred pain from other regions, like your liver. A heart condition can give you

The chest muscles, puffed out by this body-building technique.

referred pain in your shoulder. Therefore you must keep a record of your general health, noting such signs as a chesty cough or great alterations in your resting heart-beat (pulse rate) to help your doctor make an accurate diagnosis of your problem.

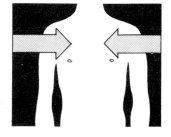

Injury to the pectorals

The pectoral muscles can be injured suddenly, by a direct blow while the muscles are contracting, or by a blocked movement during contraction, or by a sudden over-stretch. Direct blows can occur in sports like lacrosse, where the ball travels through the air, and combat sports like karate and judo. Your shoulder can be wrenched or blocked during combat sports, causing tears in the pectorals.

The pectorals may also suffer overuse injuries, for instance if you do prolonged sessions of service practice in tennis, or throwing the javelin, or rowing. As the muscles tire, they become inefficient, and tighten, making them vulnerable to tears in their fibres.

What you feel

In a sudden injury, you feel a sharp pain over your chest as your shoulder movement is wrenched or blocked, and you then feel pain when you work the muscles by drawing your arm forward and in, or when you stretch them by extending your shoulder backwards. In an overuse injury, the pain over your chest comes on gradually. It may start only after exercise at first, but you gradually begin to feel it during the exercise which caused the strain, if you try to continue with it. The pain becomes progressively worse, until you feel it on any movements which contract or stretch the muscles.

The pain of a sudden injury may be sharp at first, and then may subside to an ache, but it may become more severe if you try to continue with your sport. The pain of the overuse injury can develop to a severe stage, if you do not rest from painful activities. Once the pain is severe, you are likely to feel it when you take deep breaths or cough.

You can usually identify the sore area in the pectoral muscles, if you press over the painful part with your fingers. You can feel a tender spot, and you may also be able to feel a small area of fluid swelling, if some of the muscle fibres near the surface of the muscle have been torn.

231

What has happened

A severe wrenching injury can tear the pectoralis major tendon right through, making the muscle 'bunch up', pulling away from your shoulder. A more minor injury may tear or strain some of the muscle fibres either on the front of your chest, or where the muscle is attached to your breast-bone, ribs or collar-bone. A direct blow to the chest may crack one or more of your ribs, as well as injuring your chest muscles.

Self-help measures for chest injuries

- Apply ice (p. 15) over the injured area.
- Keep your arm close to your side and still. If the injury is close to your shoulder, and the joint feels sore, you may feel more comfortable if you support your arm in a sling.
- You must refer to your doctor or local casualty department as quickly as possible after a severe traumatic injury, for an assessment of the extent of the damage.
- As soon as the initial pain has subsided, and your practitioner allows you to exercise the injured muscles, you should start stretching them passively, doing three or four stretching exercises (p. 233) two or three times a day.
- Once you can stretch your pectorals fully, without pain, you can do the strengthening exercises (p. 233), gradually building up the amount you do. You must remember to start and finish a strengthening session with stretching exercises.
- If you suffer no setbacks of increasing pain or tightness as you progress with your stretching and strengthening exercises, you can gradually try out the movements needed for your sport, and then resume practising your sport.

How long?

You should be able to start the stretching exercises within a few hours of a minor injury to your pectorals, progressing to strengthening exercises within three to seven days. For a more severe injury, you should try to start the stretching exercises within one or two days of the injury, but you will find your flexibility limited, so you must be patient in allowing the muscles to pay out again. Strengthening exercises may have to be delayed for two to three weeks in this case. If your pectoral tendon is totally ruptured, you may need surgery to mend it, and in this case you can only start exercising the muscles when your surgeon allows.

Pectoral exercises

STRETCHING EXERCISES

1. Lie on your back, with your arm over the edge of your bed or bench, palm facing upwards, and a light weight in your hand; keeping your elbow straight, let your arm fall sideways, at right angles to your chest, until you feel the stretch over the front of your chest. Hold to a count of ten, then bring your arm back to neutral. Repeat on the other arm.

2. Place one or two pillows under your upper back, and repeat (1).

3. Lie on your back, with one or two pillows under your upper back, and a weighted bar held in your hands, palms upwards, and resting on your thighs. Letting your elbows bend slightly, take the bar over your head, until you feel the stretch across your chest. Hold to ten, then relax back to the starting position.

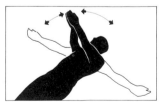

ISOMETRIC STRENGTHENING EXERCISES

(Do not do these if you have any blood pressure problems.)
1. Sit in a chair, with your hands resting palms down on your thighs; press your hands down against your thighs, holding the contraction for a count of five, then relaxing completely.
2. Hold your arms straight out in front of you, with your palms together; press your hands against each other for a count of five, then relax.
3. Hold your arms in front of you, with your palms together and your elbows slightly bent; press your palms together for a count of five, then relax.

DYNAMIC STRENGTHENING EXERCISES

1. Lie on your back on a bench, or supported by pillows, with your arms straight out sideways over the sides of the bench; with light weights in your hands, bring your arms straight up to touch your hands together above your chest, then slowly lower them sideways again. Build up to three sets of ten, then increase the weights.
2. Repeat (1), but this time turn your arms so that the backs of your hands meet above your chest.

233

Pectorals

3. Sit in a chair, with your arms straight out sideways, and weights held in your hands with your palms facing downwards; swing your arms straight forwards, so that your thumbs touch together, then swing them sideways again. Build up to three sets of ten, then increase the weights.
4. Lie on your back, with one or two pillows under your upper back, your hands by your sides, holding weights; with your palms facing each other, lift your arms straight up backwards, to touch the floor behind your head, keeping your arms about shoulder's width apart; then reverse the movement, turning your arms so that your thumbs lead the movement downwards, and the backs of your hands face each other. Build up to three sets of ten, then increase the weights.
5. Lie on your back, with one or two pillows under your upper back, and your hands by your sides, holding weights; keeping your elbows straight, swing your arms diagonally upwards and back over your head, so that your arms cross; then reverse the movement, turning your arms, so that your thumbs lead and the backs of your hands face each other. Build to three sets of ten.
6. Chins. With your hands a shoulder's width apart on a bar, and your palms facing away from you, bend your elbows to lift your body upwards to the bar, taking your chin above the bar, if possible. Start with one or two, and gradually increase the number.

The Rib Cage

You have twelve ribs, all linked to your thoracic vertebrae in your back, forming joints with the sideways struts on the vertebrae. Your upper seven ribs encircle your chest from either side, to be attached to your breast-bone (sternum). The next three ribs loop downwards over your sides, curving up in front to form a cartilage line attaching to the bottom of your breast-bone. You can feel the front edges of these ribs sloping upwards away from your stomach. Your lowest two ribs are short, with pointed, free ends, so they are called the floating ribs. You can feel them if you put your hands round your waist, just behind your sides.

Strong ligaments bind the bones together, where your ribs form joints at your front and back. Your ribs are linked to each other by muscles called the intercostals. Your pectoral muscles (p. 229) link your ribs to your shoulder girdle from the front, while a large muscle called serratus anterior joins your ribs to your shoulder blades. The diaphragm, your breathing muscle, forms a sheet linking the lower edges of your ribs, and dividing your trunk in two.

FUNCTIONS

Your ribs are a protective cage round your heart and lungs. Their joints allow movement, so that they can expand to let air in when you breathe. As your diaphragm moves down, your ribs move up and out, creating more space for the air to be breathed in; the process is reversed to expel the air that you breathe out. You can feel your rib movement clearly if you put your hands over your ribs and take deep breaths, keeping your shoulders still.

PAIN IN THE RIB CAGE

Heart or lung problems can cause pain over your chest or upper back, as can certain internal abdominal problems, which refer pain to the same regions. If you have noticed changes in your pulse-rate, a bad cough, or breathlessness, you must tell your doctor, to help his diagnosis. Damage

235

in the thoracic vertebrae can cause referred pain following the line of your ribs, as the nerves from the thoracic spine circle your chest.

Rib injuries

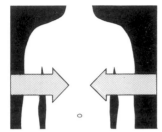

Your ribs can be injured directly by a blow, for instance if you fall onto your side, or get hit by your opponent in boxing. Indirectly, your ribs can be damaged by pressure changes in your chest while your rib movement is blocked. This can happen if you are hunched under the vertical leg press machine, when the deep breath before you push your legs against the weights can be enough to crack a rib or damage a rib joint.

The muscles over and between your ribs can be damaged by over-stretching or overwork, either as a sudden or a gradual injury. However, it is relatively rare to suffer really noticeable pain due only to a muscle injury, and often the muscle strain accompanies damage to the rib bones or joints. Stress fractures can happen in the ribs, as in all other bones, and they may be the cause of gradually increasing pain in tennis players or throwers, who stress their shoulder girdle muscles in repetitive patterns. Cracks in the ribs, due to accidents or over-stress, are usually not treated specifically nowadays. Your ribs normally heal within three weeks, provided you do not subject them to further stress, but avoid any painful activities. Ice can help to relieve the soreness.

When you are recovering from a rib cage injury, you must make sure that you gradually regain full flexibility, before you re-start your sport. You may have been protecting your ribs by limiting their movement, and you must be able to stretch out, by leaning backwards, sideways and forwards with your hands over your head, and by twisting to either side with your arms outstretched.

Complications

Rib damage can cause pain when you breathe. If this lasts for any time, you may find that your breathing pattern is inhibited, making it difficult for you to breathe deeply during exercise. Occasionally, this can result in the condition of exercise-induced asthma, although this is more often due to some allergy. If you feel wheezy, tight-chested, or breathless during activities or at rest, you must refer to your doctor for a check.

Breathing control is an important self-help measure in coping with breathing difficulties. One problem, when you become breathless, is that the feeling of constriction makes you panic, so that you try to draw more

236

breaths in, without being able to breathe out fully. This increases your breathlessness, as you are no longer breathing in oxygen efficiently, and it may make you pass out. Simple breathing exercises can counteract this difficulty. While you are sitting at rest, put your hands over your lower ribs. Take two or three deep breaths, feeling your ribs swell out as you breathe in, and then drop back as you breathe out. Try to prolong the breath out just a little longer than you normally would. Keep your shoulders still, and do not keep on deep breathing beyond three breaths, as you may get dizzy. When you are breathing normally, try to keep the same pattern of breathing out slightly longer than you breathe in. This is basic breathing control.

When you have mastered it at rest, you can try using it while jogging. Pace yourself, perhaps taking a breath in over two or three steps, then breathe out over three or four. Once you are used to using this breathing pattern, you should be able to superimpose it whenever you feel breathless, so that you re-establish an efficient breathing pattern quickly. When you are breathless, you can help your breathing by leaning your hands against a support or on your knees, to fix your shoulders, either sitting or standing. This ensures that your shoulders keep relatively still, allowing maximum rib movement for breathing.

The Neck
(Cervical spine)

Bones

There are seven vertebrae in the neck, six of which are shaped like the other spinal vertebrae (p. 189), with a cylindrical block at the front, and a fine triangular structure behind. The top vertebra, the atlas, is different, because it consists of a ring of bone, with two flat ledges to support your skull. The vertebrae are much smaller and finer than in the rest of the spine. The other main difference is that the sideways struts in the neck do not jut out, but form a ring of bone, joined to the side of the vertebral body.

Soft tissues

The strong ligament that binds the front of the vertebrae through the spine reaches right up to the base of your skull. Finer ligaments run vertically down the back and sides of the vertebrae, to link them together from the second vertebra down. Discs (p. 190) separate each vertebra, except between the atlas and the second vertebra. Tiny muscles also provide vertical links down the back and sides of the vertebrae. Bigger muscles link your neck with your shoulder girdle. Your trapezius, on each side of the neck, forms the soft contour spreading out over your shoulders.

FUNCTIONS

Your neck can move freely forwards, backwards and sideways. Twisting is the only limited movement in the neck (cervical) region, and this is compensated for by the freedom of rotation in the thoracic region immediately below. The neck forms the main support for your skull, so its movements allow you to turn your head, so that you can see in various directions, or move your head away from danger. Your shoulder movements co-ordinate with your neck movements, because of the muscular links. The muscles may hold your neck still, for instance when you extend your arms in shaping up for a dive. Or your neck may move at the same time as your shoulders, as when you serve in tennis, turning your head to watch the ball as you throw it up.

Like the rest of the spine, your neck encloses and protects your spinal cord, which emerges from your brain through a hole in your skull, and then extends downwards in the canal formed by the bone struts at the back of the vertebral blocks.

NECK PAIN

Inflammatory joint disease can cause pain in the neck joints. You can have neck pain related to certain viral infections. Influenza often causes aching and stiffness on one or both sides of your neck. Pain can be referred to your neck from internal regions, such as your diaphragm or breathing muscle. You must try to keep a record of your neck pain, including other joint pains you may have noticed, and details of your general health, to help your doctor diagnose the cause of your pain accurately.

Neck injuries

You can hurt your neck through a sudden traumatic injury, for instance if you hit your head in a fall from a height, or if your head or neck is wrenched. This type of accident can happen in sports like riding, gymnastics, diving, rugby, judo and boxing.

If the injury is severe, and there is a chance that the neck might have broken, the victim must be kept still, as there is a risk of total paralysis. For less severe strains, you can apply ice (p. 15) to relieve the worst of the discomfort. If possible, the neck should be supported, for instance by a folded newspaper wrapped around it and held in place by a towel or scarf. You should then refer to your doctor or local casualty department as quickly as possible, in case you need to have X-rays taken.

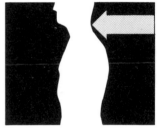

Your neck can also be injured by gradual, overuse strains. Too much strain on your neck muscles through a long bout of tennis practice, throwing the javelin, archery, or hand-stands in gymnastics can cause this type of gradually increasing pain.

What you feel
This is experienced as an increasingly noticeable pain, usually only on one side of your neck. It gets worse when you turn your head in certain ways, or lift your arm from the shoulder. You may be able to continue your sport, feeling only twinges on awkward movements, or you may find that the pain becomes continuous, even hurting at night.

239

The actual damage may vary from an injury to one or more of the neck joints, involving a strain or tear in ligaments, joint capsule, or small muscle, to gross damage to one or more of the discs. The muscles over the damaged joint usually go into spasm to protect the joint from more harm, and you feel tightness and soreness in the trapezius on the injured side. Occasionally, neck joint problems happen following an injury to the neck muscles, because the injured muscle, becoming taut, pulls against the joints and distorts them. Accurate diagnosis of neck injuries is a matter for the specialists, and the problem should be treated, before you try to resume your sport.

What you should do

Following an injury, your specialist may recommend you to do specific neck exercises, to make your neck joints stronger and more flexible. Once you have recovered, you should include some neck exercises in your warm-up before doing sport, and, if possible, as a general daily routine. At no stage should you do any movements which cause pain, during or after the exercise. If you do a daily routine of exercises, you should choose two or three strengthening and mobilizing exercises (p. 241), and repeat each of them about three times, three times a day. Do not force any movements that feel specially stiff: you risk causing damage, or suffering secondary symptoms like dizziness or arm pain.

While your neck is painful, your specialist may give you a supporting collar to wear, made of hard or soft material. If you wear a hard collar, you should not drive a car. You should try to rest your neck as much as possible. If you do not wear a support at night, you may find it comfortable to bunch up your pillow in the middle, and place it under your neck, with another pillow under your head. If you sit in an easy chair, make sure your whole back is well supported, and keep your arms and shoulders level. Try to avoid twisting your head and neck.

If you have to drive, experiment with your car seat: you may find that you have less discomfort if you are close to the steering wheel. If you have a wing mirror as well as an interior mirror, try to alternate between the two, so that you are not constantly turning your head in the same direction. The same principles apply to managing at work. If you sit at a desk, arrange it so that you do not have to lean far in any one direction, but you can reach all necessary items without strain, on either side of you. Try to support your arms, rather than keeping them extended, and try not to hold your head bent in one particular position for long periods of time. To counteract stiffness, it is useful to do simple neck mobilizing exercises (p. 242) at frequent intervals during the day. You should not lift or carry heavy loads while you have neck pain, especially not over your shoulders or above your head. If you do heavy manual work, you must have time off until you recover. Once you return to heavy work, you must remember to try to even out the loading on your spine by carrying loads on each shoulder in turn, or lifting with both arms, or each arm alternately.

Be aware of your postural habits. You may have a tendency to lean your head to one side. Long-distance runners sometimes hold their heads sideways, and tense up their shoulders during running. Swimmers often breathe on the same side all the time. Scullers and oarsmen may always look over the same shoulder when they steer. These habits can contribute to neck problems, so you should try to correct them by varying your neck movements, trying to use your neck in symmetrical, balanced patterns.

Neck exercises

ISOMETRIC STRENGTHENING EXERCISES

1. Sitting or standing, place one hand against your forehead; press your head against your hand, blocking any movement. Hold for a count of three, then relax completely.

2. Place your hand against the side of your head, and press your head against your hand, holding the contraction for a count of three, then relaxing. Repeat for the other side of your head.

241

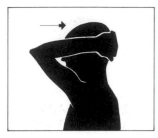

3. Put your hands on the back of your head, and press your head back against your hands, blocking any movement, and holding the contraction for a count of three.

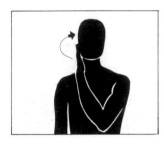

4. Put your hand against the side of your chin, and try to turn your head against the resistance of your hand, holding the contraction for a count of three. Repeat, turning your head the other way against your hand.

MOBILIZING EXERCISES

1. Sitting or standing, gently bend your head forward to touch your breast-bone with your chin, then lift your chin up until the back of your head touches your neck. Repeat five to ten times, in a rhythmical, continuous movement.

2. Bend your head to one side, trying to touch your ear to your shoulder, in a rhythmical continuous movement, starting with five times to each side in turn, building up to ten times.

242

3. Turn your head from side to side, rhythmically, starting with five turning movements, building up to ten.

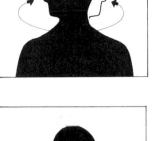

4. Tuck your chin down onto your chest, and gently turn your head from side to side, keeping your chin in contact with your chest. Start with five turning movements, building up to ten.

DYNAMIC STRENGTHENING EXERCISES

1. Lie on your stomach over the end of a couch or bench, so that your head and neck are over the end, while the rest of your body is comfortably supported. Arrange a halter and weight over your head, so that it will not slip when you move. Lift your head upwards a little way, keeping your shoulders still, hold for a count of three, then gently lower down. Start with a very light weight, gradually increasing it, and build up from five movements to three sets of ten.

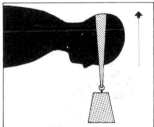

2. Lie on your back with your head and neck over the end of the bench, and the halter and weight over your forehead. Lift your head forward a little way, keeping your shoulders still, hold for a count of three, then lower back. Build up to three sets of ten, gradually increasing the weight.

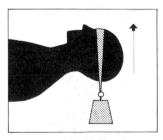

3. Lie on your side, and arrange the weight so that you lift it sideways. Then repeat the exercise lying on your other side.

243

If your sport requires special strength in your neck, you should do more strenuous strengthening exercises. However, you should not do these if you have any neck pain, problems with blood pressure, or headaches or dizziness.

1. Head-stand: kneel on the ground, with a cushion in front of you; rest your forehead on the cushion, with your hands flat on the ground, just below shoulder level, so that your weight is on your head, hands and knees. Gradually straighten your knees and lift your hips behind you so that your weight rests on your head, hands, and feet. Start with three movements, build up to ten, sitting up between each exercise.

2. Kneeling on your hands and knees, put your head down on the cushion, and gradually lift your arms away from the floor, so that you are balancing on your head and your knees. Hold the position for a count of three. Start with three, building up to ten.

3. Practise heading a light ball in every direction, with your forehead. If you play football, gradually build up until you can easily head a football.

4. Lying on your back, with your knees bent, feet flat on the floor, press the back of your head against the floor, and gradually lift your seat upwards, so that you are resting on your feet, and the top of the back of your head. Steady yourself with your hands at first, then try to balance on your head and feet only. Hold the position for a count of three. Start with three, and build up to ten.

Complications

As in the rest of the spine (p. 207), a neck problem can cause referred symptoms. You may feel pain, tingling or numbness down your arm, into your hand. The symptoms may form a continuous line down your arm to your hand, or only one part of your arm may be affected, in which case it may be more difficult to relate the symptoms to your neck problem. A ligament strain, or minor damage to a disc, will cause intermittent referred symptoms, which you can relieve by altering the position of your neck, perhaps stretching your neck away from the affected arm. A major disc problem causes unremitting pain. In either case, you should ask your doctor for specialist help, and you should not do any sport or strenuous activities until you have recovered.

Headaches and dizziness can also be caused by neck problems, either through spasm in the neck muscles, or because your injury is interfering with the flow of your circulation between your vertebrae. The pain is usually lessened if you rest your neck, and take care not to strain it with awkward postures or movements, but you must refer to your doctor for help.

OSTEOARTHRITIS

Wear-and-tear arthritis can happen in the neck joints, causing pain in your neck, with or without referred symptoms in your arms. It is important to maintain as much mobility and strength in your neck as you comfortably can, while avoiding stressing the joints with heavy loading or strenuous sports. Your doctor will advise you on the type and amount of exercise you should be doing, on the basis of your symptoms and the changes visible on your X-rays.

The Shoulder Joint

Bones

The shoulder is a ball-and-socket joint, formed between the side of your shoulder-blade (scapula) and the top of your arm-bone (humerus). The shoulder-blade forms a flattened, circular disc opposite the top of the arm-bone, and this disc is made into a cup-shape by a ridge of soft-tissue all round its edge. The top of the arm-bone is rounded, conforming to the receiving surface on the shoulder-blade. But the two bones are not tightly bound together, and the joint surface over the top of the arm-bone is much larger than the receiving surface at the side of the shoulder-blade. This means that the shoulder joint is quite different from the hip joint, although the two are parallel in structure, both being ball-and-socket joints, and both linking the limbs to your trunk.

Over the top of the shoulder you have an arch of bone which is separate from the shoulder joint structurally, but functionally linked to it. The acromion process is a wedge of bone at the end of the spine of the shoulder-blade, a ridge which you can feel clearly across the back of your shoulder. The acromion forms the hard tip you can feel over the top of your shoulder, and it joins onto the end of your collar-bone (clavicle), just above the front of the shoulder. The spine of the shoulder-blade and the collar-bone form a V-shape, with the point of the V over your shoulder.

As the shoulder is padded with thick muscles, it is hard to feel the bones forming the joint. There are also a lot of nerves crossing the joint, which make it uncomfortable to press too hard over the bones. If you put your hand round the top of your arm-bone, so that your thumb is in your armpit, and lift your arm out sideways, you can feel the rounded end of the arm-bone with your thumb, if you move your elbow backwards and forwards.

Soft tissues

The shoulder joint is enclosed in a very loose capsule, or retaining bag of tissue, which covers the whole of the round head of the arm-bone, and attaches it to the outer rim of the receiving surface on the shoulder-blade.

246

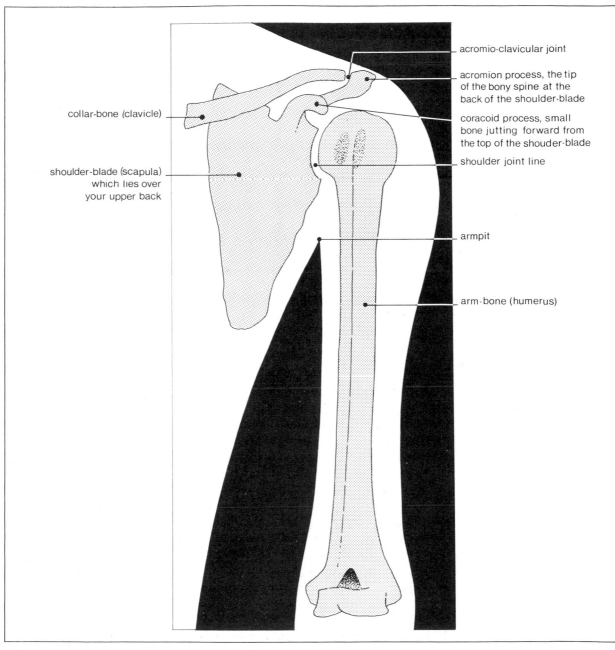

acromio-clavicular joint

acromion process, the tip of the bony spine at the back of the shoulder-blade

coracoid process, small bone jutting forward from the top of the shoulder-blade

shoulder joint line

collar-bone (clavicle)

shoulder-blade (scapula) which lies over your upper back

armpit

arm-bone (humerus)

Left shoulder joint, from in front.

247

Shoulder

The capsule is thickened into protective ligaments over the front of the shoulder, but the joint's main protection is given by the tendons which cross the joint over its back, top and front. Your biceps tendon, which crosses the front of your shoulder, actually passes through the joint structure, adding another stabilizing force to the joint. The least protected part of the joint is its underside, in your armpit. When your arm is by your side, the joint capsule folds downwards in a loose pouch. When you lift your arm sideways, this slack is taken up, and the capsule is put on the stretch, but there are no thickened bands of ligaments or tendons limiting this movement or protecting the joint from excessive strain in this direction.

The soft, rounded contour of your shoulder is formed by the deltoid muscle, which spreads right over the front, back and top of the joint. This large muscle makes it difficult to feel the smaller structures lying closer to the joint.

Separating the tendons round the shoulder from each other and from the joint structure are numerous bursae, or fluid-filled sacs. These provide friction-free movement between the tendons and the underlying tissues.

FUNCTIONS

Your shoulder is the most mobile joint in your body. You can lift your arm forwards, backwards, sideways, and above your head. Your shoulder also twists, allowing you to place your hands behind your head or back. By combining all the available movements at the joint, you can achieve a full circular swinging movement, called circumduction, at the shoulder.

When you lift your arm straight out sideways, you can see your bulky deltoid muscle contract to produce the movement, and you can feel the muscle working if you put your hand over it. If you then take your arm forwards, keeping your elbow up in the air, you can feel the front part of your deltoid working over the front of your shoulder. If you swing your arm backwards with your elbow held up, you can feel the back portion of your deltoid contracting. When you hold your arm at your side, with your elbow bent to a right angle, and press your hand inwards towards your stomach against an immovable resistance, you can feel the rotator muscles on the front of your shoulder working isometrically. If you press your hand away from your body against a resistance, with your elbow bent, you can feel the contraction of the rotator muscles on the back of the shoulder, if you put your other hand over your shoulder.

In most movements of your shoulder, there is a complex interaction between the working muscles contracting and relaxing to produce the very wide range of movement possible. The shoulder joint does not work in isolation when you move your arm. The whole shoulder girdle has to move in harmony, so any arm movements involve not only the shoulder, but a movement of the shoulder-blade relative to the back of your ribs, and a less distinct, but important, movement in the joints between your collar-bone and the breast-bone and acromion process at either end of it. If you stand with your back to a mirror, and look over your shoulder, you can see your shoulder-blades moving forward round your chest as you straighten your arms in front of you. Your shoulder-blades slide backwards towards your spine as you bring your arms back behind you, extending your shoulders.

The combination of power and mobility in your shoulder allows you to throw forcefully, so you can project a shot or discus, and bowl hard and fast in cricket. The service and smash strokes in tennis take your shoulder through a full arc, twisting the joint as you turn the racket behind your neck, then exerting a powerful thrust through the joint as you strike the ball. In combat sports, your shoulder mobility allows you to reach in various directions to grasp or hit your opponent. In judo and wrestling, shoulder power lets you pull or push your opponent down.

Your shoulder can withstand strong forces which tend to pull it apart, or distract it. In gymnastics, hanging from the rings or high bar pulls the shoulder apart through the drag of your body-weight plus the effect of gravity. Because of the great mobility in your shoulders, you can do the so-called 'dislocation' movement, swinging your body in complete arcs, while you hold the bar or rings, keeping your hands a fixed distance apart. Your shoulders can also withstand great compression forces. When you do a hand-stand, your shoulders support your body-weight plus the effect of gravity. A single hand-stand places the total load through one shoulder. Powerlifters similarly support large compression forces through their shoulders when they lift weights overhead in snatch or press exercises.

PAIN IN THE SHOULDER

A gradual pain in one or both shoulders can have a variety of causes. To help your doctor diagnose it accurately, you have to record exactly when the pain came on; what you were doing when you first felt it; whether it hurts at night or when you are resting; whether it gets worse or eases according to identifiable causes; whether it only comes on during or after sport, or whether you feel the pain at other times. Shoulder pain can be caused by an inflammatory arthritis or joint disease. It can also be

249

referred from other parts of your body, for instance from a neck problem giving referred symptoms into the shoulder, or from a condition affecting your diaphragm, your main breathing muscle. Although you might feel the pain was specifically in your shoulder joint, there might be nothing wrong with the joint at all. One of the more serious problems which can cause shoulder pain is a heart condition, and sometimes your first warning of a heart problem is a pain which comes on, without a recognizable cause, in your left shoulder.

Shoulder injuries

STRAINS

The muscles and tendons over the shoulder can be injured by wrenching and twisting strains, by over-stretching and overuse, and by a forceful block to a movement while the muscles are contracting. The damage may be sudden and traumatic, or gradual and progressive.

Traumatic injuries to the shoulder may occur in contact and combat sports, riding, gymnastics and diving. You may fall awkwardly onto your hand or elbow, wrenching your shoulder. An opponent may knock your arm, for instance in a rugby tackle, or block your throw in basketball. You may over-balance while doing a hand-stand in gymnastics. Overuse injuries are normally associated with sports in which you use your shoulder repetitively or continuously. Competitive swimmers produce about eighty per cent of their stroke power through their arms, and their arduous training may overwork the shoulder muscles and tendons. An extra long, or unaccustomed, training session of tennis serving, shot putting, archery, or cricket bowling, may similarly over-strain the muscles and tendons, which become inefficient through fatigue.

What you feel

In a traumatic injury, you feel a sudden pain over your shoulder, which may be severe. You probably have to stop your sport, although, if it is a very minor injury, you may find that the pain subsides quickly and allows you to finish your game or session. In a gradual, overuse injury, the pain is usually only very slight to begin with. You feel it on specific movements at the shoulder, and it gradually gets worse, if you continue to do your sport.

In either case, once the damage has occurred, you feel that pain whenever you move your shoulder, making the injured muscle or tendon contract or stretch out. You may be able to feel a tender spot where the tissues are injured, if you press over your shoulder with your other hand, although the bulk of your deltoid muscle makes it difficult to feel some of the individual tendons lying under its thickest parts. If the injury is over the front of your shoulder, contracting the muscles and tendons to take your arm forward, or turn it inwards, causes pain, and you feel a pull when you take your arm backwards and stretch the same muscles and tendons. An injury to the muscles and tendons at the back of the shoulder causes pain when you contract the muscles to take the arm backwards, or turn it outwards, or when you stretch them as you take your arm forwards. An injury to the deltoid muscles over the top of the shoulder is painful if you take your arm out sideways against a resistance.

What has happened

In this type of injury, you strain or partly tear some muscles or tendon fibres in the affected area. You may also damage some of the ligaments protecting your shoulder. If you continue with your sport, and feel pain over the injury, you will do further damage to the injured tissues. If you use your shoulder awkwardly, trying to avoid hurting it, you will suffer from an almost immediate weakening in the muscles which are no longer being worked normally. The shoulder then loses the stability it owes to those muscles, and with this, its normal function and range of movement. This in itself sets up a cycle of progressive weakness and associated pain.

Self-help measures for shoulder strains

• First-aid for the traumatic shoulder injury consists of ice applications (p. 15), and, if the pain is severe, support in a sling. You should then go as quickly as possible to the local casualty department or your doctor, for an assessment of the extent of the damage. It may be necessary for X-rays to be taken, if there is a risk that you might have cracked or broken one of the bones at the shoulder.

• For the overuse injury, you should refer to your doctor as soon as possible after you become aware of the pain, so that he can make an accurate diagnosis of the problem. If the pain has become severe, you can safely apply ice to soothe it.

• As soon as the acute pain subsides, your specialist will probably advise you to start remedial exercises. If a specific muscle or tendon has been diagnosed as strained, you will start with gentle passive stretching exercises for the muscle group (p. 261). If the injury is at the front of the shoulder, you do the exercises which take the arm backwards, creating a 'pulling' sensation over the joint. For an injury at the back of the shoulder, you do the exercises which pull the arm forward. What you should feel when you do the exercises is a slight pulling feeling over the

251

injured area, and you hold this stretch position absolutely still for a count of ten. You should repeat the stretching exercises about three times every hour, if you possibly can, or do at least six stretching exercises twice a day, if you do not have time to do more.

• When you start the stretching exercises, you should also begin to do isometric and strengthening exercises (p. 256), but avoiding any exercises which cause pain. Choose up to six exercises, and do them once or twice a day, as time permits. If you can, it is best to do exercises in front of a mirror, to stop yourself 'cheating', by bending your trunk instead of using your shoulder.

• While your shoulder is painful, you should not try to continue with your sport, and you should try to avoid any painful movements, while exercising the joint specifically as much as possible. Once you have regained full flexibility in the injured muscles, and your shoulder feels strong because of the strengthening exercises, you can progress to the more demanding functional strengthening exercises, starting with a few at a time, and gradually increasing the amount you do (p. 263). You must remember to maintain flexibility by stretching your shoulder muscles before and after any strengthening session.

• When you are confident that you can do the functional exercises without pain, you can gradually resume your sport. Recovery from a shoulder strain may take only a week to ten days, if the injury was minor, and you started the rehabilitation process quickly. However, if you do not make sure that you have stretched and strengthened the joint thoroughly following the injury, you risk having niggling recurrences for a long time after the original injury, or, worse, you may find that your shoulder gradually stiffens up, while becoming weak, so that after a few months you have a real functional disability. Recovery after a severe injury may take six weeks or longer. Your guide to progress is any pain you feel, or your increasing ability to use your shoulder normally. If you do suffer from increasing pain as you exercise the shoulder more, you must refer back to your doctor for further checks, to assess what is causing the setbacks, and whether there might be any complications underlying your shoulder pain.

BICEPS TENDON TEAR

The biceps tendon, which passes through the shoulder joint, and then joins the bulky biceps muscle at the front of the shoulder, can be strained, like the other tendons around the shoulder. However, a severe strain can tear it completely, causing particular problems in the shoulder. This injury can happen when a strong contraction of the biceps is blocked, for

252

instance if you are trying to make a hard throw, and an opponent pulls your arm suddenly backwards. Or it may happen when excessive loads create too much pressure in the muscle, for instance when a gymnast holds the crucifix position, holding his body-weight through the isometric holding power of his shoulder muscles.

What you feel is a sudden snap in the tendon, which may be very painful as it happens, or which may cause pain only afterwards. You see the bulky biceps muscle bunch up, leaving a noticeable gap between the muscle and the shoulder. You may also see some bruising and swelling over the front of the shoulder.

First-aid consists of ice applications (p. 15), and a sling for support if the shoulder is very painful. As soon as possible, you should refer to the local casualty department, or your doctor. You may be referred to an orthopaedic specialist, with a view to having surgery to mend the broken tendon, and re-attach it to the bone, or stitch its two ends together, depending on the exact way in which it has torn. The specialist may decide not to mend the tendon, but to allow the injury to heal naturally. Good functional recovery will be regained in the shoulder, although the tendon will not heal to its original state, and there may always be a slight weakness in the biceps muscle function.

Whether you have surgery or not, recovery consists of following a graduated programme of exercises to regain strength and flexibility in the shoulder. Your specialist will advise you on exactly when to start exercising the shoulder, and what exercises you should do. Generally, you start with gentle passive stretching for the front of the shoulder, avoiding causing any increasing pain. Strengthening starts with the isometric exercises (p. 256) and any of the dynamic strengthening exercises (p. 258) which you can do without pain. As with the simple shoulder strain, you progress gradually with the amount of movement and strengthening work you do, until you are fit to start with functional strengthening work, which leads up to re-starting sport. You should recover sufficiently to be able to do most normal and sporting activities without problems. However, you may have to accept that your shoulder might not regain enough power for highly demanding exercises, like the gymnast's crucifix.

BURSITIS

The shoulder has many large bursae for friction-free movement between the tendons and their underlying tissues. Any of these bursae may become inflamed, either because you have been using your shoulder awkwardly during some activity, or as the result of an injury to a tendon or one of the other joint structures, which has caused irritation over the bursa.

An inflamed bursa causes pain whenever your shoulder moves in such a way as to catch the bursa or irritate it. Bursitis over the top of the shoulder causes pain when you stretch your arm out sideways, and when you twist it, especially inwards, turning your palm down. Bursitis at the back of the shoulder causes pain when you twist your arm in either direction. You may also be aware of a 'snapping' feeling at a particular point in your shoulder movement.

It is difficult for you to differentiate between the pain of bursitis and that caused by a muscle or tendon strain. The main difference is that the muscular strain gives pain when the muscle is worked or stretched, whereas the bursitis is painful in relation to shoulder movement, even when this is done in a completely relaxed way, for instance, if you let your arms swing drifting over the water surface in a swimming pool. The strained tendon or muscle may be painful in different ways, according to the position of your arm when the tissues are worked or stretched, and the amount of load the muscle or tendon works against when it is contracting. The bursitis may be getting more sharply painful, if the condition is getting worse, but you always feel its pain in the same place, whenever the bursa is caught in a position that irritates it.

You must avoid any painful movements, for a period of two to three weeks, to allow the inflamed bursa to ease. Your doctor may give you anti-inflammatory injections or tablets to help the healing process. It is essential that you do not re-start your sport too soon, as the bursa will develop into a chronic niggling problem if you do. When you have allowed your shoulder enough rest for the inflammation to die down, you should do a programme of mobilizing and strengthening exercises for your shoulder for about a week or two, starting with easy exercises, in small quantities, and gradually increasing the amount you do. Once you can do the functional exercises without pain, you are safe to re-start your sport.

If, however, you do develop a recurrent problem with shoulder bursitis, or if the condition is very severe to start with, your doctor may refer you to an orthopaedic specialist with a view to having the painful bursa removed surgically. After the operation, your surgeon will tell you when to start exercising your shoulder, and you will follow the recovery process involving gradually strengthening and loosening the joint.

SHOULDER DISLOCATION

Dislocation of a joint means that one bone comes out of its retaining structures, causing pain, deformity and disability. At the shoulder, the top of the arm-bone (humerus) springs out of its 'socket' of soft-tissue ligaments and its capsule. The shoulder is particularly vulnerable to this injury, because it is such a loose, mobile joint, and because in many sports it is subjected to violent wrenching strains. The only part of the shoulder that is protected by a bony structure is the top, which is covered by the arch formed between the collar-bone and the top ridge of the shoulder-blade. The top of the arm-bone may be pushed out forwards, downwards, or backwards. When it is wrenched out violently, the rounded head of the bone tears through the joint capsule and its ligaments, and through the surrounding muscles or tendons. If this happens, but the bone slips back into place immediately, the injury is called a subluxation.

This type of injury can occur if you fall on your hand at an angle from a height. When your arm is outstretched, your shoulder can easily be wrenched out of joint by an opponent's tackle in rugby, judo or wrestling. In swimmers, the injury may happen under relatively minor pressure, because the shoulder muscles over one side of the joint have been over-developed by continuous training. In back-stroke swimmers the front of the shoulder is relatively weak, so the head of the arm-bone may slide forwards, while the opposite subluxation may happen to crawl swimmers.

What you feel

When your shoulder is wrenched out of joint, you feel the sensation of it being out of place, and the injury is very painful. If the arm-bone stays out of place, you feel its rounded head protruding, with a gap left at the shoulder. If the bone pops back into place, the joint feels almost normal again, but you may still feel a loose gap just below the top of the shoulder.

Treatment

When the injury happens violently, you should apply ice over your shoulder (p. 15), and support your arm in a comfortable position in a sling. You should not try to manipulate the joint back into place, but you should go to your doctor or casualty department for treatment.

If the injury has happened to you frequently, your doctor will probably refer you to an orthopaedic specialist. Surgery may be needed to restore stability in your shoulder.

After a shoulder operation, or after the initial phase of pain and disability, you must strengthen the shoulder specifically, before attempting your sport again. Start with the isometric exercises (p. 256), and the simpler dynamic exercises (p. 258), avoiding any which cause pain. Try to do two half-hour sessions a day, and do a few isometric exercises every

255

hour during your normal activities. Once the shoulder is stronger, you can start doing the stretching and mobilizing exercises. You should only resume your sport when you have regained full power and mobility in your shoulder, and your specialist declares you fit.

You must maintain a daily routine of shoulder strengthening exercises (p. 258), as this injury is very likely to keep happening. You may have to accept that you will be unable to continue high-risk sports like rugby, if the injury does recur, as even surgical repair is unlikely to make the joint strong enough against violent wrenching, although it normally gives enough stability for sports like swimming.

Shoulder exercises

ISOMETRIC STRENGTHENING EXERCISES

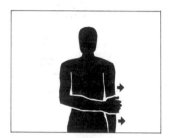

1. Keeping your injured arm straight by your side, while you are sitting or standing, place your other hand just above the outside of your elbow. Using this hand to block any movement, press your injured arm outwards, away from your side to increase the muscle tension at your shoulder. Hold the contraction for a count of five, then relax completely.

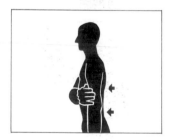

2. With your injured arm by your side, place your other hand on the front of your arm, just above your elbow. Blocking the movement with your hand, press your arm forwards for a count of five, then relax.

3. With your injured arm by your side, place your other hand on the back of your arm, just above the elbow. Blocking the movement with your hand, press your arm backwards for a count of five, then relax.

4. Repeat (1), (2) and (3) with your arm held out sideways at an angle of ninety degrees to your body.

5. With your injured arm by your side, and your elbow bent to a right angle, place your other hand against the palm of the hand on your injured arm. Blocking the movement with your other hand, press the palm of your hand inwards, without letting your elbow move, as though you were trying to take your forearm across your stomach. Hold the contraction for a count of five, then relax completely.

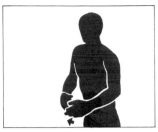

6. With your arm at your side, and the elbow bent, place your other hand against the back of your hand. Keeping your elbow at your side, try to press your hand outwards, against the resistance of the other hand. Hold the contraction for a count of five, then relax completely.

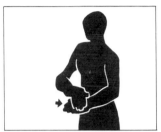

7. With your injured arm held out sideways, at right angles to your body, and your elbow bent, so that your hand is up in the air, press your other hand against your palm, to block the movement as you try to press your hand downwards, as if trying to turn your arm at the shoulder, and not allowing your elbow to change its position. Hold to five, then relax.

8. With your arm held sideways, elbow bent, place your other hand to resist the backward turning movement by pressing against the back of your hand. Hold to five, then relax.

9. With your arm held up by your head, and the elbow bent over your head, press your other hand against your palm, to resist the forward turning movement. Hold to five, then relax.

10. With your arm over your head, press against the back of your hand, to resist the backward turning movement, for a count of five.

1. Sitting or standing, raise both arms straight out sideways, hold for a count of three, then slowly lower. Start with three sets of five lifts, build up to three sets of ten, then do the exercise with light weights in your hands, gradually increasing the weights.

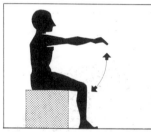

2. Sitting or standing, lift both arms straight forward, hold for a count of three, then slowly lower. Build up to three sets of ten, then add in weights.

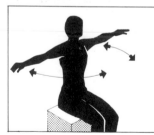

3. Sit or stand with your arms held straight out sideways; take your arms straight forwards, to touch your hands, then stretch them out sideways again. Build up to three sets of ten, then add in weights.

4. Sitting or standing, lift both arms straight forward above your head, keeping your arms close to your head, slowly lower. Build up to three sets of ten, then add in weights.

258

5. Sitting or standing, lift up both arms, bending your elbows to touch the palms of your hands on the back of your head, then lower your arms, bending them so that you touch your lower back with the backs of your hands. Start with twenty movements in quick succession, then add in weights.

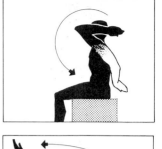

6. Lying on your back, with your injured arm held across your body so that your hand rests on the opposite hip, lift your arm straight upwards and slightly sideways, turning it so that the palm of your hand faces towards your head, so that your arm stretches back to lie beside your head. Slowly lower. Build up to three sets of ten, then add in weights.

7. Lying on your back, at the edge of a couch or bed, so that your arm lies over the side, keeping your elbow straight, take your arm up and across your body, to cross the other shoulder. Start the movement with your palm facing upwards, and turn your arm as you lift it, so that your palm faces downward at the end of the movement. Slowly lower back. Build up to three sets of ten, then add in weights.

8. Shoulder pull. Using a weights machine or pulley system, using gradually increasing weights, pull the bar downwards, hold for a count of three, then slowly control the return movement. Build up to three sets of ten.

9. Dips. On a weights machine, or sitting between two chairs or parallel bars, lift yourself up by pushing on your hands; or push the machine handles downwards; hold for a count of three, then slowly return to the starting position. Build up to three sets of ten.

10. Shoulder press. With a weighted bar held behind your neck on your shoulders, straighten your arms upwards in the air, hold for a count of three, then slowly lower. Start with light weights, building up to three sets of ten, then gradually increase the weights.

1. Lying on your back with your hands clasped together, elbows straight, swing your arms upwards above your head, starting with twenty rhythmical swings forwards and back, and building up to fifty.

2. Lying on your back with a bar held between your hands, and a weight strapped to the centre of the bar; swing the bar back over your head, rhythmically trying to swing your arms back a little further with each movement. Start with twenty swinging movements, and build up to fifty.

3. Rig up a pulley system from a strong fixed point, either a hook in a wall, or perhaps over the top of a door; holding one end of the pulley rope in each hand, stretch your uninjured arm up, with your injured arm held down, and shorten the rope so that it is taut in this position. Then rapidly pull downwards on the rope with each hand in turn to help your injured arm to lift upwards a little more with each movement. Start with one minute of pulley work, and gradually increase to ten minutes.

4. With a weight in each hand, swing your arms easily forwards and backwards; then sideways and across your body; and finally round, describing large circles in the air. Start with twenty swings in each direction, building up to fifty.

5. Draw a straight line on the floor, fifteen centimetres away from a wall, and parallel to it. Stand with your toes against the line, facing the wall. Reach up as high as you can, to touch your fingers to the wall. Hold a pencil so that you can mark the wall, showing how high you can reach with each hand. Practise reaching up the wall from the same position each day, trying to reach further up each time with your injured arm.

6. Standing with your legs apart, keeping your elbows straight, swing your arms forward and back to clap your hands in front of your chest and behind your back. Start with twenty free swinging movements, and build up to fifty.

260

7. Holding a towel or cord behind your back, with one hand holding one end behind your head, and the lower end held in your other hand behind your back, pull at each end in turn to pull the towel up and down your back. Change hands to reverse the positions. Start with twenty quick movements, increasing to fifty. Use a fairly long towel at first, and gradually try to shorten your grip, to increase your shoulder movement.

8. Hold a towel or cord in both hands in front of you; swing your arms back over your head, keeping the towel taut, then swing back, ten times. Start with a long towel, and gradually shorten your grip.

STRETCHING EXERCISES

1. Biceps and the front of the shoulder. Clasp your hands behind your back, keeping your elbows straight. Lift your arms back behind you, until you feel the stretch over the front of your shoulder. Hold this position for a count of ten, then gently relax.

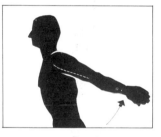

2. Triceps. Lift your arm straight up in the air, then bend your elbow so that your hand is behind your head. With your other hand, pull your elbow towards your head, until you feel the stretch at the back of your arm. Hold this position for a count of ten, then relax.

3. With your arm bent over your head, pull your wrist sideways with your other hand. As you pull your arm over your head, bend sideways in the same direction, until you feel the stretch across the underside of your shoulder. Hold to ten, then relax.

261

Shoulder

4. Hang from a bar by your hands, and let your shoulders relax completely. Hold the position for as long as you are comfortable, then step down.

5. Lying under a low bar, just further than an arm's length from the floor, take your weight on your hands by grasping the bar, keeping your body stretched straight out in front of you. Relax your shoulders completely, so that you feel the stretch over your upper trunk and the back of your shoulder-joints. Hold the position for as long as you are comfortable.

6. Keeping your elbows straight, clasp your hands together above your head. Stretch your arms backwards, hold for a count of ten, then relax.

7. Hold a lightly weighted bar up above your head, with your elbows straight and your hands a shoulder's width apart. Stretch your arms backwards, hold for ten, then relax completely.

DYNAMIC STRENGTHENING EXERCISES

1. Press-ups. Start by kneeling on your hands and knees, then bend and straighten your elbows to do the press-ups. As soon as you are strong enough, do the full press-up, with your legs straight. Start with three, and build up to thirty.

2. Backward press-ups. With your legs straight out in front of you, and your hips off the floor, so that you are leaning back on your hands, bend and straighten your elbows. Start with three, build to three sets of ten.

3. Chins. Hanging from a bar, pull yourself up to touch your chin to the bar, then let your arms straighten fully before repeating the movement. Start with three, building up to three sets of ten.

4. Hanging from a bar, pull yourself up to touch the back of your head gently to the bar. Start with three, build up to three sets of ten.

5. Crab-walking. Resting your weight backwards on your feet and hands, 'walks' forwards, backwards and sideways. Start with fifteen seconds, and build up to three minutes.

6. Wheelbarrow. With a partner holding your feet in the air, walk forwards, backwards and sideways on your hands. Without a partner, you can rest your feet up on a solid surface, and simply move around on your hands as far as you can, while keeping your feet on the support. Start with ten seconds of movement, building up to three minutes.

7. Throw and catch a light ball with both hands, then one at a time, trying to increase the height of your throws gradually.

8. Throw and catch a tennis-ball against a wall, overarm, underarm and sidearm. You should gradually increase your distance from the wall, so that you have to throw harder.

9. Using a light racket or bat, push a ball along the ground against a wall, in quick succession, gradually increasing your distance from the wall.

10. Shadow play. Practise the movements of your sport without a racket or ball. Swing an imaginary racket, stick or bat, preferably in front of a mirror so that you can check your technique and see that the movement is correct. Or practise the shooting movements for basketball or netball, or underarm throws from either side if you are a rugby player. Progress to doing the movements with a light weight or implement, then with your normal equipment, before trying a controlled practice session.

Complications

ACROMIO-CLAVICULAR JOINT STRAIN

After a shoulder injury, you may find that you have localized pain over the top of the shoulder, and soreness if you carry a heavy weight in your hand. This may mean that when you injured your shoulder, you also injured the joint between your collar-bone and the ridge on your shoulder-blade. The damage done may vary from a strain of the ligaments binding the joint, to a total tear of the ligaments, but the problem may not be evident until the pain in your shoulder has subsided. If the injury is severe, you may feel the separation between the two bones over the top of your shoulder. You must refer to your doctor, as the condition can last a long time, if it is not treated. It may be necessary to have the joint repaired surgically, although more often it simply needs an injection or physiotherapy treatment. Once the problem has been diagnosed and treated, you have to start on a graduated programme of exercises, gradually strengthening and then mobilizing the shoulder, without forcing it through pain.

CHRONIC STIFFNESS

If you do not make a complete recovery from a shoulder injury, but you re-start your sport too soon, or if you suffer repeated injuries to your shoulder, the joint may get gradually stiffer, because you are no longer able to use it fully. You may not notice this happening, until you reach the stage when you cannot lift your arm above your head. As the joint stiffens, it is also weakened. As soon as you notice this happening, you must start doing mobilizing exercises (p. 260), and isometric and simple dynamic strengthening exercises (p. 256). You may have to work through pain in your shoulder, but it is essential to reverse the process of progressive stiffness and weakness. You should also refer to your doctor for a check, just in case there is some underlying medical reason for the stiffness, apart from simple loss of function.

The Arm Muscles

Front arm muscles

STRUCTURE

Biceps brachii forms the bulging fleshy muscle on the front of the upper arm, and it extends from two attachment tendons from the top of your shoulder-blade, along the front of your arm, to a tendon which you can feel at the front of your elbow, which is attached to the top of your radius bone. Brachialis lies under the biceps, and extends from your arm-bone (humerus) to the top of your ulna, just under the elbow.

FUNCTIONS

Biceps and brachialis bend your arm at the elbow. Biceps also pulls your arm forward at the shoulder, and turns your forearm outwards below your elbow in the movement called supination. Both muscles work when you pull yourself up to 'chin' a high bar, or when you play a forehand stroke in a racket game. Biceps works, turning your forearm, when you hit a top-spin backhand.

ARM PAIN

A neck problem can cause pain over the front of your arm. Gradual pain may also be caused by spasm in the arm muscles over a stress fracture, perhaps following long repetitive sessions of fast bowling in cricket, tennis serving, or hand-springs in gymnastics. You should record details of apparently separate symptoms, like neck stiffness or pain, and your activities immediately before the pain came on, to help your doctor make an accurate diagnosis.

INJURIES

Biceps and brachialis can be injured suddenly or gradually, by over-stretching or overwork. Your arm may be wrenched back with your elbow straight, straining the muscles, for instance in wrestling. In javelin

265

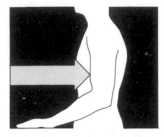

throwing you can over-stretch the muscles as you take your arm back in the wind-up. In racket sports you can strain the muscles simply through excessive repetitive practice, or through faulty technique.

What you feel is pain and tenderness over the muscles, which then hurt if you bend your elbow against a resistance, or stretch them by straightening your elbow and extending your arm backwards from your shoulder.

What you should do is to apply ice (p. 15) over your arm, if it is very sore. Almost immediately, you should start stretching the muscles, within pain limits, by clasping your hands behind your back, keeping your elbows straight, and gradually taking your arms backwards, holding the position when you reach the limit of the stretch. Repeat the exercise about three times every hour. When your arm is no longer painful on normal movement, you should do some strengthening exercises: hold a light weight in your hand, with your arm outstretched, bend your elbow quickly to touch your hand to your shoulder, and slowly straighten your elbow fully again. Build up to three sets of ten, once a day, and then gradually increase the weight loading. Remember to stretch the muscles before and after any strengthening work, and as the first part of your warm-up, when you resume your sport. If you avoid any painful activities, your recovery may take between one and six weeks, depending on the severity of the injury.

Back arm muscles

STRUCTURE

Triceps has three upper tendons, one attached to the shoulder-blade, just below the shoulder joint, and two on the back of your arm-bone. It forms the fleshy bulk on the back of your upper arm, and its lower end tendon is attached to the olecranon process, the top of your ulna. If you feel the bump of bone formed by the ulna at the back of your elbow, you can feel the triceps tendon in the space above it, when you straighten your elbow from bent, with your other hand over the back of the joint.

FUNCTIONS

Triceps straightens your elbow. It provides arm power in throwing events, and holds your arm when you do a hand-stand. If you bend your elbows while balancing on your hands, triceps controls the movement against gravity.

266

ARM PAIN

Pain on the back of the arm can be referred from a neck problem, or it can be muscular spasm over a stress fracture in the arm-bone, just like pain over the front of your arm.

INJURIES

You can injure your triceps muscle suddenly or gradually, by over-stretching it, for instance with an excessive back-swing on backhand strokes in racket games, or by overworking it, perhaps by doing hand-springs in gymnastics, or flicking your elbow hard in throwing events.

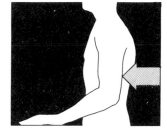

What you feel is pain and tenderness over the back of your arm, and your muscles hurt when you straighten your elbow against a resistance, or stretch them by bending your elbow.

You can apply ice (p. 15) to relieve the soreness, and you must start stretching your triceps as soon as any severe pain has subsided. With your arm above your head, elbow bent, pull your elbow behind your head with your other hand holding the stretched position, within the limits of pain, for a count of ten. Try to do this three times every hour.

When your arm is not sore on stretching and normal activities, you can do some strengthening exercises. Hold a light weight in your hand, with your elbow bent horizontally, and your arm forward: straighten your elbow, and swing your arm away from your opposite shoulder until it is straight out to your side. Build up to three sets of ten, then gradually increase the weights. The most testing exercise for your triceps is the press-up (p. 262). Remember to stretch your triceps before and after any demanding exercises, and as a warm-up before you do your sport. Recovery from a triceps strain, like the biceps injury, takes anything from a few days to several weeks, according to the severity of the initial injury. You should re-start your sport very gradually, when you are sure the arm is no longer painful.

The Elbow Joint

STRUCTURE

Bones

The lower end of your arm-bone is rounded and widened, to form a junction with the top of your inner forearm bone (ulna) and the outer bone (radius). The top of the ulna forms a hook, which fits in to a dent on the back of your arm, when the elbow is straight. If you bend your elbow, you can see and feel the end of the ulna jutting out on the inner side of your elbow. Next to the ulna, you can feel the tip of your arm-bone, forming the 'funny-bone' on the innermost side of your elbow.

Soft tissues

A fluid-filled capsule surrounds the three bones, and forms especially strong ligaments along the inner and outer sides of the joint. Where the bones lock into each other during elbow movements, you have fat pads to cushion the contact, the largest being over the back of the arm-bone where the ulna fits into it. Your elbow flexor muscles lie over the front of the joint: you can feel the biceps tendon when you bend the joint. On the inner side, the common flexor tendon is attached to the tip of the arm-bone. The common extensor tendon forms the bulky part on the outer edge of your elbow. At the back of the joint, you can feel the triceps tendon which attaches to the top of your ulna, and stands out when you straighten the joint.

FUNCTIONS

Your elbow is a hinge joint, so it simply bends and straightens. When you twist your arm, the movement happens in your shoulder and the joints linking the forearm bones, called the radio-ulnar joints. Rotating the forearm bones allows you to turn your hand palm downwards (pronation), or to face the palm upwards (supination). Your elbow provides a relatively stable link between your mobile shoulder joint and your adaptable hand.

268

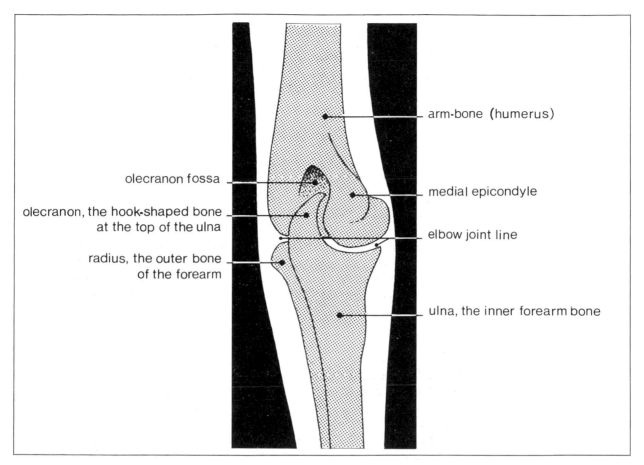

olecranon fossa

olecranon, the hook-shaped bone
at the top of the ulna

radius, the outer bone
of the forearm

arm-bone (humerus)

medial epicondyle

elbow joint line

ulna, the inner forearm bone

*Left elbow, seen from inner
side.*

ELBOW PAIN

The elbow can be affected by inflammatory arthritis, or by pain referred
from a neck problem. You must keep an accurate record of how the pain
started, and whether you noticed any other symptoms, such as pain in
other joints, like your wrists or ankles, or stiffness in your neck. Your
doctor can then decide on appropriate investigations, and treatment if
necessary.

Elbow injuries

TRAUMA

You can injure your elbow by falling on it, wrenching or twisting it.

269

Elbow trauma is a risk in sports like rugby, wrestling and gymnastics. You may notice immediate pain, swelling and bruising, or the signs of damage may come on some time after the injury, causing stiffness and gradually increasing pain which you can relate directly to the injury. You can apply ice to relieve the pain and swelling. You must refer to your doctor or local casualty department for a check, and you should avoid stressing the elbow at all until you have been declared fit. If you force movement in an injured elbow, you risk suffering complications in the joint, which can cause long-term disability. If your elbow is stiff after a traumatic injury, you must regain flexibility and strength gradually, in very easy stages.

INJURY TO THE BACK OF THE ELBOW

You can strain the triceps tendon at the back of the elbow through overuse, for instance if you do too much javelin throwing or tennis serving practice, or through a sudden wrenching injury, if you over-balance while doing a hand-stand, or someone blocks your movement of straightening your elbow.

The tendon strain usually heals quickly if you apply ice to it (p. 15), stretch it passively (p. 261) and avoid doing activities which stress or hurt the tendon. However, a fairly common complication of this problem is inflammation in the fat pad which lies under the tendon. This can happen if you try to continue sport despite the tendon pain. It can come on as the result of impingement of the ulna against the fat pad, if you repeatedly straighten your elbow hard, for instance if you do a long session of javelin throwing, or hand-springs in gymnastics. Once the inflammation has started, you feel pain whenever you straighten out your elbow as far as it will go, as you reproduce the impingement. You must refer to your doctor for specialist advice.

Apart from treatment to reduce the localized inflammation, it may be necessary for you to alter your elbow mechanics through remedial exercises, if your sport involves straightening your elbow hard. One way to reduce the range of straightening movement in your elbow is to shorten the muscles on the front of your arm. You can do this isometrically if you sit at a desk or table with your hand under the desk, and your elbow bent: push your hand against the desk, feeling your biceps tense up for a count of ten before you relax. Dynamically, you can do arm curling exercises with gradually increasing weights, bending your elbow fully, but not allowing it to straighten. If you do a few isometric exercises hourly, and a daily session of dynamic strengthening work for biceps, starting with about ten minutes and building up to half an hour, within six to eight weeks you will find that your elbow straightening movement will be slightly shortened, so that the top of your ulna no longer drives hard into the arm-bone. If you gradually practise the movements of your sport, you should find that this shortening of range prevents a recurrence of the impingement problem, and allows you to go back to your sport.

THE OUTER SIDE OF THE ELBOW: TENNIS ELBOW

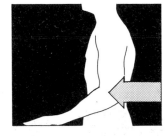

The common extensor tendon on the outer side of the elbow fans out to form the muscles which lie on the back of your forearm and hand, and which straighten your fingers back, and pull your wrist backwards. The common tendon at the elbow can be strained by activities which over-work or over-stretch the forearm muscles, like hard gripping move-ments, or excessive wrist movements. You may grip your racket handle too tightly, or use your wrist incorrectly in certain strokes, especially the backhand. Tennis elbow, or strain of the common extensor tendon, is not confined to tennis players. Other sports, and many everyday activities, can cause it.

What you feel is a gradually increasing pain over your outer elbow, which becomes severe on certain movements which stress the tendon. If the condition is allowed to develop, you may feel pain over the elbow all the time, and you may find undemanding activities like writing difficult. If you press over the tendon, it feels sore.

What you should do is to avoid any painful activities, and refer to your doctor. There are various treatments, and the sooner you receive help, the better. The longer you continue with aggravating activities, the harder the problem becomes to treat.

Self-help measures for tennis elbow

• Apply ice or contrast baths (p. 15) to relieve the soreness and stimulate the circulation in your elbow.
• Try to analyse the cause of the injury. If it was brought on by a particular practice session, take care not to repeat it in future. If you had just bought a new racket, it could be the wrong weight or balance for you. Check for grip sizing by squeezing a narrow object, like a pencil, while you move your wrist backwards and forwards, and then gripping a thick handle. If the narrow or wide grip causes pain over the elbow, you should enlarge or decrease your racket handle, as appropriate. If your racket is head-heavy, you should try out a more lightly balanced one, as a heavy racket head places a drag on your wrist, and can accentuate faulty wrist technique.

271

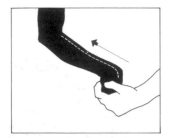

- Stretch your forearm extensor muscles: bend your wrist and fingers with your other hand, bending your elbow slightly at the same time, until you feel the stretch over the back of your forearm. Hold the position for a count of ten. Repeat the exercise frequently each day, especially after you have applied ice over the tendon.
- Avoid stressing the tendon until it is not sore, and your doctor pronounces you fit to resume sport. Re-start very gradually, practising gripping at first, and then playing shadow strokes (without the ball) if you play a racket sport, before you go back to striking the ball and playing a full game. Make sure you warm-up with arm movements and shadow play before you go on court. Stop playing, and apply ice over the tendon, if the pain returns.
- There are splints and forearm bands designed to ease tennis elbow. If you find that one of these helps, it is worth wearing, but you should not try to re-start sport until the tendon pain has eased without a support.
- If your tennis elbow problem persists or recurs severely, you must refer back to your doctor. It may be necessary for you to have surgery to cure the condition, if other treaments have failed.

THE INNER SIDE OF THE ELBOW: GOLFER'S ELBOW

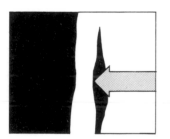

This is a similar problem to tennis elbow, except that the common flexor tendon, on the inside of the elbow, is affected. This tendon fans out over the front of your forearm, forming the muscles which bend your wrist and your fingers.

It is not a problem exclusive to golfers. You can get it by over-straining your wrist, either by bending it repetitively, or twisting it sideways. This may be the result of faulty technique in racket sports, or an unaccustomed activity using your wrist, or an unusually prolonged practice session of a particular stroke or throw.

What you feel is a gradually increasing pain over the inner side of your elbow, related to certain movements at your elbow or wrist. What has happened is that the strain in your forearm muscles has produced a localized strain at the point where the muscles join together into a common tendon which fixes to your arm-bone. Every time you repeat the stress over the tendon by using your forearm muscles, you feel the pain, and the tendon feels tight when you stretch the forearm, and tender if you touch it.

You should refer to your doctor for a check. Once the problem is diagnosed, it is not usually necessary to treat it specifically, as it is rarely as severe or persistent as tennis elbow.

272

Self-help measures for golfer's elbow

- Apply ice (p. 15) over the tendon if it is very sore, once a day.
- Avoid stressing the tendon, and rest from your sport if necessary.
- Stretch the front of the forearm by stretching your arm out in front of you with your elbow straight, palm facing away from you (fingers pointing up or down); with your other hand, pull your fingers backwards until you feel the stretch over the front of your forearm, then hold the position for a count of ten. Repeat the stretching exercise frequently during each day.
- Try to find the cause of the problem, and correct it if it involves a bad training session, faulty technique, or inappropriate equipment.
- Once your elbow is no longer painful, and you can stretch your forearm muscles fully, you should resume your sport gradually, remembering to stretch your forearm before and after each session.

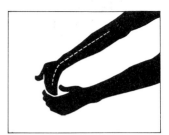

INNER ELBOW STRAIN: THE MEDIAL LIGAMENT

If your sport involves twisting your elbow, or stretching its inner side, you can strain the medial ligament, which binds that side. This can happen in combat sports like wrestling, if your opponent wrenches your elbow. It happens frequently to javelin throwers, especially if you throw incorrectly. The inner elbow can be 'pulled apart' at each throw, straining the ligament.

This causes pain when the ligament is stressed, but you can usually grip strongly and use your wrist without pain. In this it differs from golfer's elbow. You have to rest your elbow from painful activities for at least ten days. Ice applications can relieve any soreness. As the elbow is less sore, when the ligament stops feeling tender to touch, you can start doing gentle strengthening and mobilizing exercises for your arm (p. 258). You must try to analyse the cause of the injury, and correct your technique, if necessary, to avoid a recurrence.

Complications

MYOSITIS OSSIFICANS

If you over-stress your elbow too soon after an injury, there is a risk that you may get new bone formation around the joint. This may happen if you have had severe bruising with internal bleeding, or it may be a reaction to heavy weights exercises, or forced movements over a stiff elbow. To minimize this risk, it is important not to try to speed up

273

recovery from an injury by rubbing the joint hard, or by doing weights exercises or strenuous mobilizing exercises. The correct progression during recovery should not cause any pain over your elbow, and you should regain mobility in the joint in easy stages. On no account should you try to resume a sport which involves loading your elbow before you have fully recovered from an injury, and your specialist declares you fit to resume.

ULNAR NERVE DAMAGE

The ulnar nerve winds round the inner side of your arm-bone at your elbow, and causes the uncomfortable sensations when you hit your 'funny bone'. Certain injuries to the elbow may also damage the nerve, so that you feel sensations of tingling or pain in the path of the nerve down the inner side of your forearm on certain movements. If the problem persists, you must refer back to your doctor, as it may be necessary for you to have surgery to correct any continuing friction over the nerve following your injury.

REFERRED PAIN FROM YOUR NECK

A neck problem can cause referred pain, and simulate the symptoms of injury in your arm, elbow and forearm (p. 244). Sometimes you can have both a referred problem and a localized injury. If your symptoms persist following an arm injury, and you have noticed stiffness or pain in your neck, you should refer back to your doctor, in case you need specific treatment to your neck as well as to your arm.

DISLOCATION OF THE UPPER RADIO-ULNAR JOINT

The two bones which form the lower part of your elbow are linked together by a circular ligament which winds round the top of the radius. A severe injury may make the top of the radius jump out of its retaining band, giving pain just below the elbow, on the outer side of the forearm. Sometimes the problem is repetitive, as the band becomes loosened. This injury tends to happen to children, especially if they have very mobile elbows, which 'bend backwards'. It may take a violent force to dislodge the radius, perhaps through hand-springs in gymnastics, but if the problem is repetitive, the bone may dislocate with minor strains. You should refer to your doctor for advice, as surgery may be needed to regain stability in the joint. Usually, however, the problem subsides spontaneously, provided you avoid activities which place excessive strain on your elbows and forearms.

The Forearm Muscles

STRUCTURE AND FUNCTIONS

The muscles on the front of the forearm arise in a single tendon from the inner side of the elbow, and fan out across the forearm, into the palm of your hand, ending in your fingers. These are the muscles closest to the skin, and underneath them you have a deeper group of muscles following a similar line along the forearm, into your fingers, but starting just below the elbow.

The front forearm muscles bend your fingers and thumb into your palm, bend your wrist, and help to move your wrist sideways in either direction. As you do these movements, you can see the tendons standing out on the front of your wrist, and you can feel the muscles working, if you put your other hand over the upper part of your forearm. The muscles also turn your forearm to face your palm downwards.

The muscles on the back of your forearm act to extend the wrist and fingers backwards, straightening the fingers. The main muscle group starts in a tendon, called the common extensor tendon, on the outer side of your elbow. It forms the fleshy bulge over your elbow. When you straighten your fingers and draw your wrist backwards, you can see the extensor tendons standing out on the back of your hand, and the muscles working on the back of your forearm. These muscles also work to hold your wrist stable when you grip, so if you clench your fist, you see the extensor muscles working on the back of your forearm. The extensor tendons which lie to the sides of your forearm also help to bend your wrist sideways. If you hold your hand straight out, and put your other hand round your wrist, you can feel the tendons working when you move your hand in a 'karate chop' movement.

FOREARM PAIN

This can be due to referred symptoms from a neck problem, or referred pain following an elbow injury.

Forearm injuries

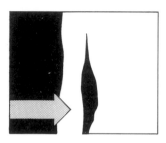

TENDON STRAINS

Overuse, over-stretching, and faulty techniques can contribute to forearm tendon strains. You feel a sudden or gradual pain in the injured muscle or tendon, which then hurts whenever you use it or stretch it, and which is sore if you press it.

Strains to the front of the forearm are treated in the same way as 'golfer's elbow' (p. 272), while the back of the forearm follows the pattern of 'tennis elbow' (p. 271). You must avoid painful activities. If the strain does not show any improvement within a few days, you must check back with your doctor, in case there is some underlying complication.

TENOSYNOVITIS

Where the forearm tendons pass close to your wrist, they are protected by synovial sheaths, or fluid-filled envelopes, which help the tendons to move freely under the bindings which keep them close to your wrist. The synovial coverings extend into your palm and fingers, but they only cover your wrist on the back: this is why the tendons on the back of your hand are so much more prominent.

With overuse, either due to repetitive wrist movements, or to hard gripping, the sheaths can become inflamed over the front or back of your wrist. Racket games players may suffer due to a change of technique involving more wrist movement, or a change of racket with a smaller or larger handle. Oarsmen can get the condition over the wrist of their turning hand, perhaps because they are doing longer outings, or have changed to a blade with a bigger or smaller handle than normal.

What you feel is pain when you use or stretch the injured area. Tenosynovitis may coincide with a strain of the tendon inside the sheath. What makes it different from a tendon strain is that you can see a defined area of swelling over the sheath, following the line of the tendon, and when you move your wrist the sheath makes a crackling noise, called crepitus. If you put your hand over the sheath as you move your wrist, you feel a grating sensation.

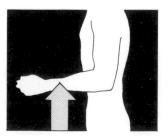

You have to rest your wrist when you have tenosynovitis over any of its tendons. Your doctor may give you a splint, to hold your wrist still while allowing a limited amount of finger movement. If it is very sore, ice applications can help bring relief (p. 15). You must avoid any movements which cause pain, for at least two or three weeks. While you are resting, you should try to analyse the cause of the problem. If you are aware of changing your technique, you must try to modify it again. If your wrist has hurt noticeably more on gripping wide objects than narrow, or vice versa, you must make sure that you adjust the handle you have to grasp in your sport to the appropriate size, when you make your gradual return to sport. Once you no longer feel the pain and grating over the tendon, you can resume your sport in easy stages, provided you remove the cause of the problem.

If the condition does not settle within three weeks, despite rest, you must refer back to your doctor. For a severe tenosynovitis, it may be necessary to have an operation to release the inflamed tissue. Your doctor has to define whether this is necessary, or whether you have some complication underlying your continuing pain.

The Wrist Joint

Eight small carpal bones lie between the longer bones of the palm of your hand (metacarpals) and the lower ends of your radius and ulna. The wrist is therefore a complex of tiny joints. Each bone is joined on to the next by a capsule and ligaments, although the ligaments on the front (palm side) of the wrist are much stronger than on the back. The end of your radius links directly with the carpal bones in a fluid-filled joint, but your ulna is separated from the carpals by a disc made of fibrocartilage.

If you hold your hand up in front of you, you can feel and see the pointed end of your ulna on the back of the inner (little finger) side of your wrist. Just above that, towards your hand, on the front of your wrist you can feel a prominent tiny bone, your pisiform. On the thumb side of your wrist you can feel the pointed styloid process on the end of your radius, just under the tendon which lies along the side of your thumb base.

FUNCTIONS

You can bend your wrist forward, flexing it, when you bend your hand towards your forearm. You can bend it backwards, into extension. It bends sideways in each direction, although there is more movement in the direction of the little finger than towards the thumb side. By combining all these movements, you can circle your wrist.

Your wrist co-ordinates with your hand, forearm and elbow movements. When you grip an object in your hand, your grip loosens when you bend your wrist forwards. This is why cocking the wrist is so important in most racket sports, and why excessive forward-backward wrist movement is inefficient technique. Ball handling games like volleyball and basketball can involve powerful thrusting movements through your wrists. Archery and fencing require good co-ordination through your shoulder, elbow, wrist and hand.

WRIST PAIN

Inflammatory joint disease, which may spread to involve many of your

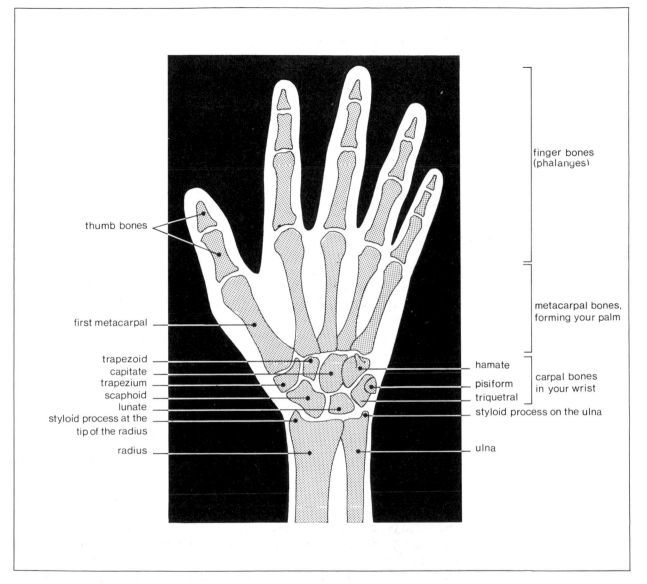

finger bones
(phalanges)

metacarpal bones,
forming your palm

carpal bones
in your wrist

thumb bones

first metacarpal

trapezoid
capitate
trapezium
scaphoid
lunate
styloid process at the
tip of the radius
radius

hamate
pisiform
triquetral
styloid process on the ulna

ulna

joints, often shows up first as unexplained pain and swelling in your wrists. A neck problem can cause referred pain in your wrist, although you are likely to feel pain in your forearm or arm as well. You must try to record how your pain started, any other apparently unrelated pains you may have noticed, and any problems with your general health, to help your doctor make an accurate diagnosis of your problem.

Wrist and hand bones, left hand, seen from palm.

279

THE GANGLION

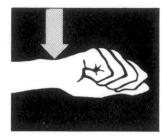

A ganglion is a well-defined, fluid-filled swelling, which can rise out of the synovial sheath protecting a tendon, or from the synovial tissue over a joint. When it happens on the back of the wrist, you see a round, soft, egg-like protrusion on the back of the joint. It does not necessarily cause pain, although it may limit full movement in the joint, because you can no longer stretch the back of the wrist fully. Sometimes it can cause quite severe pain when you use your wrist.

The ganglion may be caused by an injury to the tendons on the back of the wrist, or a sprain to the joint itself. It happens most commonly on the back of the joint, but can happen over the front. Sometimes, the ganglion appears without any obvious reason, or it may be associated with simple overuse, from an unaccustomed activity involving wrist movements.

If the ganglion causes problems, you must refer to your doctor, so that he can check whether it is a simple ganglion, or something more serious, like a tumour. If the ganglion does not hurt or limit your activities, there is no need to have treatment for it. If treatment is needed, the usual course is to remove the ganglion surgically, and then immobilize the wrist in a splint or plaster cast for about three weeks, before you gradually resume your normal activities. The ganglion does tend to recur, but this may be prevented if you take care not to stress your wrist until it has recovered fully from the surgery.

Wrist injuries

SPRAIN

You can injure your wrist by falling on it, or landing on your hand, wrenching the joint. An unexpected movement, like late release when throwing the javelin, or a bad mis-hit in a racket sport, can jar your wrist. Cumulative stress can cause a more gradual strain in the joint, for instance when you do repetitive practice of a particular stroke in a racket game, when the stroke is newly learned, or your technique is faulty.

What you feel is pain in your wrist, which may hurt on all wrist movements, or only on movements in a certain direction. You may be able to find a tender spot by pressing over your wrist. What happens in a sprain is that you injure a ligament, or several ligaments, within the wrist. You may also strain one or more of the tendons lying close to the joint. There may be visible swelling or bruising if the joint capsule is damaged.

What you should do in the first instance is to apply ice over the painful area, or do contrast baths to stimulate the circulation (p. 15). If the injury is at all severe, you must check with your doctor or local casualty department, in case you have fractured one of the wrist bones. You must then rest the injured wrist from any painful activities, until it is fully healed. You may have to wear a wrist support, splint, or even a plaster cast to ensure that you do not risk straining the joint while it is healing. You must not take risks by 'trying out' the joint, before it has healed. The only way you can check whether the injury has healed is to note which movements cause pain when you first notice the injury, and if there are any tender spots. When you have rested the wrist for the time your doctor has recommended, which may range from ten days to three weeks or longer, you can check whether those same movements still cause pain, and whether the tender spots are still sore to press. If those pains have gone, you can start exercising your wrist gradually until you can move it and use it without pain, and then you can start practising the movements needed for your sport, until you are confident you can do them without any inhibition. If you find, on testing, that your wrist still hurts on certain movements, you must continue to rest it, and check back with your doctor in case there is some complication.

Wrist and hand exercises are listed on p. 286.

Complications

HIDDEN FRACTURE

A fracture in a wrist bone may be missed when the doctor first examines your wrist, as the bones are small but thick, so that X-rays do not always pick up the line of the crack. The scaphoid bone under the base of your thumb is a common place to have one of these 'hidden' fractures, but they can happen in the other bones. If you have had a severe traumatic injury to your wrist, like a direct blow, fall, or jarring force, and you have long-lasting pain in the joint, you must check with your doctor, in case you need to be referred to an orthopaedic specialist for diagnosis and treatment.

NERVE COMPRESSION

The nerves which supply sensation and motor impulses into your hand are bound down by retaining bands where they cross the front of your wrist into your hand. They are held particularly tightly just beyond the crease that separates your wrist from your hand, where there is a dip

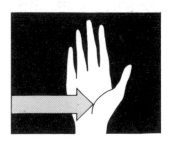

281

between the raised parts of your palm at the bases of your thumb and your little finger.

If this area is subjected to constant or deep pressure, you may damage the conductivity of the nerve crossing the wrist. This can happen if you grip hard against the handlebars of your bicycle, or if you do long sessions balancing on your hands on the parallel bars in gymnastics. Your racket handle can rub against the palm of your hand, especially if the butt end is enlarged. Sometimes the problem arises after you have injured the front of your wrist, by straining the tendons, or bruising the area in a fall. Then the injured tissues may swell, causing congestion in the part of the palm bound down in its retaining ligament, and the nerves may be affected. When this problem happens to the nerve which crosses the centre of your wrist, it is called the 'carpal tunnel syndrome', because the retaining band forms a kind of tunnel through which the nerve passes. The problem can also happen in other parts of your palm, for instance under the fleshy pad which leads to your little finger.

What you feel is numbness or tingling, which you may experience while you are doing the activity causing the nerve compression, or which may come on slowly afterwards. In the carpal tunnel syndrome, the tingling spreads up the outer side of your palm, into the middle and index fingers, and sometimes into your thumb. If the nerve on the outer part of your palm is affected, you usually feel the sensation changes spreading up your palm into your little and ring fingers.

What you must do is to stop your activity as soon as you notice the symptoms. Apply ice (p. 15) to reduce the soreness and any swelling. To check whether you have a nerve compression syndrome, you can press hard over the palm of your hand with your other thumb. When you touch the relevant area, you will re-create the tingling or numbness that you noticed previously. Apart from this test, you should avoid any movements or activities which reproduce the symptoms. If the problem is severe, so that you notice pain or tingling in your palm even when you are not using your hand, you must check with your doctor, who may refer you to an orthopaedic specialist. For yourself, you must try to analyse the cause of the problem. Check the implements you have been using. If you can see that they rub your hand, because they are too wide or too narrow, try to adjust them accordingly. If you are aware of having done too much of an activity involving gripping, make sure you do not repeat the mistake.

You should not resume your sport until your doctor allows, and you are quite sure that you can no longer reproduce your symptoms when you press into your palm. Start gradually, and if you notice any recurrence, check your equipment again, and rest until you have fully recovered.

The Hand

Your hand consist of five metacarpal bones, which form your palm and the base part of your thumb, and which form joints with your upper four wrist bones and with your finger bones. Your knuckles are the rounded ends of the metacarpal bones. Your thumb has only two bones over its metacarpal, while your other fingers each have three.

Your metacarpals are not strongly bound to each other, although they are linked by ligaments and small muscles lying between the bones. If you hold the knuckle of your little finger, you can rock it backwards and forwards freely, independently of the ring finger bones next to it. The joints between the metacarpals and the wrist and finger bones are much firmer within their binding capsules and ligaments.

FUNCTIONS

The thumb has a special function in your hand, because it can swing right across your palm, owing to the structure of the joint between its metacarpal bone and the trapezium bone in the wrist. This is what allows you to grip objects. By contrast, there is very little movement between your wrist bones and the other four metacarpals. These joints simply contribute to the overall movements in your wrist, and you cannot create movement in them at will.

Your thumb bones bend and straighten. However, you can bend and straighten your fingers at their joints with their metacarpals, as well as bending them to either side, and circling them. In the joints between the finger bones themselves, you can simply bend and straighten. The combination of movements in these complex joints in your hand make it possible for you to cup your hands to catch a ball; grip with your fingers; enclose objects within your whole hand; punch, grasp, or thrust away an opponent in combat sports; perform fine movements like writing, sewing, or moving chessmen; and balance on your hands in gymnastics, on the floor or on apparatus.

HAND PAIN

Inflammatory arthritic conditions can cause unexplained pain in your

283

hands. Pain can be referred from a neck problem, although you normally feel some pain down your arm as well as in your hand. Occasionally, a circulatory problem can cause pain in your hand. You should try to record how your pain started, whether it hurts only on certain movements, and whether you have had any other pains or symptoms, to help your doctor make an accurate diagnosis of your problem.

Hand injuries

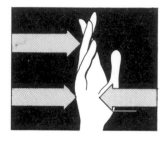

You can injure your hands by a direct blow or force. In boxing, you can damage your knuckles in hard punching if your technique is bad, or your hand taping faulty. A poor entry into the water in high diving can badly jar your hands. The butt end of your racket can drive into your palm if you jar your racket against the wall in squash.

Your hands can also be injured by wrenching or twisting forces. This can happen in combat sports like wrestling or judo. Your stick may be twisted in your hand by a tackle in hockey. You may miss your hold on the bars in gymnastics. You can catch your fingers over the end of the blade handle when your rowing or sculling boat lurches.

The damage done ranges from a fracture of one or more of the bones in your palm or fingers, to complete dislocation of one or more of the hand joints, to rupture in a tendon, to more minor strains of the hand ligaments or tendons. Correct diagnosis is essential to correct treatment of the hand, so you must refer to your doctor or casualty department as quickly as possible. It may be obvious that the injury is severe. Swelling and soreness when you touch your hand may indicate that a bone is broken. A dislocated joint may remain out of shape. A rupture in an extensor tendon on the back of one of your fingers may leave you with a 'mallet finger', in which you cannot straighten the tip of the finger. When a flexor tendon is ruptured, on the front of a finger, you can no longer bend the finger properly, especially at its tip. However, the initial injury may not seem that bad, so that the more severe damage only shows up later on, when it delays your recovery by giving you continuing problems with pain and loss of function. If you are in any doubt about a hand injury, you should refer back to your doctor, in case you need to be referred to an orthopaedic specialist.

Self-help measures for hand injuries

• First-aid at the moment of injury consists of applying ice over your

284

hand, or dipping it in a bowl of iced water (p. 15). If it is very painful, you should support your wrist and fingers in cotton wool covered by a crepe bandage (p. 11) taking care not to wrench your hand. You should then support your arm in a sling, with the hand up (p. 12) if it is very swollen. You must see your doctor or go to the casualty department immediately, to check the extent of the damage, and to have appropriate treatment.

- While you are recovering from the injury, you must not do any painful movements with your hand. This may mean that you cannot swim for fitness training, although you can do circuit exercises or ride a static bicycle without using the injured hand. You must make sure you move your elbow and shoulder actively as much as possible, especially if your hand is to be held still in a cast for any length of time. Secondary stiffness in the rest of your arm is avoidable, and it will delay your recovery, if you allow it to happen.
- Control any swelling by keeping your hand up as much as possible, bending your elbow to keep the hand at shoulder height, if you do not wear a sling for support. If you have a removable splint, apply ice each day, or do contrast baths, to stimulate the circulation and reduce the swelling.
- Once your hand has recovered sufficiently, and your doctor allows you to move it, you should start doing the simple hand and wrist exercises (p. 286). Gradually you should progress to using your hand more, and then trying the more demanding functional exercises (p. 288). Do not do any exercises which cause pain. Start with a few at a time, and gradually increase the number you do.
- Before resuming your sport, make sure you are properly prepared. If you box, check that you know how to tape your hands correctly, to protect the joints from stress as you punch. If you have calloused hands from gymnastics or rowing, pare down the hard skin with a skin-scraper. You can remove some of the excess skin with a proprietary skin-removing lotion. If the skin is broken, keep the wound clean, and protect it with sterile dressings. Try to keep your skin pliable and soft with a daily application of hand cream.
- If your sport involves implements, make sure that the handle is the right size for your hand, and covered in an appropriate binding, giving the right amount of grip, without friction. In racket sports, you should be able to spread your fingers comfortably along the racket handle, with about one finger's width between your thumb and fingers. Your fingers should not touch each other, nor should they reach your thumb, but equally they should not be spread uncomfortably apart by too wide a grip.

285

- If your sport involves powerful hand movements, like rock climbing, you must make sure you have regained full mobility and power to the necessary level, before you re-start your sport. Otherwise, you are safe to start your sport gradually as soon as your hand is no longer painful, tender or swollen, and you have regained good, normal function in it.

Wrist and hand exercises

MOBILIZING AND STRENGTHENING EXERCISES

1. With your hands flat on a table, palms down, spread your fingers out sideways, then bring them together again, keeping your fingers in contact with the table, and trying to spread them as far apart as possible. Repeat ten times, three times over.

2. With the backs of your hands resting on a table, wrists level, touch your thumb to the tip of each finger in turn, as quickly as you can. See how many times you can do this without making a mistake and touching the wrong finger tip in the sequence, and try to increase your speed and accuracy.

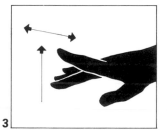

3. With your hands flat on a table, palms down, and your fingers slightly spread, lift each finger in turn, take it to each side three times, then lower, keeping your other fingers as still as possible on the table. Repeat ten times.

4. With your hands in front of you, palms facing each other, and your elbows bent to a right angle, clench your fists as tight as you can for a count of three, then straighten your fingers and stretch them away from you as hard as you can. Repeat ten times, increasing to thirty.

5. Resting your forearms on a table, with your wrists free over the edge, bend and straighten your wrists as far as you can ten times; then bend your wrists from side to side; then rotate your wrists in circles. Keep your fingers relaxed, and keep your forearms in contact with the table.

6. Place two boxes about thirty centimetres apart, with small objects like paper clips, bits of paper, and marbles in one. Using a pair of tweezers, or a pincer paper clip, transfer the small objects into the second box. Start by holding the tweezers between your thumb and forefinger, then thumb and middle finger, thumb and ring finger, and finally thumb and little finger. To make the exercise harder, place the boxes further apart.

7. With your forearm resting on a table, palm upwards, loop a strong elastic band round your thumb and index finger. Extend thumb and finger to stretch the band to the limit, ten times, building up to twenty. Repeat between the thumb and each of the other fingers in turn, then repeat the exercise with your other hand.

8. With your hand facing upwards, forearm on the table, loop the elastic bands over the front of each finger in turn, holding the other end in your other hand, or fixing it to a hook or fixture. Bend your finger to stretch the elastic band to its limit, starting with ten, building up to twenty times.

9. Put the palms of your hands together, with your fingers pointing upwards. Keeping your fingers together, gently press your wrists downwards, until you feel the stretch over the front of your wrists. Hold the position for a count of ten, and repeat the exercise three times.

10. Practise squeezing a squash ball as hard as you can, then stretching your fingers. Then squeeze a larger rubber ball for wide grip, stretching afterwards.

11. Gripping first the squash ball, then the larger one, practise moving your wrists around, bending, straightening and circling, while you grip as hard as you can. Try holding the grip for ten seconds at first, and increase the time.

12. With your forearms resting on a table, and your wrists free over the edge, holding a light weight in your hands, lift your hands upwards as far as you can, keeping your forearms still, hold for a count of three, then lower. Build up to three sets of ten, then increase the weights.

13. Repeat (12), but turning your hands from side to side.

14. Attach a weight on a rope to the centre of a bar of wood, about thirty centimetres long. With your hands at each end of the bar, palms facing down, turn your wrists alternately to wind the rope around the bar and raise the weight of the bar. Then unwind by twisting your wrists in the opposite direction.

15. Repeat (14), with our palms upwards on the bar. Repeat the movement three times, building up to twenty.

287

1. Throw and catch a ball against a wall or to a partner, throwing across a short distance, and gradually moving further away. Use a small ball, then a large one, then progress to using a heavier ball. Throw with both hands, then each in turn.

2. Throw a ball or object sideways, against a wall or to a partner, then backwards, using overarm and underarm throws.

3. Using an old racket or rounded stick about four centimetres in diameter, hit a ball against a wall from a distance of about six metres. Use as heavy a ball as will still bounce on the ground, and gradually increase your distance from the wall.

4. Using a normal squash or tennis racket, in the squash court or against a wall, starting about three metres from the wall, practise hitting volleys in succession, gradually moving back as you hit each stroke, and starting from the beginning if you make a mistake. Count how many you can do, and try to increase the number.

5. Kneeling on hands and knees, with your palms flat on the floor, 'walk' your hands around in front of you and to each side, without losing your balance.

6. On your hands and knees, resting on your clenched knuckles, straighten out each leg behind you in turn, keeping your balance, and keeping your fists still. Start by holding the position for fifteen seconds. Then try to increase the time.

7. Balance your feet up on the edge of a couch or chair, with your body straight, balancing on your hands, palms flat on the floor. Keeping your body straight, 'walk' your hands forwards and to each side as far as you can without losing your balance. Start with fifteen second walks, gradually increasing the time.

8. Balancing on your hands in a handstand, walk around on your hands, starting with a timed walk, and trying to increase your original time.

9. Hook your fingers over the top of a fixed door or a hanging bar (do not grip with your thumb). Hold your balance as long as possible. Then try to pull yourself up, starting with three pulls, gradually increasing the number. If your hands get tired, step down, let them relax downwards, then start again.

10. With your hands hooked over wall-bars or a hanging bar, 'walk' up the wall-bars, or along the hanging bar, using only your hands. Start with a few movements, and gradually increase the number.

Index

ABDOMINAL MUSCLES (stomach muscles), 221–228
structure and functions, 221–223; pain, 223; injury, 224; self-help measures, 225; complications, 226–228
ABDOMINAL EXERCISES
strengthening exercises, 199–200; stretching exercises, 206, nos 1, 3, 5, 7
Abductor muscles (hip), 185–188
Acetabulum (part of hip joint), 168
ACHILLES TENDON
structure and function, 70; injuries, 73–74
Acromio-clavicular joint
structure, 246; injury, 264
ADDUCTOR MUSCLE EXERCISES
stretching exercises, 156; isometric strengthening exercises, 157; strengthening exercises, 158; functional exercises, 159
ADDUCTORS (inner thigh muscles), 150–160
structure and functions, 150–152; pain, 152; injuries, 152–154; self-help measures, 154–156; exercises, 156–160; complications, 160
Alternative training, 8
ANKLE, 35–49
structure and functions, 35–36; pain and swelling, 37; injuries, 37–40; self-help first-aid measures, 40–41; phasing your recovery, 41–43; exercises, 44–47; complications, 47
ANKLE EXERCISES
balance exercises, 44; isometric exercises, 45; dynamic exercises, 46
ANKLE INJURIES
inversion strain, 37; eversion strain, 39; dorsiflexion strain, 40; plantarflexion strain, 40
Ankle sprain, 37–40
Ankylosing spondylitis
inflammatory joint disease, 180; foot pain as symptom, 22

Anterior tibial muscles (shin muscles)
structure, 52; injuries, 57–60
Appendicitis, cause of stomach pain, 223
Arches (in the foot), 20
ARM MUSCLES
front arm muscles, 265–266; back arm muscles, 266–267
Arnica, 16
Arthritis
see osteoarthritis
Arthroscopy, 103, 109, 120
Avulsion fracture
of fibular malleolus in ankle, 38; fifth metatarsal base in foot, 39; tibial tubercle, 68; pelvic bone, 135; seat-bone, 149; pubic bone, 160; lesser trochanter on thigh-bone, 167; pelvic bones, iliac crests, 226

BACK, see spine, lumbar, thoracic, cervical
BACK ARM MUSCLES
structure and functions, 266–267; pain, 267; injuries, 267; self-help measures, 267
Back exercises
see Trunk exercises, 196–206
Balance exercises, for ankle, 44
Balance mechanisms, 37
Bandages, 10–12
Beer gut, effect on posture, 177
Biceps brachii (muscle on the front of the arm), 265–266
Biceps tendon, injury, 252–253
Big toe
structure, 20; injuries, 26–27
Bio-mechanics (foot movement patterns)
relating to foot problems, 30; relating to shin problems, 54, 59, 62
Black toe-nails, 28
Bladder problems, cause of groin pain, 178
Blisters
treatment, 17; in the foot, 29
Blood bruise (haematoma), over shin-bone, 63

Blood tests, 4
Bone scan, 4
for tibial stress fracture, 65
Bone tumour, 52, 129, 139
Bony outgrowth (exostosis), complication in ankle injury, 49
Brachialis (muscle on the front of the arm), 265
Brain damage, 9
Breathing
part played by abdominal muscles in, 222; problems following rib injuries, 236; breathing exercises, 236
Bruising, 14, 16
Bunion (hallux valgus), 27
Burn, 17
ice burn, 15
Bursitis
in the heel, 24; over the knee-cap, 95; under the iliotibial tract, 104; popliteal bursitis, 107; under hamstring tendons, 149; under hip flexor tendons, 165; round the hip, 170; round the shoulder, 253

CALF (and Achilles tendon), 70–79
structure and functions, 70; pain, 70; varicose veins, 72; injuries, 73–75; self-help measures, 75–76; exercises, 77–79; complication, 79
CALF EXERCISES
stretching, 77; strengthening, 78; dynamic, 78–79
CALF INJURIES
Achilles tendon, at insertion onto heel-bone and just above heel-bone, 73; Achilles tendon rupture, 74; partial rupture, 75; gastrocnemius tendon injury, 75
Cardiac resuscitation, 8–10
Carpal bones (wrist bones), 278
Carpal tunnel syndrome (nerve pressure in the wrist), 281
Cartilages (menisci)
buffers in the knee, 81; injury to, in the knee, 108

Cervical spine, *see* neck, 238–245
'Charley-horse' (injury to thigh muscles), 129
Chartered physiotherapists, 4
Chest muscle exercises
  stretching exercises, 233; isometric strengthening exercises, 233; dynamic strengthening exercises, 233–234
CHEST MUSCLES (pectorals), 229–234
  structure and functions, 229; pain, 229; injury, 231; self-help measures, 232; exercises, 233–234
Chondromalacia patellae, 91
'Cinema Sign', 91
Circuit exercises, 8
Circulation, check in bandaging, 11
Circulatory problems
  in the calf, 70; thigh, 129; hamstrings, 139
Circumduction (shoulder movement), 248
Clarke's sign, 93
Clavicle (collar-bone), 246
'Clicking'
  in the ankle, 48; hip, 171
Collar-bone (clavicle), 246
Common flexor tendon (in the elbow)
  structure, 268; injury: 'golfer's elbow', 272
Compartment syndrome
  in anterior tibial muscles, 59; posterior tibial muscles, 62
Contrast baths (hot-and-cold treatments), 15
Cramp, 6
  in the calf, 72, 76
Creams, for massage and first-aid, 16
Cruciate ligaments (knee)
  structure, 82; injury, 119
Crutches, 13
Cryotherapy (ice applications), 15
Cysts, *see* bursitis

Death in sport, 8–10
Dehydration, 6
Deltoid (arm muscle), 248
Diaphragm (breathing muscle)
  as cause of pain, 239, 250; structure, 235
Diet, 6
Discs, intervertebral (spinal discs)
  structure, 190; damage to, 194, 207; prolapse, 208
Dislocation
  knee-cap, 97; shoulder, 254–255;

radio-ulnar joint, 274
Dizziness (in neck problems), 240
Dorsiflexion
  ankle movement, 36; ankle injury, 40
Double-leg-raising exercise, dangers of, 162–164
Dressings, for wounds, 16–18
DYNAMIC and FUNCTIONAL EXERCISES, 7
  for the ankle, 46; calf, 78; knee, 118, 124; hamstrings, 147; front-thigh muscles, 118; adductors, 159; hip abductors, 188; chest muscles, 233; neck, 243; shoulder, 262; wrist and hand, 288

ELBOW INJURIES
  trauma, 270; back of the elbow, 270; tennis elbow, 271; inner elbow, 272
ELBOW JOINT, 268–274
  structure and functions, 268; pain, 269; injuries, 270; complications, 273
Elevation, to control swelling, 14
  for the foot, 30; ankle, 41; shin muscles, 59; calf, 75; knee, 85; hand, 285
Epiphysis (damage in knee injury), 103
Epiphysis, slipped (hip condition), 170
Epiphysitis
  in the heel-bone, 25; hip-bone (iliac crest), 227
Eversion
  foot movement, 22; ankle injury, 39–40
Exostosis (bony outgrowth), complication of ankle injury, 49
Extrinsic injuries, 4

Fatigue, 5
Femur (thigh-bone)
  structure, 80, 126, 136, 150, 161, 168
Fibula (outer leg bone)
  structure, 35, 50; injuries, 38–40, 54–57
First-aid kit, 18
Fluid intake, 6
FOOT, 20–34
  structure and function, 20–22; pain (causes), 22; injuries, 22–30; self-help measures for foot injuries, 30–31; foot exercises, 31–34
FOOT EXERCISES, 31–34
  strengthening the small foot muscles, 31–32; strengthening and

mobilizing exercises, 33; stretching exercises, 34
FOOT INJURIES
  ligament strains, 22–23; stress fractures, 23–24; heel bruise, 24; bursitis, 24; heel spur, 25; epiphysitis of heel-bone, 25; plantar fasciitis, 25; 'spring' ligament strain, 26; metatarsalgia, 26; sesamoiditis, 26; hallux rigidus, 27; bunion, 27; hammer toes, 28; tenosynovitis, 28; black toe-nails, 28; skin conditions, 29
FOREARM INJURIES
  tendon strains, 276; tenosynovitis, 276
FOREARM MUSCLES, 275–277
  structure and functions, 275; pain, 275; injuries, 276
FRONT ARM MUSCLES
  structure and functions, 265; pain, 265; injuries, 265; self-help measures, 266
FRONT-OF-THE-THIGH MUSCLES, 126–135
  structure and functions, 126–128; pain, 128; injuries, 129; self-help measures, 132; stretching exercises, 133; complications, 134
Functional exercises, 7
  see also dynamic exercises

Ganglion, in the wrist, 280
Gastrocnemius (calf muscle)
  structure, 70; tendon injury, 75
Glands (lymph), 14
  cause of groin pain, 152
Glutei (seat muscles)
  structure, 136, 185; action on hip, 168
Gluteus maximus (seat muscle)
  structure, 136, 104
Gluteus medius (hip abductor muscle), 185
'Golfer's elbow' (injury to the common flexor tendon), 272
Gravity, force of, influence on swelling, 14
Grip
  in racket sports, 271, 276, 285
GROIN
  pain, 152, 163, 178; friction injury, 180; *see also* adductor muscles
Gynaecology, problems causing stomach pain, 223

Haematoma (blood bruise), over shin-bone, 63

Hallux rigidus (big toe stiffness), 27
Hallux valgus (bunion), 27
Hammer toes, 28
HAMSTRINGS, 136–149
    structure and functions, 80, 136–139,
        168; pain at the back of the thigh,
        139; injuries, 139–141; self-help
        measures, 142; hamstring exercises,
        144–149; complications, 149
HAMSTRING EXERCISES
    in cruciate ligament tears, 121–124;
        stretching exercises, 144; isometric
        strengthening exercises, 145;
        dynamic strengthening exercises,
        147; functional exercises, 148
HAND
    structure and functions, 283; injuries,
        284; self-help measures, 285;
        exercises, 286
HAND EXERCISES (and wrist)
    mobilizing and strengthening
        exercises, 286; advanced dynamic
        exercises, 288
Hard skin
    on feet, 29; on hands, 285
Head injury, 9
Headaches, in neck problems, 244
Heart conditions
    cause of chest pain, 229, 235; cause of
        shoulder pain, 229, 250
Heart stoppage, 9
Heat applications, 16
Heel bruise, 24
Heel spur, 25
Heel-tabs, 74
Heparinoid cream, 16
Hernia, abdomen, 227
    from straight-leg-raising exercises,
        162; inguinal h., 163
High-heeled shoes, effect on posture, 177
HIP ABDUCTORS (side of seat muscles),
    185–188
    structure and functions, 168, 185;
        injury, 186; exercises, 187;
        complications, 188
HIP ABDUCTOR EXERCISES
    stretching exercises, 187;
        strengthening exercises, 187;
        dynamic exercises, 188
Hip-bone (ilium), 168, 176
HIP EXERCISES
    mobilizing exercises, 173;
        strengthening exercises, 174;
        stretching exercises, see thigh
        muscle; groups and back extensor
        stretches, 173

HIP FLEXORS (muscles at top of thigh),
    161–167
    structure and functions, 161–164,
        168; pain in the groin, 163; injuries,
        164; self-help measures, 165;
        complications, 167
HIP FLEXOR stretching exercise, 166
HIP INJURIES
    Perthes' disease, 170; slipped
        epiphysis, 170; bursitis, 170;
        'snapping' hip, 171; osteoarthritis,
        171
HIP JOINT, 168–175
    structure and functions, 168–169;
        pain, 169; injuries, 170–172;
        exercises, 173–175
'Housemaid's knee', 95

Ice applications (cryotherapy), 15
Iliacus (hip flexor muscle), 161
Iliopsoas (top-of-the-thigh muscles),
    161
Iliotibial tract (band)
    structure, 82, 126; injury, 104
Ilium (hip-bone), 168, 176
Illness, 5
Immobilization: support for injuries, 10
Infections
    viral, 9; in skin wounds, 17; foot, 29
Inflammatory joint disease, as cause of
    pain, 5
Inflatable splints, 10
Inguinal hernia, 163
Inner thigh muscles (adductors),
    150–160
Insoles and inserts for shoes, 30
Intermittent claudication, cause of calf
    pain, 72
Interval training, 8
Intrinsic injuries, 4
Inversion
    foot movement, 22; ankle injury,
        37–39
ISOMETRIC EXERCISES
    for the ankle, 45; knee, 112, 122;
        hamstrings, 122, 145; front-thigh
        muscles, 112; adductors, 157; chest
        muscles, 233; neck, 241; shoulder,
        256; front-arm muscles (biceps),
        270

'Jumper's knee' (patellar tendon strain),
    87

KNEE, 80–125
    structure and functions, 80–84; pain,

84; swelling, 84; first-aid for the
        swollen knee, 85; injuries, 86–124;
        complications, 124–125
KNEE EXERCISES
    straight-leg exercises, 112; mobilizing
        exercises to bend the knee, 113;
        strengthening exercises, 116;
        dynamic exercises, 118; cruciate
        tear instability exercises, 121–124
KNEE INJURIES
    pain at the front of the knee, 87–100;
        pain on the inner side of the knee,
        100–103; pain on the outer side of
        the knee, 103–107; pain at the back
        of the knee, 107; damage inside the
        knee, 108–125
Knee-cap (patella)
    structure, 80; knee-cap pain, 91;
        knee-cap dislocation, 97

Laminectomy (back operation), 208
Lateral ligament (ankle)
    structure, 35; injuries, 37
Lateral ligament (knee)
    structure, 82; injury, 103
Ligament strains
    foot, 22; ankle, 37, 47; knee, 100, 103,
        119; elbow, 273; wrist, 280
Linea Alba, 221
Liver problems
    cause of stomach pain, 223; cause of
        chest pain, 229
'Locking'
    in the ankle, 48; in the knee, 109
'Loose bodies'
    in the ankle, 48; in the knee, 124
Low back pain, see lumbar spine,
    189–212
LUMBAR SPINE (lower spine), 189–212
    effect of straight-leg-raising on, 162;
        structure and functions, 189–192;
        pain, 192; injuries, 192–195;
        self-help measures, 195; trunk
        exercises, 196–206; complications,
        207–212
LUMBAR SPINE INJURIES
    causes, 192; what you feel, 193; what
        has happened, 194; self-help
        measures, 195
Lymph glands, 14
    cause of groin pain, 152

Malleoli
    structure, 35; injuries, 38–39
'Mallet finger', 284
'March fracture', 23

Massage, 16
Medial ligament (ankle)
    structure, 35; injuries, 39, 40
Medial ligament (elbow)
    injury, 273
Medial ligament (knee)
    structure, 82; injury, 100
Menisci (cartilages)
    buffers in the knee, 81; injury to, in
    the knee, 108
Menstruation, effect on pelvic joints,
    181
Metacarpal bones (hand), 278, 283
Metatarsalgia, 26
MOBILIZING EXERCISES, 7
    for the foot, 33; ankle, 46; knee, 113;
    hip, 173; spine, 202; neck, 242;
    shoulder, 260; wrist and hand, 286
Morton's foot, 20, 23
Mouth-to-mouth or to-nose
    resuscitation, 8
'Muscle pump', 72
Muscular spasm, see Spasm over stress
    fractures
Myositis ossificans
    in thigh muscles, 134; at the elbow,
    273

Navel (umbilicus), 221
NECK (cervical spine), 238–245
    structure and functions, 238; pain,
    239; injuries, 239–241; exercises,
    241–244; complications, 244–245
NECK EXERCISES
    isometric strengthening exercises,
    241–242; mobilizing exercises,
    242–243; dynamic strengthening
    exercises, 243; demanding
    strengthening exercises, 244
Nerve pressure, 281

Oblique stomach muscles, 221
Orthopaedic surgery, see surgery
Osgood-Schlatter's disease, 68
Osteitis pubis (groin injury), 179
OSTEOARTHRITIS
    in ankle, 49; knee-cap joint, 91; knee
    joint, 124; hip joint, 171; lumbar
    spine, 211; neck, 245
Osteoarthrosis, see osteoarthritis
Osteochondral fracture (complication of
    ankle injury), 48
Osteochondritis (in the knee-cap), 90
Osteophytes (in spinal osteoarthritis),
    211
Overuse injuries, 4

Pain, as a warning, 5–6
Paralysis, danger in spinal injuries, 10,
    195, 239
Patella (knee-cap)
    structure, 80; injury, 91, 97
PATELLAR TENDON
    structure and functions, 67, 82, 98,
    126; injury, 87–90; 'Q' angle, 98
PECTORAL EXERCISES
    stretching exercises, 233; isometric
    strengthening exercises, 233;
    dynamic strengthening exercises,
    233–234
Pectoral muscles, see chest muscles,
    229–234
Pellegrini-Stieda's disease, 102
PELVIS, 176–183
    structure and functions, 176–178;
    pelvic problems, 178–183;
    complication, 'short leg syndrome',
    183
Peronei (shin muscles), injuries, 56
Perthes' Disease, 170
Physiotherapist, chartered, 4
Plantar fasciitis
    in ankylosing spondylitis, 22; foot
    injury, 25
Plantarflexion
    ankle movement, 36; ankle injury, 40
Plaster-of-Paris cast, 12
Pleurisy, cause of chest pain, 216
Podiatrist
    helping foot problems, 18, 30; for
    shin problems, 54, 59, 62; for knee
    problems, 94, 99, 105
Popliteus (knee muscle), 106
Posture
    hip functions in posture, 169; and the
    pelvis, 177; lumbar spine (lower
    back), 191; thoracic spine, 215;
    stomach muscles, 223; neck, 241
Pregnancy
    effect on posture, 177; on pelvic
    joints, 181
Progression
    in training, 5; in rehabilitation, 7
Pronation
    foot movement, 22; forearm
    movement, 268
Proprioception
    in the foot, 22; in the ankle, 37; in the
    knee, 94
Prostate problems, cause of groin pain,
    178
Protective clothing and equipment, 5
Psoas major (hip flexor muscle), 161

Pubis, see symphysis pubis, 176
Pulse, checking, 9

'Q' angle, formed by patellar tendon,
    98
QUADRICEPS MUSCLE GROUP (thigh
    muscles)
    front-of-thigh muscles, 126–135;
    injuries, 129; function in relation to
    knee, 82–83, 91, 97; isometric
    strengthening exercises, 112;
    strengthening exercises, 116–117;
    dynamic exercises, 118–119;
    stretching exercises, 133

Racket handle, measuring for size, 285
Racket size, 5
Radio-ulnar joints (in the forearm)
    structure, 268; dislocation of, 274
Radius (forearm bone), 268
Recovery position, 10
Rectus abdominis (stomach muscle), 221
Rectus femoris (thigh muscle), 126
REFERRED PAIN
    from low back, 207; from mid-back,
    217; from neck, 244
Resuscitation, 8
RIB CAGE, 235–237
    structure and functions, 235; pain,
    235; injuries, 236; complications,
    236–237
Ribs
    structure, 214, 235; fracture in chest
    injuries, 232
'Rider's strain', 154
Risks in sport, 5
Rules in sport, 5
'Runner's Knee', see knee-cap pain, 91

SACRO-ILIAC JOINT
    (part of pelvis), 176; pain, 180;
    injuries, 181–182; self-help
    measures, 182
Sacrum (pelvic bone), 176, 190
Saddle friction (groin injury), 180
Safety equipment, 5
Sartorius muscle (part of front-of-thigh
    muscles), 126
Scheuermann's Disease, 220
Sciatic nerve, causing pain at the back of
    the thigh, 139, 207
Sciatica (referred pain), 207
Scoliosis (twisted spine), 178
Serratus anterior (upper back muscle),
    235
Sesamoiditis, 26

Sever's disease, *see* epiphysitis of the heel-bone, 25
SHIN, 50–69
    structure and functions, 50–52; pain, 52; ankle tendon injuries, 52–54; outer leg injuries, 54–57; muscle and tendon injuries around the shin-bone, 57–63; injuries to the shin-bone, 63–69
'Shin soreness', 57
'Shin splints', 57
Shoes, 5, 22, 27, 28, 29, 74, 177
'Short-leg syndrome', 183
Shoulder blades, 214, 246
SHOULDER EXERCISES
    isometric strengthening exercises, 256–257; strengthening exercises, 258–259; mobilizing exercises, 260; stretching exercises, 261; dynamic strengthening exercises, 262
Shoulder girdle, 249
SHOULDER INJURIES
    strains, 250; biceps tendon tear, 252; bursitis, 253; dislocation, 254
SHOULDER JOINT, 246–264
    structure and functions, 246–249; pain, 249; injuries, 250–256; self-help measures, 251, 253, 255; exercises, 256–264; complications, 264
Shuttle runs, 47, 79
Sinding-Larsen-Johannson syndrome, 90
Skin problems
    foot, 29; hard skin on hands, 285
Slings (triangular bandages), 12–13
Slipped epiphysis
    childhood hip problem, 170; knee pain as symptom, 84
'Snapping'
    of iliotibial tract over thigh-bone, 104; snapping hip, 171
Soleus (calf muscle), 70
Spasm (over stress fractures)
    in the calf, 79; shin, 58; thigh-bone, 134, 149, 152; arm, 265, 267
Spinal cord
    major damage, 10; structure, 192, 239
Spine
    lumbar, 189–212; thoracic, 213–220; cervical (neck), 238–245
Splints, 10
Spondylolisthesis, 210
Spondylolysis, 210
Sprained ankle, 37–40
Sprained wrist, 280

'Spring' ligament
    structure, 20; injury, 26
Spur (heel), 25
Sternum (breast-bone), 235
Stiffness, chronic, in the shoulder, 264
Stitch, 223
Stomach muscles, *see* Abdominal muscles, 221–228
Strapping (taping), 10, 43
STRENGTHENING EXERCISES, 7
    for the foot, 31; shin problems, 60, 62; knee, 112, 116, 122; hamstrings, 122, 145, 147; front-thigh muscles, 112, 116; adductors, 157, 158; hip, 174; hip abductors, 187; back and abdomen, 196–202; shoulder, 256, 258; front arm muscles, 266, 270; back arm muscles, 267; wrist and hand, 286
Stress fractures
    in the foot, 23; shin, 58, 64, 79; fibula, 54; thigh-bone, 134, 149, 152; lumbar spine, 209; thoracic spine, 219; ribs, 236; arm, 265
STRETCHING EXERCISES, 5, 7
    for the foot, 34; shin, 58, 61, 69; calf, 77; knee (*see* thigh muscle stretches); front-thigh muscles, 133; hamstrings, 144; adductors, 156; hip flexors, 166; hip abductors, 187; spine and abdomen, 206; chest muscles, 233; shoulder, 261; front arm muscles, back arm muscles, *see* shoulder stretches; back forearm, 272; front forearm, 273
Subperiosteal haematoma (over shin-bone), 63
Supination
    foot movement, 22; forearm movement, 268
SURGERY
    for the foot, 25, 26, 27; ankle, 48, 49; leg, 57; anterior tibials, 59; tibial tubercle, 68; Achilles tendon, 75; knee injuries, 90, 94, 96, 100, 101, 109, 120, 124; front-thigh muscles, 130, 134; hamstring tear, 140; adductor tear, 153, 160; inguinal hernia, 163; pubic joint, 179; back, 208, 211; abdominal hernia, 228; pectoral tear, 232; shoulder injuries, 253, 254, 256; elbow injuries, 272, 274, 277; wrist problems, 280
Swelling, 10, 14

Swimming, as alternative training, 8
Symphysis pubis (pelvic joint)
    structure, 176; injuries, 179–180

Taping (strapping), 10–12
    for the ankle, 43
Temperature, raised by infection, 9
'Tennis elbow' (injury to the common extensor tendon), 271
Tenosynovitis
    in foot tendons, 28; ankle tendons, 53; forearm tendons, 276
Tetanus, immunization, need for, 16
THORACIC SPINE (upper back), 213–220
    structure and functions, 213–216; pain, 216; injuries, 216–218; self-help measures, 218; complications, 219–220
Thrombosis, cause of calf pain, 72
Tibia (shin-bone)
    structure, 35, 50, 80; injuries (stress fracture), 64
Tibial tuberosity (tubercle), 67–69
Tibialis anterior (shin muscle)
    structure, 52; injuries, 58–60
Toe-nails, 28
Training, gradual progression in fitness, 7
Transversus (stomach muscle), 222
Trapezius (neck muscle), 238
Traumatic injuries, 4
Trendelenburg sign, 185
Triangular bandages (slings), 12–13
Triceps (muscle on the back of the arm), 266–267
    tendon injury, 267, 270
TRUNK EXERCISES
    strengthening exercises, 196–202; mobility exercises, 202–205; stretching exercises, 206
Tuberculosis
    cause of hip pain, 169; cause of spinal pain, 192
Tumour (bone), 52, 129, 139

Ulna (forearm bone), structure, 268
Ulnar nerve, damage to, 274
Umbilicus (navel), 221
Unconsciousness, 9–10
Upper back, *see* thoracic spine, 213–220

Varicose veins, 72
Vastus medialis (inner quadriceps muscle)

Vastus medialis – *contd.*
 structure, 126; importance for knee
  stability, 91–95
Vertebrae
 lumbar, 189; thoracic, 213; neck
  (cervical), 238
Viral infection
 cause of chest pain, 216; cause of neck
  pain, 239

Walking, foot movements, 20–22

Warm-up, 5
Water
 in avoiding cramp, 6; in first-aid, 16,
  19
Weight-lifting, protecting your back,
 178
Weight-resistance, in strengthening
 exercises, 7
Wobble board, for balance exercises,
 44
Wounds, 16–17

WRIST AND HAND EXERCISES
 mobilizing and strengthening
  exercises, 286; advanced dynamic
  exercises, 288
WRIST JOINT
 structure and functions, 278; pain,
  278; injuries, 280; complications,
  281; exercises, 286

X-rays, 4